Moving by the Spirit

THE ANTHROPOLOGY OF CHRISTIANITY
Edited by Joel Robbins

1. *Christian Moderns: Freedom and Fetish in the Mission Encounter,* by Webb Keane
2. *A Problem of Presence: Beyond Scripture in an African Church,* by Matthew Engelke
3. *Reason to Believe: Cultural Agency in Latin American Evangelicalism,* by David Smilde
4. *Chanting Down the New Jerusalem: Calypso, Christianity, and Capitalism in the Caribbean,* by Francio Guadeloupe
5. *In God's Image: The Metaculture of Fijian Christianity,* by Matt Tomlinson
6. *Converting Words: Maya in the Age of the Cross,* by William F. Hanks
7. *City of God: Christian Citizenship in Postwar Guatemala,* by Kevin O'Neill
8. *Death in a Church of Life: Moral Passion during Botswana's Time of AIDS,* by Frederick Klaits
9. *Eastern Christians in Anthropological Perspective,* edited by Chris Hann and Hermann Goltz
10. *Studying Global Pentecostalism: Theories and Methods,* by Allan Anderson, Michael Bergunder, Andre Droogers, and Cornelis van der Laan
11. *Holy Hustlers, Schism, and Prophecy: Apostolic Reformation in Botswana,* by Richard Werbner
12. *Moral Ambition: Mobilization and Social Outreach in Evangelical Megachurches,* by Omri Elisha
13. *Spirits of Protestantism: Medicine, Healing, and Liberal Christianity,* by Pamela E. Klassen
14. *The Saint in the Banyan Tree: Christianity and Caste Society in India,* by David Mosse
15. *God's Agents: Biblical Publicity in Contemporary England,* by Matthew Engelke
16. *Critical Christianity: Translation and Denominational Conflict in Papua New Guinea,* by Courtney Handman
17. *Sensational Movies: Video, Vision, and Christianity in Ghana,* by Birgit Meyer
18. *Christianity, Islam, and Orisa Religion: Three Traditions in Comparison and Interaction,* by J. D. Y. Peel
19. *Praying and Preying: Christianity in Indigenous Amazonia,* by Aparecida Vilaça
20. *To Be Cared For: The Power of Conversion and Foreignness of Belonging in an Indian Slum,* by Nathaniel Roberts
21. *A Diagram for Fire: Miracles and Variation in an American Charismatic Movement,* by Jon Bialecki
22. *Moving by the Spirit: Pentecostal Social Life on the Zambian Copperbelt,* by Naomi Haynes

Moving by the Spirit

*Pentecostal Social Life on
the Zambian Copperbelt*

Naomi Haynes

UNIVERSITY OF CALIFORNIA PRESS

University of California Press, one of the most
distinguished university presses in the United States,
enriches lives around the world by advancing scholarship
in the humanities, social sciences, and natural sciences. Its
activities are supported by the UC Press Foundation and
by philanthropic contributions from individuals and
institutions. For more information, visit www.ucpress.edu.

University of California Press
Oakland, California

© 2017 by The Regents of the University of California

Library of Congress Cataloging-in-Publication Data

Names: Haynes, Naomi, author.
Title: Moving by the spirit : Pentecostal social life on
 the Zambian Copperbelt / Naomi Haynes.
Other titles: Anthropology of Christianity ; 22.
Description: Oakland, California : University of
 California Press, [2017] | Series: The anthropology of
 Christianity ; 22 | Includes bibliographical references
 and index.
Identifiers: LCCN 2016040501 (print) | LCCN
 2016042777 (ebook) | ISBN 9780520294240
 (cloth : alk. paper) | ISBN 9780520294257
 (pbk. : alk. paper) | ISBN 9780520967434 (ebook)
Subjects: LCSH: Pentecostals—Zambia—Copperbelt
 Province—Social life and customs. | Pentecostalism—
 Social aspects—Zambia—Copperbelt Province.
Classification: LCC BR1644.5.Z33 H39 2017 (print) |
 LCC BR1644.5.Z33 (ebook) | DDC 270.8/2096894—
 dc23
LC record available at https://lccn.loc.gov/2016040501

Manufactured in the United States of America

24 23 22 21 20 19 18 17
10 9 8 7 6 5 4 3 2 1

For my parents

The problem, of course, is to uncover the rules, regularities, and reproductive logics that underpin our current condition—a condition that is of necessity global, although always global in a variety of local ways, shapes, and forms. . . . What I have in mind is the relation between intentionality, contingency, and routine in the making of lives under the shadow of the global system—shadows Africa seems to epitomize in the most dramatic way, precisely as the *kolossos* of our world. What is the backdrop against which the work of production or maintenance of life or of a semblance of life is done? What are the materials that individuals work from, draw on, might even take for granted, in any case, consistently use?
—Achille Mbembe, "Africa in Theory"

Contents

List of Illustrations	*xi*
Acknowledgments	*xiii*
Note on Bemba Orthography and Pseudonyms	*xvii*
Prologue: A Breakthrough for Mr. Zulu	*xix*
Introduction: Pentecostalism as Promise, Pentecostalism as Problem	*1*
1. Boom and Bust, Revival and Renewal	*19*
2. Making Moving Happen	*37*
3. Becoming Pentecostal on the Copperbelt	*57*
4. Ritual and the (Un)making of the Pentecostal Relational World	*74*
5. Prosperity, Charisma, and the Problem of Gender	*92*
6. On the Potential and Problems of Pentecostal Exchange	*110*
7. Mending Mother's Kitchen	*127*
8. The Circulation of Copperbelt Saints	*147*
Conclusion: Worlds That Flourish	*159*
Notes	*167*
References Cited	*177*
Index	*191*

Illustrations

1. An unfinished plot with a "cabin" in the back / 25
2. Pouring cement for the floor of the Freedom Bible Church chapel, 2013 / 32
3. Outside Key of David in 2013 / 35
4. Bana Vincent at home, 2008 / 44
5. Bana Kondwani and her new "kitchen unit" / 51
6. Believers crammed into a house for a meeting / 79
7. Receiving line at Key of David with Pastor and Mrs. Mwanza / 81
8. Church member during the Key of David thanksgiving service / 111
9. The inside of a Key of David tithing envelope / 120
10. Template for the invitation card for Mrs. Mwanza's kitchen party / 129
11. "African print" outfits worn by kitchen mending committee members / 135

Acknowledgments

Conventionally, this part of a book begins with observations about the many debts one incurs when writing a monograph. Anthropologically speaking, this is not a bad way to go, at least insofar as debt implies a relationship. My experience of researching and writing this book over the last nine years has been enhanced by many relationships, more than I can enumerate here, though I will do my best.

The people who deserve the most thanks are my friends and informants on the Copperbelt. In particular, I am grateful to the pastors and other church leaders, especially my host family, whose real names I cannot use here. The same goes for the dozens of others who have welcomed me into their homes, fed me *nshima* or made me tea, and patiently answered my unending questions. *Natotela sana*. Dinewe Musoni, Chisengo Musukwa, and Rachel Nakamba have been very good research assistants. Thanks as well are due to the Kufunas, who have been my family from the moment I first set foot in Zambia. Finally, a huge debt of gratitude is owed Patricia Kalabwe, Gift Musalu, and Phalany and Mukumbi Kabesha, who have been friends indeed.

Funding for my research on the Copperbelt has been provided by the Institute for International, Comparative, and Area Studies and the Friends of the International Center, both at the University of California, San Diego; the Wenner-Gren Foundation; the Fulbright Foundation; the British Academy; the Carnegie Trust for the Universities of Scotland; and the Moray Endowment Fund at the University of Edinburgh.

Thanks to each of these organizations for their invaluable support. An earlier version of chapter 4 was published as "Egalitarianism and Hierarchy in Copperbelt Religious Practice: On the Social Work of Pentecostal Ritual" in *Religion* 42(2): 273–92. An earlier version of chapter 6 was published as "On the Potential and Problems of Pentecostal Exchange" in *American Anthropologist* 115(1): 85–95.

Portions of this book were presented at the University of Bergen, the University of Zambia, the London School of Economics, the University of St. Andrews, and the University of Cambridge. Each of these audiences had a hand to play in strengthening the argument. My analysis has also benefited from conversations with numerous colleagues and mentors, including Jon Bialecki, Tom Boylston, Alice Street, Jamie Cross, Jason Hickel, Katherine Miller, Joseph Webster, Magnus Course, Maya Mayblin, Rebecca Marsland, Laura Jeffery, Jonathan Spencer, Andreas Bandak, Girish Daswani, Courtney Handman, Rupert Stasch, Suzanne Brenner, Robert Cancel, Thomas Csordas, Brian Howell, Simon Coleman, Matthew Engelke, Annelin Eriksen, Olaf Smedal, Knut Rio, Austin Cheyeka, Rijk van Dijk, Linda van de Kamp, Adriaan van Klinken, Ruy Blanes, Maxim Bolt, Juliette Gilbert, China Scherz, and an anonymous reviewer for the University of California Press. Leanne Williams read large chunks of the manuscript in draft form and helped to improve it significantly. Reed Malcolm was gracious and encouraging as he shepherded the manuscript through the review process. Finally, special thanks are due to Joel Robbins, who has supported this project (and me) for years, who figured out what the kitchen mending was about well before I did, and whose thought has been the guiding inspiration behind much of what I have written here.

I'm also very grateful for the care and companionship of my friends outside of anthropology, whose kindness, good humor, and perspective have made my life richer and more balanced. Thanks here go to the Luttrell family, Lauren and Nathan Edwards, Quinn Riebock Cruz, Rachel McDonald Brown, Gemma Stoddart, and Elise Korherans. As they say on the Copperbelt, *tulaumfwana sana*.

My family has likewise been a great support to me over the many (many!) years I have devoted to understanding Copperbelt Pentecostalism. My grandparents, Richard and Ellen Haynes, and the late John and Ruby Kinsala have all contributed to the creativity and curiosity that made this book possible. My siblings, Joseph, David, and John Haynes and Rachel Reuter, are each accomplished in their own creative fields and are excellent people to boot. Thanks for being my friends. I am also grateful for the kindness of my mother- and father-in-law, Alice and Mingde Zhu, and my brother-in-law Peter, who have welcomed me into their home and lives. Last on the family roll call are my parents, Neil and Toni Haynes, to whom this book is dedicated, and without whom writing it would not have not been possible. People have often asked me how my parents feel about me traipsing all over the world, and I've always been able to say that I have their full support, for which I am very grateful.

And finally, there is my husband, Norman Zhu. His love has been the greatest surprise of my life, and the joy he has brought me has infused everything—including the writing of this book—with brightness. Thank you for everything, HB. 我爱你

A Note on Bemba Orthography and Pseudonyms

The Copperbelt lingua franca is known as "Town Bemba," an urban variety of CiBemba with a large lexical input from English, as well as other regional Bantu languages (Spitulnik and Kashoki 2001). Town Bemba also has a simplified grammar. In this book, I follow the Bemba spelling conventions of Rev. E. Hoch's *Bemba Pocket Dictionary* (Hoch 1960) whenever possible. Verbs are usually given in the infinitive form. Plural nouns are written without the preceding vowel, just as they are spoken (e.g., *bafyashi, fitenge*, rather than *abafyashi, ifitenge*).

The International Phonetic Alphabet symbol "ŋ" is used for the "ng" sound (as in "sing"), in addition to the twenty-six letters of the English alphabet. Pronunciation is relatively straightforward, with the exception of the letter "c," which in Bemba always makes the "ch" sound as in "church" or "child." Bemba uses the cardinal vowels (i.e., a, e, i, o, u) and they do not usually coalesce.

All individuals and congregations, as well as the township at the center of this study, have been given pseudonyms. I have tried to choose individual pseudonyms that reflect the variety of names given to and used by my informants, drawing on different Zambian languages as well as English. Some people on the Copperbelt use the titles "Mr." or "Mrs." as well as their Bemba equivalent of "Ba" and "Bana." In my writing, I also use the latter for women's teknonyms, along with "Bashi" for men's teknonyms. While others may write these as one word—for example, Banamusonda, Bashijoshua—for the sake of clarity I have chosen to

xvii

separate them. I use "Bana" rather than simply "Na" as a marker of respect, just as I did in the field (the prefix "Ba" adds a level of formality and distance). Most of my informants were older than I was, whether in terms of calendrical or social age (i.e., as an unmarried, childless woman, I was considered younger than those who had attained a more mature social status, even if I was older in calendrical age), and addressing them in more formal terms was therefore appropriate.

Prologue

A BREAKTHROUGH FOR MR. ZULU

In October of 2008, in the gathering heat that precedes the rainy season on the Zambian Copperbelt, Mrs. Zulu stopped going to church. Up to that point she and her husband had been prominent members of Key of David, a Pentecostal congregation located in a burgeoning middle-class township that I call Nsofu. Rumors as to why Mrs. Zulu stayed away from church spread rapidly. Many Pentecostal believers thought the trouble had followed a wedding held at Key of David earlier in the year, an event in which Mrs. Zulu had played a central role. Right up to the day of the wedding, members of the church struggled to put together the necessary funds, and as a result Mrs. Zulu had been caught in the middle of some nasty discussions about money. Soon afterward, she stopped attending church services.

As the weeks went by and Mrs. Zulu still did not return, Key of David members prepared to hold a conference. A white fabric banner was tacked to the church's plank fence, announcing the theme of the gathering as "There is a Way Out!" A Nigerian pastor had been invited as a guest speaker, and the wait for his arrival was filled with discussions of his expected spiritual power—Nigerians, people said, really knew how to pray. Anticipating a large crowd, Pastor Mwanza, the leader of Key of David, borrowed extra chairs from another Pentecostal congregation. Last-minute improvements were made to the church building, and the women of Key of David spent an entire afternoon sweeping and polishing the floor. Special invitations were given to Pentecostal leaders from around Nsofu, and extra sofas, including those that usually filled the Mwanzas' living room, were brought in to accommodate the visiting clergy, who would be given seats of honor (and extra comfort) in the front of the church.

The conference was a massive success. A large crowd of believers from across the township gathered night after night to sing and dance enthusiastically, freeing their hips and swinging handkerchiefs in the air. To everyone's surprise, on the penultimate night of the conference Mrs. Zulu appeared at Key of David. Although she sat in the back of the room, her presence was conspicuous, particularly because the other women had arranged ahead of time to wear matching Key of David polo shirts and *fitenge* (sing. *citenge*), the two-meter pieces of cloth that are worn as wrap skirts across Africa. Since Mrs. Zulu had not been present when this decision was made, she had come dressed in a navy blue pantsuit, an outfit that emphasized her distance from the rest of the Key of David women.

Despite the awkwardness of her unexpected appearance, Mrs. Zulu's decision to attend the conference seemed like a gesture of goodwill. That this was indeed the case was confirmed when she went to the front of the church at the end of the meeting and embraced the pastor's wife, Mrs. Mwanza. After this very public return, Mrs. Zulu resumed her position at Key of David alongside her husband. She even took on a new leadership role with the women, helping to plan a large "kitchen mending" party organized in Mrs. Mwanza's honor.

When I left the field in July of 2009, an uneasy truce hung between Mr. and Mrs. Zulu and Mr. and Mrs. Mwanza. However, a few years later the conflict between the couples flared up again, and this time the results were more dramatic. After a protracted dispute over a baby shower for Mrs. Zulu, which drew in many members of the church, the couple left Key of David for good and began attending another Pentecostal congregation in a neighboring township. Mr. and Mrs. Zulu knew the pastor of this church, a Bible college classmate of Pastor Mwanza, and he welcomed them into his fold. In a short time both Mr. and Mrs. Zulu came to occupy leadership positions in their new congregation, with Mr. Zulu serving as an elder, as he had done at Key of David, and his wife heading up the women's ministry. The Zulus' split with the Mwanzas was thoroughgoing and unfriendly to the extreme, and Mrs. Zulu told me that if they met in town they would not even greet one another. On the Copperbelt, greeting is the most basic of all social exchanges, and the refusal to do so (*ukukana ukuposha*) is therefore a potent index of conflict, the rejection of even the most minimal of ties.

When I returned to Nsofu in 2013, I spent a great deal of time talking to current and former Key of David members about the Zulus' departure from their church. One such conversation took place when I joined Bana Karen on a trip to the local hospital, where she was scheduled to bring her young daughter to the under-five clinic. It was June, and the dry season dust hung thick in the air, refracting the afternoon sunlight. Bana Karen was a friend of Mrs. Zulu's. She was also a member of Key of David and regarded Pastor Mwanza as her spiritual "father." This left her caught in the middle of their conflict, and after the Zulus left Key of David Bana Karen was angry and hurt. She shared these feelings with me as we waited for her daughter to be weighed, standing together in a long line of patient mothers and fussy babies. In Bana Karen's opinion, Mr. and Mrs. Zulu were wrong to break with Key of David, a church they had helped to start nearly ten years before. They should have stayed in the place where they had laid their spiritual foundation, she explained, as that would have led to a greater blessing for their family.

Hearing her mention of blessing, I remembered something Mrs. Zulu had told me a few days before. You know, I told Bana Karen, turning to face her in the shade of the hospital alcove, Mrs. Zulu told me that after her family left Key of David they had a "breakthrough." For Copperbelt believers a breakthrough is an important religious event, a "deeply felt [experience] of protection and success" (Englund 2007: 490) that produces a marked change in circumstances. In Mrs. Zulu's telling, leaving Key of David and joining a new church had brought about a clear shift in the family's situation; most notably, her husband had been promoted at work and was now a mine foreman. The news that the Zulus had experienced a breakthrough after leaving Key of David caused Bana Karen to quickly change her tone. If leaving had brought them a blessing, she reasoned out loud, then perhaps their departure from Key of David was part of a divine plan. Sometimes, Bana Karen observed, adjusting the *citenge* that secured her daughter on her back, God moves you from one place to another. It's like when you've been working on a contract and it runs out, she explained: when the contract is up, it's time to go elsewhere.

The story of the Mr. and Mrs. Zulu's changing relationship with, and eventual departure from, their Pentecostal church highlights several themes that are central to this book. For Mr. and Mrs. Zulu, Bana Karen, and Pentecostal believers like them, religious adherence is structured by miraculous transformations like a promotion to mine foreman. While such breakthroughs would likely be compelling to anyone anywhere, on the Copperbelt they are invested with a particular local significance because of their connection to what people there call "moving." Moving is a value, an animating idea that reverberates through the symbols and social structures of the Copperbelt. When people in Nsofu say that "things are moving" (*fintu filesela*), they are referring to measurable progress according to a variety of interlocking metrics, most notably economic achievement. Pentecostalism provides new ways of making moving happen, including new frameworks by which it can be measured. For the Zulu family, this meant not only a breakthrough in the form of better employment, but also a religious "promotion" of sorts when Mrs. Zulu was put in charge of the women's ministry in their new church.

Moving doesn't always happen for believers, however. Just as the presence of moving in the form of a breakthrough can indicate that a believer is where she should be—connected, in other words, to the right congregation and pastor—the absence of moving can be interpreted as a failure of Pentecostal social ties. Under these circumstances believers may feel that, as Bana Karen put it, it is time to go elsewhere, time to transfer their allegiance to one of the dozens of other churches and fellowships in Nsofu. As old members leave a congregation, new members soon take their place, and this shifting matrix of affiliation highlights both the promise and precariousness of the relationships through which believers seek to move "by the Spirit." The analysis that follows is focused on these efforts, how they work, the problems they create, and they way they structure Pentecostal social life on the Zambian Copperbelt.

DEMOCRATIC
REPUBLIC
OF CONGO
N
TANZANIA
ANGOLA
Chililabombwe
Chingola
Mufulira
Kitwe
Ndola
Luanshya
COPPERBELT
Lunga
MALAWI
Luangwa
ZAMBIA
MOZAMBIQUE
Kafue
Lusaka
NAMIBIA
Zambezi
ZIMBABWE
BOTSWANA
0
100
200 mi
0
100
200
300 km

Introduction

*Pentecostalism as Promise,
Pentecostalism as Problem*

Reality demands
that we also mention this:
Life goes on

—Wislawa Szymborska, "Reality Demands"

Pentecostalism is a form of Christianity that emphasizes the immediate experience of the Holy Spirit through practices such as prophecy and healing. On the Zambian Copperbelt, Pentecostalism is at the heart of a dynamic process of social creativity that I refer to as "moving by the Spirit." My aim in this book is to tease out the particular qualities of this process, to show how Pentecostalism fits into the broader repertoire of tools and strategies through which people on the Copperbelt "[make] life possible," to use Achille Mbembe's phrase (Shipley 2010: 659). To those familiar with the literature on Pentecostal expansion in Africa, this may seem like a strange focus. Because of its emphasis on individualism and consumption, Pentecostalism has often—and in my view far too easily—been characterized as a socially corrosive force, a handmaiden of neoliberalism. This book calls such arguments into question. Building on an important body of ethnographic work that has focused on Pentecostalism's social productivity, its capacity to create and strengthen interpersonal and institutional ties (e.g., Englund 2007, van Dijk 2009, Engelke 2010, Lindhardt 2010), my analysis explores how Copperbelt Pentecostals draw on their religion in order to act in and on the world. As we saw in the example of Mr. Zulu, these efforts turn on a distinct metric of value, a uniquely Pentecostal way of measuring and experiencing moving. It is only in the light of this Pentecostal model of moving, which I call "moving by the Spirit," that we are able to properly interpret not only the widespread popularity of Pentecostalism in Zambia, but also, and more importantly, its particular local traits.

In the following chapters I examine the promise (and problems) of Pentecostal adherence in the kind of community where it most often flourishes: a densely populated neighborhood in the heart of an extraction economy. The primary site of my ethnography is Nsofu, a township with a population of about twenty-five thousand people located on the outskirts of the city of Kitwe.[1] I will describe Nsofu in detail in chapter 1. First, however, my task in this introduction is to situate my argument within some broad currents of anthropological thought. Before turning to this task, I must make one important point about the scope of my discussion.

Although this book is about Pentecostalism, what I offer here is by no means a complete treatment of Copperbelt Pentecostal theology or practice. To do these topics justice would require another book. There may be those who are troubled by my focus on how Pentecostalism makes life possible in the here-and-now. At its worst this book could be read as a reductionist argument in which Pentecostal religious life emerges as purely instrumental, disconnected from other elements of Christianity like God and salvation, heaven and hell. Let me be clear that this is not the case. For the vast majority of believers, commitment to the Christian God (*Lesa*) is the driving force of their religious lives; in other words, their Pentecostal adherence is directly tied to concerns that we can readily define as central to Christian theology. By choosing not to focus on these topics in my analysis, my goal is not to paper over the very real religious commitments of Copperbelt believers, but rather to show how these commitments shape social relationships.

I have chosen this approach for two reasons. First, thanks to the efforts of scholars working throughout Africa, we already have a very robust picture of Pentecostal history, theology, and practice on the continent (e.g., Meyer 1999, Marshall 2009, Maxwell 2006, Daswani 2015). It would therefore not be terribly helpful to reproduce this picture here. Second and more significantly, while the social processes that I explore in what follows do not represent the entirety of believers' religious lives, my analysis will demonstrate that they are nevertheless extremely important to people in Nsofu. While it would be wrong to reduce their commitment to Pentecostalism to these processes, then, it would be equally mistaken to write about believers' religious adherence without giving the relational aspects of Pentecostalism a prominent position. This is what I have tried to do here. The first step in this approach is to look at the ways in which the relational components of Pentecostalism have been denied by analyses that have treated it as a socially corrosive, rather than socially productive, religion.

NEOLIBERALISM, PENTECOSTALISM, AND THE TENACITY OF SOCIAL LIFE

Central to much anthropological research in the past two decades is the notion that life has changed dramatically as neoliberal ideas have come to shape social and economic policy across the globe (see Ganti 2014 for a review). Here I am using the term "neoliberal" to refer to changes in the relationship between the state and the market, a reduction in government's role in the economy, the rolling back of the welfare state, privatization of industry, and with it, a new emphasis on personal responsibility. Under neoliberalism, the logic of the market is extended to what were traditionally nonmarket domains, such as the family and religion (Rose 1999, Foucault 2008, Rudnyckyj 2010). Neoliberalism therefore has effects at the level of political economy, of sociality, and of subjectivity; it transforms states and markets, but also relationships and persons. On the whole, the results of these changes are understood to be negative, ranging from increased possibilities of political corruption in the light of new standards of "good governance" (D. J. Smith 2007) to the high incidence of HIV infection (Hickel 2012). Similarly, social life is also understood to have suffered under the atomizing effects of liberalization and the "institutional deficit" of the global neoliberal order (see Lash and Urry 1994).

To focus specifically on Africa for a moment, one key element of analyses of neoliberalism on the continent has been what scholars have described as the breakdown of established frameworks of meaning, a semiotic crisis generated by the paradoxes of liberalization. To wit, the "uneasy fusion of enfranchisement and exclusion" (Comaroff and Comaroff 2000: 299) and the "odd paring of dispossession and wealth creation" (Roitman 2005: 15) that characterize neoliberalism have produced an "overheating" of signs (de Boeck and Plissart 2004: 58), a "generalized condition of semiotic suspension" (Apter 2005: 283; also see Mbembe 2001: 145–49). Here most of Africa exists in a "shadow" world in which "much is unknown, hard to make out, perhaps even unknowable" (Ferguson 2006: 15–16). The Copperbelt has not been exempt from such interpretations. James Ferguson's (1999) influential study of Kitwe in the late 1980s reflects not only his informant's despair in the face of economic collapse, but also an overarching sense of inscrutability. Ferguson writes about his fieldwork as "a continuing encounter with an intractable unintelligibility," a situation in which "to understand things like the natives [was] to miss most of what was going on" (1999: 208). In Ferguson's analysis, economic breakdown was connected to more than just social breakdown; it produced a crisis of meaning.

Anthropological accounts of religion under neoliberalism have taken up a similar line of analysis, focusing again on the confusion generated by liberalization. In particular, the parallel expansion of Pentecostalism alongside the spread of neoliberal reforms has been treated as no mere coincidence, but rather as a direct response to the increasingly "spectral" quality of late capitalism (Comaroff and Comaroff 2000: 290). The most influential of these arguments has been Jean and John Comaroff's discussion of "occult economies" (Comaroff and Comaroff 1999, 2000). Comaroff and Comaroff observe that the global expansion of neoliberal capitalism at the turn of the millennium was marked by an increase of things like witchcraft accusations, Marian apparitions, rumors of zombies, and "fee-for-service" religions, among which they include the Pentecostal prosperity gospel. All of these are what they call occult economies— supernatural frameworks simultaneously focused on the "quest for new, magical means for otherwise unattainable ends . . . [and] a desire to sanction, even eradicate, people held to have accumulated assets by those very means" (Comaroff and Comaroff 2000: 316). These parallel goals might be realized through distinct discourses—for example, by accusing someone of getting rich through demonic or satanic means while at the same time joining a Pentecostal church in hopes of getting rich through the power of God (Blunt 2004, Newell 2007).

A number of objections to the occult economies argument have been raised (e.g., Green and Mesaki 2005, Marshall 2009, Haynes 2012), and there is no need to rehearse them here. My main goal in bringing up this line of interpretation is to show how one particularly prominent analytical approach to neoliberalism is related to what has historically been the dominant framework for interpreting Pentecostal expansion. If neoliberalism has been understood to exert an atomizing, socially corrosive force on places like the Copperbelt, Pentecostalism has often been cast as its religious avatar, a mechanism for breaking down relationships that stand in the way of self-realization, especially self-realization through consumption.[2] This is especially true in the light of the popularity of the prosperity or "health and wealth" gospel, a Christian movement that I describe in more detail in chapter 3. In the framework of the prosperity gospel, lavish wealth is linked to divine favor, and believers are encouraged to "trade with God" (Ukah 2005) and invest in a "heavenly bank" (Hasu 2006) in an effort to secure earthly blessings. It is because of these emphases that the prosperity gospel has been described as the point at which "Pentecostalism meets neoliberal enterprise" (Comaroff and Comaroff 2000: 314).

While ultimately I want to argue for its social productivity, I should point out that interpretations that cast Pentecostalism as socially corrosive are not completely without ethnographic support. Indeed, when one examines the rhetoric of Pentecostal preachers, it is not difficult to see why this form of Christianity has historically been treated as a religion for people who were interested in breaking at least some of their social relationships, and especially in abandoning obligations to kin.[3] For example, the retributive arm of the occult economies model suggests that Pentecostals can leverage the power of God against anyone that they believe to be causing them harm. Such actions follow from a belief in the continued influence of the powers of darkness on a believer's life, thanks to connections to nonbelieving kin, neighbors, and ancestors (van Dijk 1998, Meyer 1998). Faced with such threats, Pentecostals are encouraged to launch a spiritual counterattack—what some Copperbelt believers rightfully call "dangerous prayers"—against those who would hurt them through supernatural means. As Paul Gifford puts it in his summary of Pentecostal preaching on this topic, "The lesson [is] that if members of your family, even your mother, are responsible for your ills and are hurt by your counter-attack, don't pray for them; 'Let them die, let them die . . . !'" (2004: 105). Little wonder then that analyses of Pentecostalism have often focused on relational corrosiveness, individualization, and the "radical restructuring of the social networks and moral and ethnic matrices of the family, of kin relations, and ethnic affiliations" (de Boeck and Plissart 2004: 56).

My aim in this book is to complicate the model I have just laid out. Rather than continuing to rely on increasingly problematic metaphors of social and semiotic breakdown under neoliberalism, my analysis is focused on what Achille Mbembe describes as "the deliberate labor involved in . . . sustaining social-political life and relations, and in constituting the social-political self" (Shipley 2010: 657) in the neoliberal era. Here, Pentecostalism has a central role to play. Although, as the mention of "dangerous prayers" suggests, there are some situations in which Copperbelt believers would very much like to cut off certain social relationships; and although their religion provides them with a theological structure within which these sorts of breaks are possible, Pentecostal ideas and practices are far more frequently mobilized toward socially productive, rather than socially corrosive, ends. Indeed, the creative power of Pentecostalism is one of the things that makes this religion especially compelling to people on the Copperbelt. My analysis therefore troubles the easy connection between Pentecostalism and social corrosiveness, and between neoliberalism and social breakdown. While this book is focused on the familiar intersection of relational life, Pentecostalism, and the effects of economic crisis, then, I want to weave these strands together in a different pattern than the one that has typically been used, and in so doing provide a different picture of Pentecostalism than that which we have grown accustomed to seeing.

Let me be clear here that I do not wish to ignore the difficulties—indeed, the structural and sometimes physical violence—that have marked the neoliberal period in Africa and elsewhere. Evidence of the many problems created by neoliberal reforms is not hard to find in Zambia, and this will be clear in the discussion that follows. However, what I have found in the time I have spent on the Copperbelt is that the social effects of these economic changes have not been what the literature on Africa in particular has led us to expect. I went to Zambia for my doctoral fieldwork well acquainted with the idea that after liberalization everything would be different than it had been, and more specifically that people would find these differences unnerving or confusing. What I found in Nsofu, however, was something else. While people were frustrated by fluctuating prices and food shortages, and uncertain about the security of their jobs in the face of the 2008 global financial crisis, they were not confused about what relational life should look like, or indeed, about how to make it happen. Instead, they were carrying on as best as they could—and often carrying on rather well.

This book reflects, to the best of my ability, what I found in the field. In keeping with their creative and tenacious efforts to make the kinds of social relationships that were most important to them, my analysis is focused on how people on the Copperbelt make life possible—how, in other words, they go about "trying to create sustainable social relationships in their everyday lives through their productive, imaginative work" (J.H. Smith 2011: 20). As such, while this book represents a contribution to the anthropology of Christianity, it is my hope that it will also be seen as part of an emerging "anthropology of the good" (Robbins 2013a), an exploration of how Pentecostal adherence allows people on the Copperbelt to live their lives "pitched forward toward what they take to be a better world" (Robbins 2013a: 459). My primary concern in what follows is therefore how Pentecostals on the Copperbelt mobilize the various elements of their religion in order to make life—and, as far as they can, to make a good life—possible for themselves and their families.

Doubtless there is some extent to which this focus reflects my own vision of the world. I am an optimist by nature, and it would be foolish to assume that in a discipline like anthropology, where the analyst is so intimately bound up in the experiences of those she studies, personality would not shape the outcome of one's research. While I am sure that my disposition had some part to play in orienting my analysis, I am equally confident that a much more important factor in determining the direction of my argument was the fact that the vast majority of the people I met on the Copperbelt are forward-looking and optimistic. As I have just noted, their lives are "pitched" in a direction that often belies their circumstances. Since I first began living with Copperbelt Pentecostals more than ten years ago, their consistent commitment to the notion that the future will be better and brighter than the present has compelled my attention and demanded my intellectual engagement. To borrow an observation from Jane Guyer (1995: 5), on the Copperbelt "hope seems to spring eternal in ways that need analysis."

TOWARD AN ANTHROPOLOGY OF THE GOOD: SOCIAL LIFE AND THE REALIZATION OF VALUES

If this study is concerned with the good, how do we know what that is? It is a truism in anthropology that the good is not a universal category, and that people's visions of a good life vary across culture, time, and space. The first step in studying the good is therefore to understand what this means in a given ethnographic setting. In appealing to notions of the good I therefore have in mind a very particular kind of analytical object. Specifically, what I mean by this term is a relational model, a vision of an ideal social world. What makes this social world a good social world is its capacity to realize important values. Understanding the good therefore means understanding values, and more specifically understanding how values are connected to social life. This is our task in this section.

While the topic of values is enjoying something of a revival in contemporary anthropology (e.g., Otto and Willerslev 2013; Graeber 2001, 2013; Eriksen 2012; Robbins 2004a, 2009a; Pedersen 2008; Haynes and Hickel 2016a), there is nothing like an agreed-upon definition of what it is we mean by this term. David Graeber (2001: 1–2) has outlined three primary uses of "values" or "value" in the discipline: value in the "sociological sense" of what is good and proper; value in the economic sense of what is desirable, as well as of what something is worth; and value in the linguistic or structural sense of "meaningful difference." Graeber has argued that these three ways of approaching value are at bottom one in the same, and has unified them in a theory of action that is strongly influenced by Terry Turner (see Graeber 2001, 2013). While I do not wish to take my definition of value quite as far as Graeber does, I do agree that much of what we mean by these three uses of the term derives its significance from a unified process of valuation. I have found that the best way to get at this unity is to begin with a distinction between what I will be calling "value" as a noun and "value" as a verb, as in "to value something."

As nouns, values are most simply defined as animating ideas. Values like justice or freedom or progress set a social world in motion, enlivening relational life (Rio and Smedal 2009: 22), orienting it toward particular ends and thereby shaping local understandings of the good. By the same token, a good social world is a world in which it is possible to realize values—that is, to turn these animating ideas into symbols of themselves. By realizing a value I mean giving a value an actual or physical form that is both symbolically significant and socially recognized (Munn 1986: 3; Graeber 2013: 225). Although values may be realized in elements of material culture like houses or tapestries, my primary interest here is in how values are realized—again, given form—through social elements such as institutions, rituals, or persons. So, for instance, among the Christian Urapmin of highland Papua New Guinea, people who have been possessed by the Holy Spirit in the "Spirit disco" ritual emerge as individuals purged of sin, and this ritual therefore realizes the Urapmin Christian value of individualism, which is necessary for salvation (Robbins 2015). To take another Melanesian example, on the island of Gawa the act of giving food to a visitor from another part of the Massim realizes—gives form to—the expansion of "intersubjective spacetime" as the "fame of Gawa" extends in the gift and the memory it creates (Munn 1986).

If by values as nouns I am referring to ideas that animate social life, by value as a verb I am referring to the structuring force of such ideas. Values are realized in social forms, but not all social forms will realize a given value equally well. It follows then that those aspects of social life that most adequately realize the most important values will be the most prominent, the most "elaborately worked out" (Robbins 2009a: 66), while those that do not will not be as well developed or as often pursued. If this is true, then the rank-ordering of the various elements that make up any society—be they actions, ideas, relationships, or even other, lower-ranked values—is a product of values. The idea of value as a verb therefore refers to the way that certain animating ideas (values as nouns) shape society, transforming what is theoretically a space of open-ended potential in which sociality or subjectivity might take any number of forms into one where certain forms are both more common and more desirable—more highly valued—than others. It is because of values that social life takes place not on a level ground in which all options are open or all ways of being are equally possible, but rather in a field that is differentiated and varied, a field with topography (Kapferer 2010: 198–99). Simply put, values value.

Although I have drawn a distinction between value as a noun and value as a verb, it should be clear by now that these ideas bleed into one another quite easily. Values as nouns provide the trajectory for value as a verb, which in turn carries out the work involved in expressing values as nouns. Together these two aspects of value make up the process of value or of valuation, a process that applies to all aspects of a society. Given the overlap between values as nouns and verbs, we can say that this process is worked out at the point of articulation between ideas and social forms (Sahlins 1976: x). My use of the term "articulation" here is meant to denote both intersection and vocalization, as social forms reveal the animating ideas behind them. One of the implications of this observation is that we can read values off of social life. In other words, by paying attention to the sorts of things that anthropologists are always concerned with—rituals, relationships, and so forth—we can begin to understand the values that animate a given society. This observation is greatly indebted to the work of Louis Dumont (e.g., Dumont 1980: xlviii), who has also influenced many of the theorists cited above. While there are certainly aspects of Dumont's model that I do not take up here, the discussion that follows has been fundamentally shaped by the notion that social organization—the pattern of social life—is closely connected to values, a notion that sits at the heart of Dumont's approach (Kapferer 2010). My decision to bring Dumont into the discussion raises several issues that need to be addressed before we can move on to a brief overview of the values that are at the heart of this book.

The first issue that requires our attention is that of how values relate to one another. The notion of value suggests not only differentiation, but also rank-ordering and hierarchy. For Dumont, this hierarchy takes a very particular form, which he describes as "encompassment," and more specifically "encompassment of the contrary." In Dumont's words, encompassment is a relation "between a whole (or a set) and an element of this whole (or set): the element belongs to the set and is in this sense consubstantial or identical with it; at the same time, the element is distinct from the set or stands in opposition to it" (Dumont 1980: 240). I describe the relationship of encompassment in greater detail in chapter 5. For now it is simply necessary to sketch the contours of this relationship as part of a more general theory of value. Here, the most important thing to bear in mind is that values in a relationship of encompassment are variously identified with and opposed to one another, which can make the relationship between them difficult to navigate.

The second thing we take from Dumont's work is the observation that the position of values is not fixed. This is clear in Dumont's studies of modern Western ideology (Dumont 1977, 1986), which focus on shifts in the organization of values over time. More than a shift, in some situations there is an open contest between values that calls to mind Weber's notion of competing "value spheres" (1946: 323–59). The changing arrangement of values over time and the sometimes-vexed contest among them represent the final elements of our theory of value. The dynamic interplay of values, their competition and complementarity, opens up a field of play that not only gives social life its contours but also propels it forward. In other words, it is the interaction between values, and especially the need to keep dangerous or ambiguous values from gaining too much ground, that provides social life with its internal momentum. This means that social life is shaped by values both as individual animating ideas and as a dynamic aggregate, informing what people are trying to create as well as what they are trying to control. This play of values is "always in process, opening constantly to new modes of expression" (Kapferer 2010: 199), a point that leads us to one final observation about the role of values in this book.

Anthropological studies of Christianity that make use of values in their theoretical framing have typically focused on shifts in the arrangement of values, and on the replacement of older values with new ones (e.g., Robbins 2004a, 2009a; Eriksen 2009, 2012). This emphasis has proved quite useful in understanding conversion and the sort of radical cultural change that has been so important to the anthropology of Christianity. While I do not wish to dispute these analyses, the context of my fieldwork has necessitated a different approach. In what follows I do not argue so much for a shift in the organization of values in response to Pentecostal adherence as I do for a change in the way that established values are imagined and measured. The discussion that follows is therefore an exploration of creativity—in looking for new ways that old values might be realized. Having laid out my theory of value, I can now turn my attention to the animating idea that concerns us most in this book.

MOVING (BY THE SPIRIT)

In 2013 I returned to Nsofu after nearly four years away. Many things about the township were just as I had left them, but there had also been a number of changes. Several of my neighbors had moved to larger homes, and many more had bought cars and learned to drive. Perhaps as a result, they had put on weight—a key marker on the Copperbelt that someone is living well (*ukwikala bwino*). Babies had been born, marriages made, and children had gone to college. Remarks about these changes always pleased people in Nsofu, and I noticed that if I failed to say anything about a new car or house (I knew enough to always mention a baby), those I was speaking to would be sure to draw attention to such positive transformations. "At least," they would say, "you have found [*ukusanga*] us in a different situation than you left us." "At least things have changed." "At least things have *moved*." As I prepared to leave the field a few months later, conversations turned toward expectations for the future, and again I heard people speak of transformation. Many of my neighbors told me that when I came back to Nsofu I would find that things had improved still further. Often, they had specific changes in mind, saying that when I returned I would find that a new house had been built, that someone who had been unemployed had started working, that an unmarried woman had found a husband, or that a man taking night classes had finished his university degree. They had similar plans for me. I had finished my doctorate and become a lecturer, people were happy to hear, and in time they expected that I would found my own university.

My return to Nsofu after such a long absence meant that these sorts of conversations were especially frequent; however, upon further reflection I realized that they were not unique to this particular trip. Once I started to think through how people had responded over the years I had worked on the Copperbelt to the changes that had happened and the changes they expected, I realized what a central issue this was. People in Nsofu were constantly engaged in very subtle practices of gauging progress in themselves and in those around them, noticing who had put on a bit of weight or who was wearing a new blouse. I was always struck by how fine-grained these measurements were, by how carefully everyone was paying attention to the relative progress of those around them. Taken together, expectations of progress and the "political economy of recognition" (Guyer 2004: 147) according to which progress is measured point to a key value, an animating idea that on the Copperbelt is described as "moving" (*ukusela*). When my informants say that "things are moving" (*fintu filesela*), they are referring to a recognizable, usually visible, positive change in circumstances.[4] There are several overlapping metrics of moving, including educational advancement and progress through the life-course. Moving also refers to economic achievement, realized in visible markers of financial improvement, as seen in the above emphasis on things like cars and houses—an emphasis, incidentally, that has clear echoes in earlier ethnographies of urban Zambia (e.g., Epstein 1981, Hansen 1997).[5] Importantly, moving does not simply entail advancement as such, but is instead the result of certain kinds of social relationships, especially patronage ties, as well as lateral networks that allow for the pooling of resources, such as savings associations.

Moving is a central value for all people on the Copperbelt, and here Pentecostal believers are no exception. Indeed, relationships that facilitate moving are produced through Pentecostal adherence with particular ease. While moving in Pentecostal groups happens through relationships that are similar to the ties that help realize this value on the Copperbelt more generally, the model and metric of moving that has developed among believers is uniquely Pentecostal. I call this model "moving by the Spirit." Moving by the Spirit is, like its non-Pentecostal counterpart, primarily concerned with progress. As we have seen in the example of Mr. Zulu's breakthrough, one way in which this value is realized is through the kind of economic and social advancement that usually characterizes moving on the Copperbelt. In the theological framework of Pentecostalism, this element of moving by the Spirit finds its expression in the prosperity gospel, as the message of divine health and wealth makes it clear that there is space in Pentecostalism for moving as it has traditionally been defined—that is, for moving that is measured in expanding waistlines and promotions at work. However, moving by the Spirit is more than a Christianized version of a traditional Copperbelt value. This is because in Pentecostal moving material prosperity is always accompanied by and subordinate to spiritual development. In other words, in moving by the Spirit prosperity follows from what can broadly be termed charisma: facility with religious practices like prayer and singing, and, in rarer cases, prophecy and healing.

Even this very quick sketch gives us some insight into the expansion of Pentecostalism in urban Zambia. Pentecostalism's popularity stems from its social productivity, the ease with which it produces relationships through which people can realize moving in a new way. While Pentecostalism would therefore likely have been well received under any circumstances, it has become especially important to people on the Copperbelt in times of economic crisis. As we will see in chapter 2, economic upheaval makes it more difficult to access the relationships that make moving possible on traditional terms, and as a result alternative relational networks and models of moving become that much more attractive. That said, although there is a connection between the expansion of Pentecostalism and economic crisis, I do not think that this link represents the whole story behind the runaway growth of this religion in Zambia. This is true for two reasons.

First, the problem with focusing too much on what Joel Robbins (2009b: 56) calls "compensation and deprivation arguments" in making sense of Pentecostal expansion is that doing so turns religion into something that believers do simply because they cannot do anything else. In other words, people move by the Spirit only because traditional models of moving—which they presumably prefer—are not working. Seen from this angle, Pentecostalism performs what Ruth Marshall refers to as a "second-order process of adjustment," which implies that Africans simply "make do with religion," again, because they are unable to act in any other way (2009: 29). This view is spurious by anyone's measure, and we should be wary of any interpretation that treats Pentecostalism, whether implicitly or explicitly, as nothing more than a next-best option.

Second, even if we leave behind more vulgar arguments linking Pentecostal expansion exclusively to economic downturn, we will nevertheless miss an important component of this religion's popularity if we focus on this historical conjunction alone. Here I am referring to the longstanding cultural emphasis, documented throughout Zambia, on novelty. Ubiquitous observations in the ethnographic and historical literature of the importance attached to new clothes and tools, new modes of distinction, and relationships to new kinds of people (e.g., Powdermaker 1962: 94–96; Richards 1995: 216–17; Schuster 1979: 80) point to what James Pritchett refers to as "an almost fanatical pursuit of novelty" among Zambians (Pritchett 2001: xi). One further element of this pursuit is a quest for new metrics by which to gauge personal advancement. As Pritchett puts it, writing about the Lunda-Ndembu, "Individuality is expressed through the selection of the particular hierarchy within which one feels most capable of succeeding, the manner in which one strives to reach the top, or the construction of a new hierarchy" (Pritchett 2001: 245). In other words, one of the driving forces behind the cultural emphasis on novelty in Zambia has been the way that new connections, new fashions, and so on make what I have been calling moving possible by expanding the list of potential frameworks in which it can be realized. What is important about moving by the Spirit from this perspective is its role as a new and unique mode for realizing an established cultural value.

Pentecostalism is perhaps especially well suited to the pursuit of novel forms of moving. The Pentecostal philosopher James K. A. Smith (2010) has argued that to be a Pentecostal is to live a life oriented toward novelty, surprise, and spontaneity. The theologian Nimi Wariboko (2011:1) makes a similar point in his discussion of what he calls "the Pentecostal principle," an idea that turns on the notion of newness and "a radical openness to alternatives and surprises.".[6] The result of this emphasis, as Marshall puts it, is a "permanent dynamic of change and renewal" (Marshall 2009: 88). Taken together, these analyses point to creativity and newness as central characteristics of Pentecostalism. It is therefore not surprising that on the Copperbelt this form of Christianity represents an important source of novelty with regard to how moving is measured and realized.

While my discussion so far has focused on how Pentecostalism helps make life on the Copperbelt possible, Pentecostal adherence also presents problems for believers. Most of these problems stem from the complex relationship between prosperity and charisma, the two elements—or subvalues—that together make up moving by the Spirit. In the constellation of Copperbelt Pentecostal values, charisma must rank more highly than prosperity. One reason for this ordering is that, following some rather clear warnings in the biblical text, Pentecostals believe that they must keep their priorities straight and their motives pure if God is going to bless them.[7] To use an example that people in Nsofu often gave me, a believer shouldn't ask for a car just because he wants one, but rather so that he can drive people to church. Another reason for ranking prosperity below charisma is the special ritual efficacy, or at least efficiency, of the latter. When it comes to Pentecostal social relationships, those that are structured by charisma are especially good at helping believers to move by the Spirit.

However, the main motivation for keeping charisma above prosperity is that this ordering ensures that the relational possibilities presented by Pentecostalism are available to all believers regardless of economic status. Believers consider it a vital article of faith that when it comes to relationships that can make moving happen—especially ties to church leaders—a lay believer who is wealthy should not have any advantage over one who is not. Not surprisingly, this idea is especially important to those who are materially poor. One way to ensure that access to relationships remains democratic is to see to it that prosperity does not become too prominent, and more specifically that it does not come to dominate in the social life of a particular church. Throughout my discussion we will see that balancing the subvalues that make up moving by the Spirit is far from easy, and it is in large part the efforts of believers to keep charisma and prosperity in their proper order that give Copperbelt Pentecostalism its shape.

OUTLINE OF THE BOOK

This book examines the role of Pentecostalism in making life on the Zambian Copperbelt possible by showing how believers move by the Spirit. In chapter 1 I provide the ethnographic background for my argument. I begin by responding to James Ferguson's (1999) well-known study of Kitwe, which portrayed the Copperbelt as a place of decline and despair. In contrast to Ferguson's description, I situate the Copperbelt in a broader historical context of boom and bust, with regular cycles of prosperity as well as poverty. This is one of the main reasons for the optimism I found during my fieldwork. Chapter 1 also offers a description of Nsofu, focused on those features of township life that facilitate moving, namely economic diversity and the large number of Pentecostal churches. In addition, I trace the development of Pentecostalism in Zambia, beginning with the arrival of the first Pentecostal missionaries in the 1950s.

Building on this broad social and religious context, chapter 2 explores moving as a value, an animating idea that gives social life on the Copperbelt its shape. I show how people in Nsofu structure their relationships around the possibility of moving through two types of social ties. Most important here are relationships of patronage, or "dependence" (Ferguson 2013), which connect poorer people to those with greater economic and social resources. People also move through relationships that produce alternating indebtedness, including rotating credit associations and the "committees" that finance expensive events like weddings. In both cases moving requires asymmetry, which makes these ties particularly vulnerable to the leveling forces of economic downturn, and I conclude by describing how events like the 2008–2009 financial crisis have impacted the social world of Nsofu. It is these economic factors, coupled with a cultural emphasis on novelty, that make Pentecostalism especially compelling.

In chapter 3 I begin my analysis of Pentecostalism in Nsofu by exploring the relationships in which Pentecostal adherence embeds believers. For many people in Nsofu, Pentecostal membership is constituted by their connection to a church leader, whose superior spiritual power is able to transform what they call "stubborn situations" such as childlessness or unemployment. The other relational axis on which Pentecostal membership turns is lateral networks of collective prayer. Prayer in Pentecostal groups creates a rolling tide of ritual energy that carries everyone along with it, and like connections to church leaders, the relationships that form through prayer also have the power to effect change. The pivotal role of these relationships reveals moving by the Spirit as a central Pentecostal value, and I conclude with a discussion of how moving by the Spirit is realized in displays of charisma and prosperity.

Chapter 4 examines how the relationships formed in Pentecostal churches—both vertical ties to church leaders and horizontal ties among laypeople—are worked out through ritual. Over the course of a Sunday morning worship service, believers move toward increasingly hierarchical practices like preaching, demonstrating the primacy of ties to church leaders in the Pentecostal relational world. However, egalitarian practices like prayer nevertheless persist throughout the ritual, reminding everyone that charismatic authority is by definition unstable. At any moment, the authority of the pastor may be challenged, and his position as a spiritual leader given to someone else. This potential for charismatic hierarchy to be upended serves as an important safeguard against what one believer called "corruption." By this she was referring to the fact that Pentecostal pastors are regularly faced with the temptation to show special attention to those members of their churches who are most likely to make financial contributions to their families and ministries. From the perspective of poorer believers, in particular, this presents a problem, a problem that Pentecostals on the Copperbelt are always trying to solve. Central to this process is the need to keep charisma and prosperity, the two subvalues that make up moving by the Spirit, in their proper order, and more specifically to keep prosperity from becoming the dominant force in Pentecostal social life. The difficulty of keeping prosperity in its proper place is a central preoccupation of Copperbelt Pentecostals, and I examine their efforts toward this end in chapters 5 through 7.

Chapter 5 explores the tension between charisma and prosperity through a discussion of gender, especially as it relates to church leadership. In Pentecostal congregations on the Copperbelt, as in other parts of the world, women are generally not given the same authority as men, despite the democratic thrust of Pentecostal theology. Rather than argue, as others have done, that the subordination of women in Pentecostal groups is simply an extension of dominant ideas about gender into the church, I show that on the Copperbelt Pentecostal gender politics are a result of the need to keep prosperity in its proper place. This, I argue, following Marilyn Strathern (1988), is because prosperity and charisma represent social orientations that are both gendered and gendering. Prosperity is a female social orientation, while charisma is a male social orientation. By subordinating female leaders, then, believers are also subordinating prosperity, attempting in the process to keep it in its proper place.

Chapter 6 is also focused on the relationship between charisma and prosperity, this time through an analysis of "seed offerings," the small gifts associated with the prosperity gospel that are believed to result in large blessings for the giver. All Copperbelt Pentecostals acknowledge the power of seed offerings, but they are likewise keenly aware of the problems they raise. To wit, if the central concern of Copperbelt laypeople is that a pastor will begin to "choose" (*ukusala*), as they put it, the wealthier members of their congregations, then occasions that call for a display of wealth in the form of giving are especially problematic. Through a careful examination of the different registers through which believers interpret seed offerings, I show how believers keep prosperity in its proper place even in this socially dangerous practice. By focusing on the priestly capacities of the leaders who receive a gift on God's behalf, Pentecostals work to protect seed offerings from the taint of corruption, allowing relationships between leaders and laypeople to develop through socially productive exchange.

I examine a similar balancing act between registers in chapter 7 by focusing on a large party given for Pastor Mwanza's wife. Like seed offerings, donations to this party sparked fears of choosing, since not everyone in the congregation was able to contribute the same amount toward the event. Those who gave the most were members of a subset of Pentecostal laity that I call "super-members." These believers are both spiritually devout and materially wealthy, and as such they occupy a difficult position. On the one hand, super-members affirm the power of a church leader to help people move, power to which all members of a congregation appeal. On the other, they enjoy a degree of closeness to the pastor that, in the light of their wealth, makes other believers nervous about corruption. Although the ambivalent status of super-members made the kitchen mending a risky event, these believers also played a central role in making it ritually successful. In the run-up to the kitchen mending, super-members worked hard to protect Mrs. Mwanza from the conflict that surrounded the party. This in turn allowed her to continue in her role as the social lynchpin of the congregation and as an icon of moving by the Spirit. At great cost to themselves, super-members kept prosperity in its proper place.

While the tools that believers use to navigate the relationship between charisma and prosperity can be very effective, they sometimes fail, despite the best efforts of believers. In chapter 8, I examine what happens when Pentecostal social relationships break down after the promise of moving by the Spirit is not realized. Under these circumstances, some people decide that they no longer want to be part of Pentecostal communities, but most will simply choose to try their luck in another church, perhaps one of the new fellowships that regularly spring up in Nsofu and neighboring communities. My goal in this chapter is not to overemphasize the failures of Pentecostalism, but rather to show how the movement of believers from church to church serves as a mechanism of valuation, raising and lowering different congregations on the Copperbelt religious landscape. This analysis in turn allows us to revisit prominent social scientific arguments about schism, and to challenge these arguments by demonstrating that schism is about realizing values.

I conclude by briefly exploring those characteristics of Pentecostalism that make it especially effective at making claims about value—about what constitutes the good life. As a religion that is remarkably capable of resonating with local concerns wherever it is taken up, while at the same time critically engaging with local cultural models in a way that demands a response, Pentecostalism represents a potent framework for reimagining the terms of the good. This capacity for creative value reconfiguration or realization is, I argue, a key component of Pentecostalism's worldwide success. I close my argument by showing how the theory of value I have developed in this book responds to materialist critiques of the anthropology of Christianity by bringing together the ideological framework of Pentecostalism with the political economic context of the Copperbelt. In this analysis, Pentecostalism emerges not as an epiphenomenal manifestation of neoliberal capitalist power, but rather as a way of acting in the world, a way of making life possible.

CHAPTER 1

Boom and Bust, Revival and Renewal

The Copperbelt is, to borrow a turn of phrase from one of the reviewers of this book, one of anthropology's "longstanding laboratories" (see also Schumaker 2001: 75–116). Ethnographers have been working in this particular province of what is now Zambia for nearly a century, and have left behind an extraordinary body of work. In particular, beginning in 1937 anthropologists associated with the Rhodes-Livingstone Institute (RLI), the first social science research institute established in Africa, did pioneering studies that fundamentally shaped scholarly understanding of the region. Through their analyses of urbanization, the shifting relational patterns associated with wage labor, and the apparently fading importance of ethnic loyalties, RLI researchers fixed the Copperbelt in the anthropological imagination as a site in which to examine social change. Insofar as this is the case, for anthropologists the Copperbelt has served as an idea as much as a location. While the classic studies of the RLI and subsequent research in urban Zambia inform the discussion that follows, I do not attempt to provide a survey of Copperbelt anthropology here. This has already been very ably done both with regard to the theoretical contributions of the Manchester School (Werbner 1984) and the research culture of the RLI (Schumaker 2001). My more modest aim in this chapter is simply to capture the Copperbelt as I have found it, and more specifically to paint a picture of Nsofu, the Kitwe neighborhood that provides the context for my analysis.

Kitwe residents generally regard Nsofu as a "middle-class" township, which in Zambia means that it is a place where a sizable number of residents are in formal-sector (if not necessarily salaried) employment. While living in Nsofu is not the same as living in one of the high-status, "low-density" neighborhoods of Parklands or Riverside, it is a significant improvement on life in a shantytown or former mine townships like Buchi or Wuzakile. This means that Nsofu is an aspirational place. Poor people move to Nsofu in hopes of escaping some of the scourges of shantytown life, while those with greater means are attracted to the township because it offers the opportunity for them to construct their own homes, as it is one of the places in Kitwe where the city council is offering plots for new houses. Construction of a new home may seem like a different sort of aspiration from renting a few rooms in Nsofu, but both strategies are of a piece, part of a large-scale social project through which rich and poor alike seek to make moving happen.

Recent work on middle-class experience and identity in sub-Saharan Africa has highlighted the "uneasy privilege" (Sumich 2016: 5) that accompanies a higher class status than that enjoyed by most people on the continent. In part this unease is a function of the overabundance of qualified labor alongside a shortage of permanent jobs. A great deal of formal sector employment in places like the Copperbelt is offered on a contract basis, which translates into a lack of job security even for educated professionals (Spronk 2012: 64–76). Middle-class identity is also precarious insofar as it is increasingly propped up by debt, which finances the purchases that index economic status (James 2015). Finally, the greatest source of insecurity for the middle class is the obligation to care for an ever-widening network of kin and neighbors (Sumich 2016). As we will see in this chapter, the obligation that follows from one's status as a middle-class person is written into the very built environment of Nsofu.

My description in this chapter focuses on those features of Nsofu that make it a particularly good place to make moving happen, namely, the economic diversity of the township and its large number of Pentecostal congregations. Economic diversity is relevant because moving is most often realized through social relationships that span differences in status, particularly economic status. Similar relational asymmetries are found in Pentecostal congregations, the second aspect of Nsofu life that helps to facilitate moving. Before going on to explore these elements, however, I must first take a moment to update the Copperbelt ethnographic record, so to speak, and in so doing help to set it straight.

MANAGING *EXPECTATIONS*

It is safe to say that if anthropologists have read one book about the Copperbelt, they have read James Ferguson's *Expectations of Modernity* (1999). Ferguson carried out fieldwork in Kitwe in the late 1980s, a time of economic crisis triggered by a rapid drop in copper prices alongside a global spike in the cost of fuel. Real incomes fell dramatically during this period, as did most metrics of development. In the light of these circumstances, Ferguson's treatment focuses on the apparent reversal of the "modernist metanarrative," as he dubs the view that the Copperbelt had been on track for its own industrial revolution (see Ferguson 1999: 16). Faced instead with the prospect of lower incomes, less education, and shorter life expectancies than his informants' parents had known, the Copperbelt seemed to be heading "down, down, down," as one resident put it (Ferguson 1999: 13).

During the time of Ferguson's fieldwork, the population of the Copperbelt was shrinking, and he relates the experiences of several miners who moved to rural villages after losing their jobs in town. Over the years I've had several colleagues ask, upon hearing that I work on the Copperbelt, if anyone still lived there; the impression they had was that people had more or less cleared out when the bottom fell out of the economy in the 1980s. I'm sure that this question was asked with at least a bit of irony, but it nevertheless suggests that Ferguson's analysis has fixed the Copperbelt in the minds of many anthropologists as a place of desolation and despair. In part, this impression can be attributed to the very particular moment at which he did his fieldwork—though, as I noted in the introduction, it also reflects a disciplinary emphasis on the cultural semiotics of economic crisis. There is, however, more to the story of the Copperbelt than what *Expectations* reveals, as a quick glance at the region's subsequent economic history makes clear.

The downward turn in the Zambian economy continued for years after Ferguson finished his fieldwork. Structural adjustment measures implemented in the 1990s succeed in curbing inflation, but at tremendous human costs; the result was widespread unemployment and a massive increase in overall poverty levels, despite rising economic growth rates (Bloemen 2016). By 1998, 71 percent of the Zambian population was living below the poverty line (McCulloch et al. 2000). The Zambian writer Binwell Sinyangwe captures the mood of this period in his novella *A Cowrie of Hope* (2000: 14):

These were the nineties. The late nineties. They were lean years. They were the years of each person for himself and hope only under the shadow of the gods. No one wanted to give because no one had anything to spare. The rains were bad and so the crops and the harvest were bad too. Without what to sell from the fields people had no money. Even chiefs and headmen who usually had a grain or two more than the ordinary people, roamed the land without an *ngwee* in hand. The days were truly hard.

Eventually, however, Zambia's fortunes began to change. Between 2000 and 2005 the price of copper, Zambia's primary export, increased on the global market by 102.9 percent, owing primarily to a massive growth in demand for primary product exports in China (Zafar 2007). In 2006 China opened one of the first manufacturing special economic zones in Africa on the Copperbelt (there is another in Lusaka), further cementing the central role that Chinese investment has played in the Zambian economy since the turn of the century.[1] Between 2002 and 2005, GDP grew by 4.7 percent per annum (Central Statistical Office 2006). GDP is of course a poor measure of individual welfare, but when I first moved to the Copperbelt in 2003 I found some signs of this growth in the experiences of people I got to know in the city of Chingola. An example here is the young family of a miner I call Bashi Mumba. Bashi Mumba's wife had trained as a schoolteacher and, in an entrepreneurial move common in the aftermath of structural adjustment, had opened her own primary school in a former mining township. The couple owned a small Toyota sedan, of which they were immensely proud, and their living room contained a large television set. They were financing the tertiary education of Bana Mumba's brother, in addition to caring for their own children. The future, in short, looked very bright.

This period of steady growth was abruptly cut short by the 2008–2009 global financial crisis, an ominous phrase that people on the Copperbelt soon replaced with the shorthand English term "global." When the price of copper on the international market fell precipitously in 2008, the number of mining jobs in Zambia was reduced by 27 percent (Ndulo et al. 2009: 21). This number does not include those who were employed on a contract basis, who represent a significant number of those working in the mining sector; since contract labor was greatly reduced during the crisis, even a conservative estimate of the number of contract jobs lost dramatically increases the number of people left unemployed by the *global* (Ndulo et al. 2009: 19).[2] In addition, the value of the kwacha declined sharply during this period, depreciating by roughly 40 percent against the dollar between October 2008 and April

2009 (te Velde et al. 2010: 52).³ The primary effect of the drop in the kwacha's value was an increase in the price of imports. A sizable number of those employed in the informal sector purchase their wares outside of Zambia, and as the kwacha lost value, much of this transborder trade ground to a halt; where it did continue, increased expenses on the supply side meant much higher costs for customers. Sales on the Copperbelt, already hurt by layoffs, were further hampered by rising prices.

Since the crisis of 2008–2009, the Copperbelt economy has witnessed further periods of expansion and contraction. Returning to Nsofu in 2013 I found the vacant land surrounding the township filled with dozens of new houses in the latest styles. As we will see, ongoing construction in Nsofu ensures the continued economic diversity of the township, as partially finished houses provide ready accommodation for the community's poor. My neighbors pointed to the new houses and cars with pride, seeing in them a clear marker that their community was moving. This period of visible development was short-lived, however, and by 2015 *Forbes* reported that the kwacha was the worst performing currency in the world (Guest 2015). At the time of this writing (2016), the kwacha has recovered again, thanks primarily to an increase in copper prices.

In short, the economic history of the Copperbelt, not only since Ferguson's writing, but also well before it (Macmillan 1993), has been characterized by regular cycles of boom and bust. In an economy dominated by a single commodity it could hardly be otherwise, as the changing fortunes of the mines send regular waves of prosperity and penury rolling across neighborhoods like Nsofu. Returning to Ferguson's work, it is clear that the downturn of the 1980s did not, as he thought, trigger an upending of the modernist metanarrative, an end to Copperbelt life as the people who lived there knew it. It was simply one very difficult moment in a volatile political economy that has historically been marked as much by "ingenuity, resourcefulness, and essential optimism" (Macmillan 1993: 712) as by despair and "abjection," a key term in Ferguson's analysis. Indeed, one could argue that the periodic disruption of the Copperbelt economy fuels hopefulness in times of growth, just as moments of free fall on a roller-coaster help propel the riders up the next incline. As Owen Sichone puts it in his critique of Ferguson, "Optimism surely is based on the knowledge that others have been through decline before and survived" (2001: 379).

This sustained (and sustaining) hope for the future, the forward pitch of moving, is the subject of this book. While there has been no shortage of crisis on the Copperbelt in the thirteen years I have worked there, neither has there been a shortage of optimism. My aim in the discussion that follows is to tease out the mechanisms behind this hopefulness in a context particularly well suited to this topic of study. This brings us to a more detailed description of Nsofu.

SETTING THE SCENE: A PORTRAIT OF NSOFU

Nsofu is a rambling collection of houses situated on the outskirts of Kitwe, the largest city on the Copperbelt and the region's commercial hub.[4] From Nsofu one can just glimpse the smokestacks and cooling towers of the Nkana mine, which are more visible at night when illuminated by a blaze of floodlights. Turning your back to the mine and walking just over a mile to the other end of the township, you come to the far edge of Nsofu. To the left there is a massive power line that connects the township with the city's electric grid. Straight ahead the land quickly falls away to a broad expanse of forested savannah dotted with trees and boulders. Further on, the Kafue River winds its way south, where it will eventually plunge over the Kafue Gorge dam before joining the Zambezi. A serpentine strip of tarmac runs down the middle of Nsofu, but the remaining roads are unpaved, or were paved so long ago that they are now a jumble of stones and crumbled asphalt, rutted by wear and rain. Cutting across these roads are dozens of hard-packed footpaths, which take advantage of vacant lots and gaps between fences to create a network of shortcuts. The fastest way to get most places in Nsofu is therefore on foot, and during my fieldwork I walked several miles a day as I called on different people in the neighborhood or went to Pentecostal meetings.

Nsofu is a pleasant place. In the evenings the roads fill up with people coming home from work, some wearing the polyester blouses required for employees at the Shoprite supermarket, others in suits and ties or sensible pumps. Many have plastic bags on their arms, bearing bread for the next day's breakfast or perhaps vegetables to eat with dinner. Children play soccer and tag in the dusty streets, their school uniforms dripping on clotheslines strung alongside their houses. Women who have been to visit neighbors make their way slowly home, meandering along in the company of their hosts, who will be sure to see them a good part of the way home (*ukubashindika*). Along the tarmac, a few charcoal braziers glow in the gathering darkness, loaded with roasted maize or cassava for sale. It should be obvious from these observations that I liked Nsofu very much. I enjoyed the call of neighbors and children in

FIGURE 1. An unfinished plot with a "cabin" in the back (behind the bricks and drying clothes). The potatoes in the foreground are for sale.

the evening, the cool air rolling up from the river, and the greetings of those I passed during my morning runs along the township roads.

Some of the houses in Nsofu were formerly company housing for the mine, or homes built for government workers that have since been privatized. Others were or are being built as part of a "site and service" scheme sponsored by the Kitwe City Council, which offered plots of land with electricity and water hookups to those willing to develop them. While some of these houses have long since been completed and are ringed with fruit trees and bougainvillea, many others are not yet finished. One of the implications of this ongoing process of construction is that the township is dotted with small "cabins" built on larger plots that, if all goes well, will one day boast big houses (Nielsen 2011). Piles of cement and stacks of bricks are heaped next to front doors, and foundation slabs or trenches for footings stretch out in front of the tiny cabins, marking out the boundaries of homes that will be built someday (figure 1). Other houses are further along in the process of construction, with walls and a roof, but without windows or a connection to basic services.

The variety of housing situations in Nsofu reflects the socioeconomic diversity of the township. Some residents own their homes, but most are tenants. Rent in Nsofu is quite expensive compared with other parts of Kitwe, or indeed, with other cities on the Copperbelt. As I have already noted, many Nsofu residents are in full-time professional employment. Another significant percentage earn a living through what is locally glossed as "business": trade, often informal, in everything from agricultural products brought in from rural parts of Zambia to clothes and housewares purchased in urban centers from Lusaka to Dubai. Alongside these middle-class residents of Nsofu live others whose situations are much less secure. Included here are pensioners, some widows, and those who are unemployed or underemployed. These are the people who live in the small Nsofu cabins or stay in unfinished houses, where they pay little or no rent, but instead provide security for the owner by keeping an eye on bags of cement or loose window frames.

For Nsofu's underclass, residence in the township is precarious. Many of the neighborhood's poor are on the edge of their capacity to afford even a cabin or part of an unfinished house, and a small disruption in employment, or the unexpected expense of a funeral or an illness, can put them irrecoverably behind in payment. It is also possible that construction on a house will be completed, resulting in a hike in rent that puts it beyond the reach of those who lived there before there were windows or electricity (this is what happened to Bana Vincent, whom we will meet in the next chapter). Faced with the necessity of relocation, people try very hard to stay in Nsofu. Poorer residents said that they were afraid their children would learn "bad manners" in a township where the cost of living was lower. In many such places they would also have to contend with increased crime, as well as smaller houses, shared toilets, and an overall higher population density. A young mother named Bana Charles told me once that she had gotten used to (*ukubelela*) Nsofu, where she was living with her two young sons in her parents' home, and that she was determined not to lose her foothold in a more middle-class life. For Bana Charles this goal proved illusive, and in time I watched her, like several other informants, relocate to townships in other parts of the city. Bana Charles had followed a new husband to a more dangerous and densely populated neighborhood, where her growing household shared two small rooms without indoor plumbing. Bana Charles tried to keep a positive attitude, however, and on my last trip to Zambia she was happy to tell me that her family had moved a few blocks nearer to Nsofu. "We're heading that direction," she said, coming closer (*ukupalaminako*) bit by bit.

While part of what made Nsofu a desirable place to live was the difference in the built environment, the sense of security and of class distinction, I would argue that the primary reason that Bana Charles did not want to leave was because Nsofu offered opportunities for moving. This is not just a question of social mobility, of living in a better neighborhood. Rather, as the foregoing description makes clear, Nsofu was a place where it was possible to develop relationships with neighbors of a different social status, relationships that might in turn help to make moving happen. People of all social classes live cheek by jowl in Nsofu, as plots are small and houses are very close together. When the owner of a new house with satellite television lives next door to an underemployed carpenter and his young family, the possibility of a social connection between these two households increases. The potential for moving in Nsofu is not just a result of the township's economic diversity, however, but was also connected to its large number of Pentecostal churches. I describe these congregations in a moment, after first providing a brief account of Pentecostal expansion in Zambia.

CHRISTIAN INNOVATION IN ZAMBIA: A SHORT HISTORY

Compared with other parts of southern and central Africa, Christian missions in the British protectorate of Northern Rhodesia developed rather slowly due to the low population density in much of the territory (Taylor and Lehmann 1961: 21). Over time, however, people began to convert throughout Northern Rhodesia's rural areas, and by the early 1920s there was a significant Christian presence in many village settings. Despite this rural expansion of Christianity, converts who went to the growing cities of the Copperbelt to look for work found themselves without a church of their own. Missionaries had neglected the Copperbelt because it was understood that residence at the mines was temporary. The result of this lacuna was a spontaneous Christian movement, a new church made up of Africans from different denominational backgrounds. In 1925, this group was formally established as the Union Church of the Copperbelt, and it operated independently for nearly a decade before missionaries eventually set up their own churches in Copperbelt towns (Taylor and Lehmann 1961: 33–56).

The formation of the Union Church of the Copperbelt is just one example in a long history of Christian religious innovation in Northern Rhodesia and later Zambia. Most famous here is the Lumpa Church, founded by

Alice Lenshina in the early 1950s. Following a miraculous recovery from a coma, Lenshina claimed to have met with Jesus Christ and was baptized at the nearby Presbyterian mission. In time Lenshina's followers set up a new church outside the established mission, which they called "Lumpa" (Superior).[5] Similar groups include the Sweetheart Church, another indigenous development with Catholic roots (Hinfelaar 1994, Burlington 2004). Also important have been Jehovah's Witnesses, which historically represented "a vehicle of religious protest" (Hinfelaar 1994: 43; Assimeng 1970), and African Independent Churches, particularly those of Zimbabwean origin (Jules-Rosette 1975, Dillon-Malone 1978, Kirsch 2008). Taken together, these examples point to the parallel importance of emergent religious forms, established ecclesiastical frameworks, and transnational networks. Each of these elements is crucial to the most recent generation of Zambian religious innovators: Pentecostals.[6]

Pentecostalism first arrived in Zambia via missionaries from the Apostolic Church of Pentecost of Canada and the Pentecostal Assemblies of God Canada (PAOC), who came in 1954 and 1955, respectively (Burgess and van der Maas 2010). These missionaries were what are usually called "classical" Pentecostals, representatives of denominations founded on the heels of the 1906 Azusa Street Revival in Los Angeles. Broadly speaking, classical Pentecostalism emphasizes personal piety and holiness, as well as separation from the world, including a rejection of conspicuous consumption. Zambians talk about early Pentecostals as those who do not permit women to wear jewelry or to chemically treat their hair. Missionary-established Pentecostalism continues to play an important part in the country's religious life; in particular, the Pentecostal Assemblies of God Zambia (which was born from the PAOC mission) is now the largest Pentecostal denomination in the nation, with more than one thousand churches. However, it is telling that this very successful group has moved away from many of the emphases of classical Pentecostalism, a transformation that reflects a broader theological shift toward "neo-Pentecostalism."[7] In large part this is a shift away from ascetic holiness to the prosperity gospel (see Corten and Marshall-Fratani 2001: 7). The vanguard of this new form of Pentecostalism has been churches that are nondenominational and locally initiated. In Zambia, as in much of sub-Saharan Africa, it is neo-Pentecostalism that has served as the primary engine of Pentecostal growth since the mid-1980s.

The easiest way to track Pentecostalism's growth in Zambia is through the numbers.[8] Today, the vast majority of the roughly 13 million Zambians are Christians (95.5 percent according to the 2010 census), and more than 3.8 million could be classified as "Renewalists"—that is, as classical Pentecostals, charismatics (i.e., members of mainline denominations who engage in Pentecostal practices), and neo-Pentecostals. Of these groups the last is by far the largest, comprising more than two million Zambians (Johnson and Zurlo 2014). While these numbers are helpful, they do not tell the whole story. On the Copperbelt there are many people who would not describe themselves as Pentecostals when asked, but who nevertheless participate in Pentecostal religious activities. This may be in the context of a mainline congregation, as in the case of charismatic Catholics, or perhaps through an interdenominational prayer meeting. Add to this auxiliary Pentecostal participation the fact that mainline churches in Zambia have been increasingly "Pentecostalized" in recent years (Cheyeka 2006), borrowing ritual and aesthetic forms from Pentecostalism, and it becomes clear that on the Copperbelt local religious practice is perhaps best described as a continuum of Pentecostal participation that incorporates a large percentage of an overwhelmingly Christian population. In Nsofu, historic mission churches, as well as older and newer forms of Pentecostalism, are all features of the local religious landscape.

NSOFU'S RELIGIOUS SCENE

Like most urban neighborhoods in Zambia, Nsofu is home to dozens of churches. The biggest congregations belong to missionary-established groups, in this case, the Catholic and Seventh Day Adventist churches, and the United Church of Zambia (a denomination born from the Union Church). Smaller Christian bodies, such as the Baptist and Dutch Reformed churches, are also represented. Finally, and most importantly for our purposes, there are more than a dozen Pentecostal groups in Nsofu. The oldest Pentecostal church in the township is Life Chapel, founded in 1995 by Pastor Kalanga, who has remained at the helm of this congregation ever since. Life Chapel is also the largest of Nsofu's Pentecostal churches, with more than one hundred members in 2008. Life Chapel was connected to a transnational Pentecostal body, as were two of the other Pentecostal congregations in Nsofu. When I first began my fieldwork in 2008, the remaining Pentecostal groups in Nsofu were independent, and most of them met in private homes or rented spaces, primarily classrooms.

In addition to established churches, a significant amount of Pentecostal ritual activity in Nsofu takes place in midweek gatherings, the most popular of which are interdenominational "fellowships." These groups meet for prayer, the practice that is most emphasized here, and in fact some fellowships are simply referred to as "prayers" (*amapepo*). There will also be singing and sometimes a sermon. While fellowships do not meet on Sundays, they operate very much like churches. In particular, they often have a formalized leadership structure, or at least a designated leader, who is usually called a pastor or a prophet. This person is in charge of the group's ritual practice and also uses fellowship meetings as a platform for providing personalized religious services like prophecy and deliverance. Alongside this dense network of fellowships, there is an even looser field of Pentecostal membership in Nsofu, most commonly associated with "the mountain" on the edge of the township. This rocky hill is covered with dense forest and crowned with a mobile phone tower (it is, as far as I could tell, the highest point for over a mile). Individual believers will sometimes go to the mountain to pray, drawn by the comparative privacy of this out-of-the-way place. Up-and-coming pastors can also be found at the mountain, where believers may seek them out for prayer and where they may even hold informal meetings.

In short, Nsofu is a place that is permeated by Pentecostalism. Pastor Kalanga once told me that by his count there were forty-three pastors living in Nsofu—nearly one for every five hundred people. There are new fellowships springing up all the time, announcing their presence only by the unmistakable sound of prayer spilling out someone's front door, attracting a crowd only by word of mouth. Groups split and new churches form in a regular process of congregational mitosis. As I discuss in more detail in chapter 8, individual believers move frequently from church to church, and sometimes maintain connections to more than one group at once. The sheer density of Pentecostal congregations in Nsofu makes this easy, and if someone wanted to go to a different Pentecostal meeting each day of the week—as I did early on in my fieldwork—it would not be difficult to do so.

While I have visited dozens of Pentecostal groups in the time I have spent on the Copperbelt, my fieldwork focused on three small congregations that, at least at the beginning of my research, were all independent churches with fewer than one hundred members. I chose to focus on these groups for two reasons. First, while not all Zambian Pentecostal congregations fit this description (i.e., nondenominational and small), the vast majority do, and the churches I studied therefore provide a representative picture that can be used to help understand Pentecostalism in Zambia more generally. Second, I wanted to offer a point of contrast to most anthropological work on Pentecostalism, which has overwhelmingly focused on mega-churches rather than smaller congregations. Since the three churches that I studied represent the backbone of my ethnography, I describe them in some detail here.

Freedom Bible Church

Pastor Ephraim first started Freedom Bible Church in 2002 as a midweek interdenominational prayer meeting, and when the group grew large enough he began holding Sunday morning services as well. This move represents a common trajectory for Pentecostal groups in Nsofu. Fellowships often become churches, and in some cases that is the leader's plan from the beginning—to establish a church by establishing a fellowship first. When I arrived at Freedom Bible Church in February 2008 the group was by all accounts at its peak. Each Sunday the classroom the congregation used for worship was bursting at the seams, with latecomers forced to stand outside or in an adjacent room during the service. Church members began to talk of registering the congregation with the Kitwe City Council, the first step toward securing a plot of land for their own building. This is the great dream of all Pentecostal churches, though few are able to make it a reality.

This period of heady growth continued for the better part of a year. However, in late 2008 a scandal erupted when two women came forward, both claiming to be pregnant by Pastor Ephraim. The church leadership asked him to take a leave of absence from preaching and individual ministry—no praying for people or offering prophecy—while they figured out what to do. With their most charismatic leader out of the pulpit, the remaining members of the pastoral team did their best to keep the congregation going, but church members felt that these other pastors were less skilled and often nodded off during their sermons. By the time I left the field in July 2009, Pastor Ephraim had been restored to his position, even though the situation that had caused his removal had not to my knowledge been resolved. It seemed the church leadership felt they had to reinstate Pastor Ephraim if the congregation was to continue to function. Already scores of people had left when faced with the loss of the leader that had been the church's main attraction. While Pastor Ephraim's return to ministry seemed to stem this tide, during my doctoral fieldwork Freedom never recovered the momentum it had when I first arrived.

When I returned to Nsofu in 2013 I found that some of the dreams of the glory days of Freedom Bible Church had become reality. The

FIGURE 2. Pouring cement for the floor of the Freedom Bible Church chapel in 2013 with Pastor Ephraim and Mr. Moyo, the church administrator.

congregation had been given a plot of land on the far edge of Nsofu, near the mountain where Pastor Ephraim had once held prayer meetings. There was no money for a building, but church members had built a small chapel (*cikopa*) from timber offcuts and filled it with narrow wooden benches (figure 2). Each week a few of the most dedicated believers arrived early to sweep the chapel and hang curtains around the room, covering the rough walls with panels of mismatched polyester lace. While the church remained small, believers proudly told me of the new "branch" congregations that had been opened under the banner of Freedom Bible Church, one in a different part of Kitwe and another in a nearby rural area. In these churches Pastor Ephraim was referred to as the "bishop," as he oversaw them all, and a few of his friends jokingly referred to him as "ba Archy," a suggestion that he was or one day would be an archbishop.

Higher Calling

As with Freedom Bible Church, the popularity of the group I call Higher Calling was evident from the first time I visited. In early 2008 the average attendance at midweek prayer gathering on Wednesday mornings was over one hundred people, a significant number of whom returned on Saturdays for the weekly fast. Around two dozen Higher Calling members had also started holding church services on Sunday mornings. The group met at the home of its popular founder, Bana Mfuwe, in a chapel similar to the one that Freedom Bible Church would eventually erect on its plot: timber offcuts nailed to a long wooden frame. The interior was decorated with curtain panels, carpets, tinsel, and silk flowers. A collection of tarps and empty maize meal bags covered the roof, providing protection from the sun, but not necessarily from the rain, and members of the group sometimes held their bibles under umbrellas during particularly heavy showers.

Bana Mfuwe was without question the primary attraction at Higher Calling. She had no formal religious training but was nevertheless a gifted speaker and singer. Her sermons usually focused on encouraging members of the group to remain true to their faith and continue to expect that God would "come through" for them. As I discuss in chapter 5, Bana Mfuwe often used her own experience as proof of this promise. While the early years of her Pentecostal commitment had been rocky, she had persevered and (here Pentecostals would say, "as a result") had been blessed on every front; she dressed well, had a nice house, healthy children, and a happy marriage. Not long after I arrived in Nsofu I learned that Bana Mfuwe planned to move to South Africa, where her husband had been offered a job. When it came time for her to leave Nsofu, Bana Mfuwe held a final worship service in the Higher Calling chapel, where she announced that a widow named Bana Chilomba would take her place as head of the fellowship.

After Bana Mfuwe left, Higher Calling members dismantled their chapel and carried the materials several blocks to the home of church members Mr. and Mrs. Ntembe, where they rebuilt the structure over a freshly poured cement slab. They were not able to stay in this new location for long, though, as Mr. Ntembe lost his job a few months later, and soon after his house as well. In the absence of a central, rent-free location, the congregation found itself in a difficult situation. After searching unsuccessfully for someone who might offer his home as a new meeting place, Bana Chilomba decided that the group would use a nearby community center for midweek prayers and a school classroom for Sunday morning meetings.

All of these changes took a toll on Higher Calling membership. As with Freedom Bible Church, the removal of a popular leader was followed by a significant drop in weekly attendance. Eventually, Bana Chilomba also left Higher Calling, and when I returned to the field in 2013 the group was being led by Pastor Conrad, one of the few men who had been part of Higher Calling leadership. Every few years Bana Mfuwe would return to Nsofu to great fanfare, and her former followers would rent one of the local church buildings so that she could hold meetings. Many of those who had long since left Higher Calling attended these special events, which nourished the connection they still felt to Bana Mfuwe. All the same, in her absence the group was not what it had been.

Key of David

Key of David Pentecostal Church was led by Pastor Mwanza and his wife, both of whom had trained at a Bible college in Lusaka before moving to the Copperbelt to "plant" a church, as Pentecostals put it. During my fieldwork I lived in the Mwanza home and therefore saw a side of Key of David that I did not have access to in other churches. Members of the congregation were always stopping by to see the pastor and his wife, and much of what I learned about the all-important relationship between leaders and laypeople was picked up in the Mwanza home. Bible studies, prayer meetings, and the occasional deliverance session were held in our sitting room, giving me exceptional access to Pentecostal ritual life. I was able to ask Pastor and Mrs. Mwanza about things that I had observed in their church much more easily than I was able to follow up with other Pentecostal leaders. And finally, because I lived with the Mwanza family, I became associated with them in the minds of many Nsofu residents. This had some drawbacks, as I often suspected that people were more cautious when I was around, careful to be on their best behavior lest a prominent pastor learn of their moral shortcomings. But my association with the Mwanzas also had advantages; the inside knowledge about Pentecostal communities that I was assumed to have developed while living in a pastor's house prompted conversations that I doubt would have happened otherwise.

Key of David differed from the other two congregations in my study in several respects. While both Freedom Bible Church and Higher Calling held meetings either in private homes or rented spaces, Key of David had its own building—a large cinderblock structure positioned prominently on the tarmac road (figure 3). The Mwanzas had been able to build a church with notable speed thanks to a grant from their former

FIGURE 3. Outside Key of David in 2013 (the sign has been altered to obscure the church's real name).

Bible college. While, like the other churches in my study, Key of David had been an independent congregation when I first began to visit it, soon after I left the field in 2009 the church joined the Pentecostal Assemblies of God.

In addition to these differences in meeting space and denominational affiliation, Pastor Mwanza took great care to separate himself from some of the other Pentecostal pastors in Nsofu by advocating what he called a more "holistic" model of spiritual development. Although the core message of Pastor Mwanza's sermons was similar to that of other Nsofu pastors—he too preached about prosperity and spiritual warfare—his teachings were peppered with references to things like psychology, market research, and popular business advice. Perhaps as a result of these unique features, Key of David had a larger number of professionals than the other congregations in my study, though there were a number of members whose existence was more precarious, including some who were un- or underemployed. Although in this way the church fulfilled a desire that Pastor Mwanza often expressed for congregational diversity, we will see that differences between richer and poorer members of Key of David—and especially the influence of the former in the affairs of the church—created serious problems there. This was one reason for the turnover in church membership. While believers tended to stay at Key of David longer than they did in other Nsofu congregations, over the years a significant number of people, including prominent members like the Zulus, have left this church.

As we turn our attention to how people in Nsofu work to realize moving, it will become clear that the characteristics of township life that I have highlighted here are crucial. As we have seen, Nsofu is known as a middle-class community, but this label obscures an internal economic diversity. Importantly, the presence of poor people in Nsofu has not to my knowledge affected the view that it is an aspirational place. Nsofu's status as a middle-class township has proved to be as enduring as the optimism that has thrived despite the Copperbelt's endless cycles of boom and bust. Just as these cycles represent the key to township residents' remarkable sanguinity, so the presence of people of different economic statuses is not a detriment to aspiration, but rather its driving force. It is economic difference, in other words, that makes moving happen.

CHAPTER 2

Making Moving Happen

No matter how much you manage to do for yourself, it's not enough. If you've got a decent job with decent money, it can't do you much good, because it's got to spread so far. You're always a rich man compared with your sister or your brother or your wife's cousins. You can't ever get out of debt while there's one member of the family who has to pay a fine or get sick and go to the hospital. And so it goes on. If I get an increase, what'll it help me? Someone'll have to have it to pay tax or get a set of false teeth.

—Nadine Gordimer, *A World of Strangers*

Late one evening, after I had gone to my bedroom for the night, I heard a small commotion in the Mwanzas' living room. Kicking away the mosquito net, I climbed out of bed and tied a *citenge* over my pajamas before crossing the hallway to see what was happening. Under the yellow glow of an incandescent light bulb, Pastor and Mrs. Mwanza and their daughter Musonda were struggling to cut open a large cardboard box. Inside were a dozen glass shelves, some clinking black pipes, and a few curious pieces of plastic, painted gold. Before I could ask what all of this was, Mrs. Mwanza and her husband began fastening the pipes together to make an elaborate frame. They fitted the newly built structure with the shelves and topped it with the golden fixtures, which looked a bit like horns. By the next day the new "display," as Zambians call the shelving units popular in living rooms across the country, was covered with a collection of photographs, greeting cards from special events, and silk flowers in a glass vase.

As this example of an aptly named piece of furniture indicates, Copperbelt living rooms are important sites of display. Every morning the women in a household, wives or teenaged daughters, sweep and carefully arrange their living rooms, straightening doilies over the backs of chairs and wiping dust from the top of the television. Displays like the Mwanzas' new shelves or the cooking pots lined up in the family's kitchen are, as I have argued elsewhere (Haynes 2012), key elements of the Copperbelt social world, because display is the primary way through which people in Nsofu realize the value of moving. Returning to the theoretical framing set out in the introduction, values are realized when they are given physical form, in this case through the ownership of a new item of furniture.

In this chapter I show how moving orders social relationships in Nsofu. If social life is structured by the capacity of its various elements to realize values, then on the Copperbelt the ties that people consider most important—that is, the social ties that are most highly valued—will be those that help them realize moving. As we will see, the relationships that are most effective in this regard are ties that span differences in economic status. These differences may be relatively fixed, as in the case of class difference, or they may be temporary, as in the case of differences created through a rotating credit association. An analysis of moving reveals the dynamic processes that animate Nsofu social life on both a small and large scale, as the relationships described below evolve in conversation with the changing economic fortunes of the Copperbelt. I begin my discussion by exploring in greater detail what people in Nsofu mean when they say, "Things are moving" (*fintu filesela*).

MOVING AS A COPPERBELT VALUE

At its most basic, moving is measurable progress in a specific forward direction. Those familiar with the Copperbelt ethnographic record will recognize echoes of moving in the work of earlier anthropologists. It has resonances, for example, with the "expectations" of miners laid off in the economic downturn of the 1980s (Ferguson 1999), as well as the earlier hopes of those who came of age in the decades surrounding independence (e.g., Epstein 1961). A song from that time, which serves as an epigraph in both Ferguson's (1999) *Expectations of Modernity* and A.L. Epstein's *Politics in an Urban African Community* (1958), proclaims, "Our country is going forward / and we the people too." The Nyanja-language independence anthem, "Tiyende Pamodzi," or "Let Us Go Forward," carries a similar sentiment.

Moving is measured according to a range of metrics. In part, moving refers to progress through the life-course—to the ability to grow into an adult, which in Zambia means having children and grandchildren (e.g., Richards 1982), and usually being married as well. Moving can also refer to professional and educational advancement, to completing college or receiving a promotion like Mr. Zulu did. Finally, moving means economic progress or social mobility, especially the capacity to acquire newer, better, and larger consumer goods and to build a house and fill it with nice furniture (see James 2015 for similar observations about South Africa). Moving is taking a bus if one has been traveling on foot, a taxi if one has been using a bus, and eventually owning one's own car if one has been relying on taxis. Moving is also measured in the body, and weight gain (*ukwina*) is an important marker of success and of the lack of worry that comes when one is moving properly. In practice, all of these metrics overlap. For instance, in Zambia, as in other parts of Africa (e.g., Cole and Thomas 2009), marriage is (especially for women) related to economic security and potential advancement, and this potential is strengthened by the presence of children. Likewise, education may also be a means of securing a brighter future for oneself through access to better-paying and more prestigious employment.

If moving means going forward, its absence is characterized by a lack of advancement, or worse yet, regression. People on the Copperbelt sometimes speak of being "stuck," of not being able to move, and therefore of a need to "push," which often means running around town calling in favors, knocking on the doors of government officials, or trying to get the best price at the market. As this brief description of being stuck makes clear, the opposite of moving is not standing still. On the contrary, a person who is not moving is engulfed in a flurry of frenetic activity. Between regular expenses like school fees and rent and demands for assistance from neighbors or relatives, people often find themselves rushing from one pressing need to the next. Under these circumstances, "money never sits still" (*impiya tashileikala*), and cash is "eaten" as soon as it is acquired.[1] This is why, although most Pentecostal believers are eager to take up leadership posts in their congregations, very few will volunteer to be the group's treasurer, responsible for keeping the money collected in the offering. They are afraid that they will be tempted to borrow from the church's savings when the electric bill is due. Doing so would place them in the difficult position of having to replace the money out of resources that are already stretched thin. Faced with a steady stream of needs and demands, it is very difficult to make any progress; in other words, under such circumstances, moving is almost impossible.

If the absence of moving is characterized by frenzied activity, markers of its presence are equally paradoxical. In contrast to the rushing about associated with eating money, moving effectively slows time down by pushing back against the eroding effects of the urgent. Faced with a steady stream of demands, moving represents an intervention, a stake in the ground. Typically, this means transforming liquid assets into something more enduring, a tangible marker of progress. Here, the paradigmatic form that moving takes is the acquisition of a new item for the home, the purchase of something that is "better than eating," as people in Nsofu often put it, precisely because it cannot be eaten (see Haynes 2012: 132–33). A set of overstuffed chairs in the sitting room, an "upright" refrigerator, a new dress, or a Toyota sedan are all markers of moving. Much of the value of these goods stems from their capacity to withstand the economic vagaries of Copperbelt life. There may not be food at home, and people may have to scrounge just to put together enough cash for the evening meal, but a television or a new suit, or even something as small as an empty tin of Nestlé cocoa left on the kitchen shelf, sits above the ebb and flow of monthly salaries. These items help people maintain their social position, holding their place for them, as it were, until they can move further than they have up to that point. In other words, enduring status-marking goods ensure that even after months of eating one's money a family can pick up where they left off, can continue their efforts at moving forward from a point that has been secured for them by the purchase of a car or television set. Consumer goods are also a key metric of moving because their visibility, through conscious or conspicuous display, situates them in a social domain. Moving is not only progress, in other words, but *recognizable*—usually *visible*—progress, capable of being "graded and profiled" and "recognized in small nuances by others" (Guyer 2004: 147; also see Graeber 2013: 226–28).

As a value, moving is realized by and in individual social units, usually persons or households, but also (though less frequently) corporate groups such as congregations or countries. In other words, it is people or families who give moving physical form, who symbolize—even embody—this value, whether through an increasingly plump figure or residence in a brightly painted new house. However, this can only happen through social relationships.[2] In other words, moving does not simply connote progress as such, but rather progress that comes about through connections to others, especially one's friends.

UKUMFWANA: FRIENDSHIP AS MUTUALITY

Compared to other types of social ties, friendship is an oddly undertheorized topic in anthropology. One of the reasons for this is definitional; it is difficult to pin down just what constitutes friendship, and most attempts to mark its boundaries—for example, by relating it to sentiment or juxtaposing it to kinship—are vulnerable to ethnographic counterexamples that call those definitions into question. In response to this difficulty, Evan Killick and Amit Desai (2010) turn to the gains made in kinship studies as a result of the analytic move away from biological models and toward a paradigm of "relatedness" (Carsten 2000). What the idea of relatedness did for kinship was to open up the possibility that the latter might mean a range of different things in different places, and that attention to this multiplicity of forms and definitions stood to enrich, rather than confuse, the study of kinship. Killick and Desai propose taking a similar approach to friendship, allowing local understandings of this relationship to shape our interpretive models. This is what I aim to do in this section.

On the Copperbelt, friendship is best defined by mutuality. When someone describes a relationship with one of her close friends, she will often say, "*Tulaumfwana.*" The verb here, *ukumfwa*, means "to understand," but also to hear and listen, as well as to feel, both in the sense of feeling emotions (e.g., "I feel sad") and feeling sensations (e.g., "I feel cold"). The addition of the suffix *–na* makes the verb reflexive, and in this form the word is used to indicate agreement. *Ukumfwana* is the term used when describing the outcome of negotiations over a price in the market, as well as larger and more significant transactions, such as those of bride wealth. It also connotes fellow feeling and mutual understanding. Hugo Hinfelaar (1994: 70) defines *ukumfwana* as "perfect harmony." When someone says, "*Tulaumfwana,*" then, she means that she and her friend understand one another, that they hear and recognize each other, "mutually witnessing and mutually fabricating one another's lives" (Pritchett 2007: 8) in friendship. During my fieldwork, my closest friend was a woman I refer to as Bana Sam. While I had good relationships with many people in Nsofu, Bana Sam was the person with whom I felt the deepest connection, whom I could call my friend without any hesitation. I accompanied her to her parents' home in Northern Province when it came time for her to deliver her first child, and when my father and brother came to see me in Nsofu, Bana Sam and her family were the first people outside of the Mwanza household that we visited. Commenting on our friendship, Bana Sam's mother, Banukulu Sam, observed that her daughter and I "understood each other" (*mulaumfwana*).[3]

While the idea of *ukumfwana* captures an essential aspect of the mutuality of Copperbelt friendships, there are more tangible elements at work here as well. The Copperbelt is no different from most places in the world in that social life is worked out through exchange. The importance of giving is instilled at a young age in, for instance, the regular insistence that children not "refuse" (*ukutana*) others, but instead share a bit of whatever they are eating with those around them. Among adults, relationships are indexed first and foremost by the exchange of greetings, and, as we saw in the example of Mr. Zulu, to say that someone has refused to greet (*ukukana ukuposha*) is a shorthand way of indicating relational strife. Friends also exchange visits, calling on one another at home and eating together. Finally, in addition to greetings and hospitality, friends exchange gifts. This may mean bringing something along when going to visit, perhaps a pumpkin or other produce. It may also mean sending a child to ask (*ukulomba*; literally, "to beg") a friend for something needed at home, whether charcoal, an onion, or a bit of washing powder.

During my time in Nsofu it was not unusual for me to leave a neighbor's house with something extra in my bag, usually uncooked food, but occasionally an item of clothing or a photograph of my host. Over time these people also expected that I would give them gifts as well. I learned this primarily by making the mistake of stopping by a friend's house on my way home from buying something at the market. After we exchanged greetings my friend would turn her attention to the plastic bag in my hand, the contents vaguely visible through the thin blue film, before asking, "*Tupokelele?*"—literally, "Are we receiving?" I initially struggled to respond to such direct requests, and honestly found them rather affronting (see Durham 1995 for a similar example from Botswana), until I realized that in most cases they came from people with whom I was establishing a friendship, people who had often received (*ukupokelela*) me into their homes. In this context, it was reasonable for them to assume that if I came to the house with a parcel in hand it contained a gift.

In large part, the items exchanged between female friends, to focus exclusively on women for a moment, are incorporated into the ongoing movement of resources through the household.[4] This is certainly the case for the small things begged and borrowed from friends throughout the course of the week—the charcoal and onions mentioned above.[5]

While the products of exchange are therefore usually eaten along with most of the other resources that come into a household, there are nevertheless friendships in which exchange has results that are better than eating. To demonstrate what this looks like, I turn to the example of a friendship that developed between two of my informants, Bana Vincent and Bana Taida.

DIFFERENTIATION AND DEPENDENCE

When I first met Bana Vincent I found it impossible to determine how old she was. While her slim frame and preference for T-shirts and trousers suggested youth, her face was lined with care (figure 4). Bana Vincent's husband worked bussing tables at an Italian restaurant in one of Kitwe's high-income areas, a job that paid poorly. Since all they could afford were rooms in unfinished homes, Bana Vincent and her husband never lived in the same place for long, but were forced to "shift," as people say in Zambian English, whenever construction was completed on the place they were staying. This is how Bana Vincent came to know Bana Taida. The two women met when Bana Taida moved with her husband and family into the home where Bana Vincent and her husband had been staying. Bana Taida was a young mother and could usually be seen carrying her small son on her back, her older daughter tagging close behind. She had a kind, pretty face and a pleasant demeanor. During their chance meeting, Bana Vincent and Bana Taida discovered that they shared a common Pentecostal faith, and Bana Vincent invited Bana Taida to visit Freedom Bible Church, where she soon became a regular attendee.

In the following weeks and months the two women developed a close relationship. Once, while visiting Bana Vincent, I remarked that I had come by earlier in the week and not found her at home. She responded that if this happened again I should check Bana Taida's house; "If I'm not at home or at church, I am there," she said. Indeed, Bana Vincent visited her new friend nearly every day. They watched Pentecostal television in Bana Taida's living room, sipping tea or eating *nshima*, the maize porridge that is the cornerstone of the Zambian diet. They chatted and prayed and talked about their families. Bana Vincent told me once that she loved Bana Taida, and it was not difficult to see that this was true.

Despite their important similarities, the relationship between these two women was marked by an obvious difference in economic status. Financially speaking, Bana Taida was in a much better position than

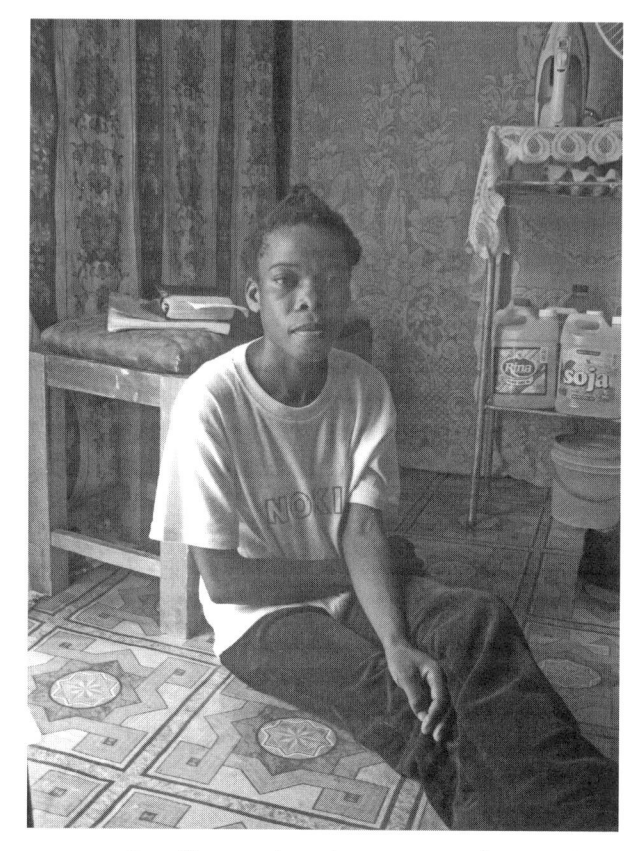

FIGURE 4. Bana Vincent at home in 2008. Her well-worn Bible and notebook full of prayers are behind her.

Bana Vincent. This was clear from their first encounter, as Bana Taida's family was moving into a house that Bana Vincent and her husband could no longer afford to rent. Bana Taida's husband had a bachelor's degree and was employed in information technology. In addition, he made some extra money repairing or refurbishing computers, which meant that their house was always a bit cluttered with circuit boards, cables, and dusty computer screens. Bana Taida was also educated, and as soon as she moved to Nsofu she began looking for work as a teacher. Eventually, Bana Taida found a job, news that was heralded at church as an answer to prayer.

Bana Taida's employment brought a change in her relationship with Bana Vincent. The two women were as close as ever, despite the fact that Bana Taida had less time to spend with her friend once she started working. In fact, it was her absence from home, coupled with the increase in her household income, which brought about the shift in their friendship. Because she would be at work all day, Bana Taida decided to employ Bana Vincent to care for her son, and to do some cooking and cleaning around the house while she was away. Bana Taida could not afford to pay much, but Bana Vincent was nevertheless optimistic about earning some money of her own. When she told me about the new arrangement, Bana Vincent explained that she hoped to be able to save her salary so that she would have money to start a small business. Her plan was to use her earnings to travel to Northwestern Province, where she had relatives, in order to buy potatoes that she could resell in Kitwe at a profit.

In this example, the combination of mutuality in friendship and asymmetry of economic status provided a chance for Bana Vincent to move. While exchange is part of all Copperbelt friendships, the specific form it takes is dictated in large part by the economic capacities of each individual. Here, Bana Vincent's friendship with Bana Taida is instructive. From the start, the fact that Bana Taida was wealthier than Bana Vincent shaped the contours of their relationship. The women primarily spent time in Bana Taida's home, which was more spacious and had a television, and this meant that when they ate together they ate at Bana Taida's house as well. Once Bana Taida started working, the asymmetry of exchange was amplified. By becoming Bana Vincent's employer, Bana Taida foregrounded the difference in their economic statuses, while at the same time providing the means for Bana Vincent to move. To be sure, exchange was never entirely one-sided. Bana Vincent worked for the money that Bana Taida gave her, just as she joined with her in praying for a job and the salvation of her husband. The mutuality that had marked their friendship from the beginning remained central to the relationship. Nevertheless, the asymmetry of their exchanges was undeniable, and this imbalance made their friendship a space within which moving became possible.

The connection between asymmetry and moving is even clearer in the case of some male friendships. While ties between women may entail the movement of gifts in a direction that disproportionately favors one person, these exchanges involve only the resources that a woman has at her disposal, namely the money she earns and whatever money she may receive from her husband, other male companion, or relatives. While Bana Taida had always helped her friend, it wasn't until she started working that she was able to support Bana Vincent in a way that made moving possible. Men, in contrast, are more likely to be working in formal sector employment, and also more likely to have relationships with people who are similarly employed. Although I do not have as much firsthand knowledge of male friendships, I have observed that men on the Copperbelt rely on connections to those with greater access to wealth and power, on friends who are in a position to become patrons. A man may call such a person his "*busa*," a term for "friend" that connotes familiarity and closeness, and they may walk down the street holding hands. A relationship with someone who is positioned to provide significant financial support or an employment reference is often the key to advancement in the competitive and complex political economy of the Copperbelt. Here again, mutuality and asymmetry come together in friendships that help individuals realize moving.

It is not difficult to see that the sorts of exchanges I have been describing here are predicated on an economic gradient. In the examples I have just outlined, a relationship with someone higher up on the economic ladder serves as a mechanism for advancement. Understood in these terms, moving is less about getting ahead than it is about being pulled up. Importantly, because moving in these examples relies on economic difference, exchanges like those we have observed between Bana Vincent and Bana Taida are not efforts at redistribution or attempts to level the economic playing field. Instead, following Jane Guyer, I would argue that what I have described here is "not a model of 'sharing,'" but rather a system in which stratification is the engine behind the transfer of resources, and therefore of moving (Guyer 2004: 147). Here, "[rich] and poor, as well as the varying shades in between, [are] necessary distinctions in a single but multifaceted social construction" (Pritchett 2001: 244). Relationships like Bana Vincent and Bana Taida's are part of an expansive social framework that incorporates a large number of people. Patrons have patrons of their own, individuals who are positioned at an even higher point on the Copperbelt economic gradient. Asymmetrical relationships therefore concatenate, reaching both up and down to form a stair-stepped social world, a long chain of patronage ties. Seen from this perspective, economic inequality is not something to be overcome, but is instead central to the Copperbelt model of a good society.

The observation that economic stratification is key to a local understanding of the good is not a terribly comfortable one for a Western academic to make. Suggesting that hierarchy of any sort might be socially significant, let alone desirable, cuts against the grain of the liberal ideals that many scholars share, raising the specter of false consciousness or worries that the ethnographer has not fully grasped the power dynamics in play (Haynes and Hickel 2016b, Peacock 2015). However unpleasant this description may be, I am convinced that it represents a central characteristic of an ideal social world as people on the Copperbelt imagine it (Haynes 2012: 129–32). In seeking to understand social life in Nsofu, it has become clear to me that the relationships I am describing here are very important to people there not in spite of the fact that they are asymmetrical, but precisely because of their asymmetry. These ties reflect the broader paradigm of "dependence" that Ferguson has recently identified as a key component of social organization throughout southern Africa (Ferguson 2013; also see Hansen 1985, Bolt 2014, Hickel 2015, Sumich 2016, Scherz 2014). Ferguson argues that throughout the region dependence plays a vital role in the composition of the person (also see Comaroff and Comaroff 2001). On the Copperbelt this means being able to realize moving, and moving, as we have seen, can only happen through relationships with other people, and more specifically people who are in a position to pull someone up. What is compelling about these ties is therefore not hierarchy as such; in other words, we cannot say that economic asymmetry is a good in and of itself. Rather, what the language of dependence highlights is the necessity of both stratification and sociality—of economic difference *and* of relationships that span that difference.

Although in the examples we have explored so far the economic asymmetry at work is relatively enduring, there are other ways to create productive differences even in relationships that develop between people of the same economic status. In order to demonstrate how these differences are produced, I turn my attention to another Nsofu friendship.

REVOLVING DIFFERENCE, OR MAKING ASYMMETRY FROM EQUALITY

Bana Mercy was widowed in 2008 when her husband was attacked and killed on his way home from work, one of the few incidences of violent crime I have heard of in Nsofu. A few years later her firstborn son, who was seriously disabled, also died, and Bana Mercy was left alone with her young daughter. She had no regular income, and survived through occasional trade and the help of her relatives. Quiet and soft-spoken, I did not know Bana Mercy well during my doctoral fieldwork. When I returned to Nsofu in 2013, however, Bana Mercy and I developed a much closer friendship, perhaps because she had moved out of her cousin's house and into the home of one of my best friends in the field, Bana Sinkala.

Bana Sinkala was divorced, and her two teenage boys spent half of their time with her and half with their father. In her divorce settlement Bana Sinkala had been awarded an unfinished house that she and her former husband had been building in Nsofu. The windows were filled with mud bricks, awaiting glazing, and there was no electricity or indoor plumbing. With nowhere else to go and without the resources to complete construction, Bana Sinkala and her sons moved into the house as it was. She cooked her meals over a charcoal brazier, perched on a stool next to a disused freezer chest and a kitchen display cabinet, reminders of her earlier life. By confining herself to a few rooms, Bana Sinkala was able to rent out other portions of the house, and this provided her with a bit of income. In addition, a small table in front of the house was usually mounded with sweet potatoes or bags of charcoal, enterprises that generated additional cash.

Unlike the other tenants in the house, Bana Mercy shared a kitchen with Bana Sinkala, though they had separate food stores and cooked their own meals. The two women helped one another out a great deal. They kept each other company and shared the work of looking after their home. They also exchanged small gifts of money, charcoal, or maize meal. In short, they supported one another in a relationship of mutuality. As with similar exchanges between friends, these efforts at assistance were mostly part of the everyday work of living, contributions that were eaten as quickly as they were received. Beyond these small-scale transactions, however, Bana Sinkala and Bana Mercy were also involved in a network of exchange that had the potential to create moving because it created difference among those who were otherwise financially equal.

One evening, Bana Mercy and I were walking back from the prayer meeting at Freedom Bible Church. As we neared her house, we stopped to greet Bana Annie, a woman I knew through Bana Sinkala, as they were members of the same church. Bana Annie and another woman, Bana Melody, shared a roadside vegetable stand stocked with greens, tomatoes, and dried fish. That night both women were selling roasted cassava as well, and they sat huddled close to the glowing embers of their braziers, each with a *citenge* drawn tightly around her shoulders. Upon our arrival Bana Annie sent her young daughter running home. I did not know the purpose of this errand until the child caught up with us after we had bid her mother goodnight. Breathless, she ran to Bana Mercy's side and slipped a K10 note into her hand with a respectful bend of her knees.[6] Seeing the puzzled look on my face, Bana Mercy explained that she, Bana Annie, and Bana Sinkala, along with three other people, were part of a *chilimba* group, the local term for a rotating credit association.

Historically, *chilimba* in Zambia has been a dyadic arrangement, often between wage workers, who would take turns giving all or some of their salary to one another each month (Wilson 1941; Ardener 1964: 206; Hansen 1985). In contrast, the typical membership of a *chilimba* group today is between four and six individuals, and sometimes more. After this conversation with Bana Mercy, my research assistant and I surveyed roughly a dozen *chilimba* groups and found that the particular mechanism of *chilimba* varied according to the means and needs of participants. Bana Mercy told me that their group had started after Bana Sinkala learned of a new way of doing *chilimba* from other women in the market (see O'Reilly 1996). The six members of the group each put K10 into a pool every day, and every ten days two people were each given K300. Unlike traditional *chilimba*, which Bana Mercy associated with salaried workers, this model did not require large monthly payments. Instead, small contributions each day accommodated the sporadic income of those involved in small-scale trade, and a short turnaround time ensured that they saw quick results. One of the other benefits of this form of *chilimba* was that the entire cycle only took a month to complete (i.e., since two participants collected one half of the kitty every ten days, all six members of the group would collect it once in the space of one month). It was therefore possible to leave the *chilimba* rather quickly if one's financial situation changed. In addition to this newer model, many people in formal sector employment are involved in more traditional forms of *chilimba* (though the larger group size persists here as well), organized around monthly contributions that coincide with the pay cycle.

Some reports from research conducted during the 1980s and early 1990s suggested that *chilimba* was an institution in decline (Hansen 1985, Roeber 1995). These analyses described it as a financial coping strategy, a response to the "indeterminacy and uncertainty caused by social and economic change" (Hansen 1985: 70), as indeed it must have been at that time. In these treatments, *chilimba* was more about getting by than getting ahead. However, in my own fieldwork, as well as in some other studies (O'Reilly 1996, Mukuka et al. 2002), we see a different picture of *chilimba*. To wit, these discussions have emphasized its role in individual advancement, and especially in helping people purchase household items or develop small businesses. *Chilimba* here is associated with larger purchases and investments outside the ordinary flow of resources; in other words, *chilimba* is a mechanism for moving.

In an environment where money is all too easily eaten, *chilimba* allows people to amass cash in ways that it would be much more difficult for them to do on their own. As all *chilimba* participants pointed out, putting aside K10 each day, let alone K300 each month, is a challenge. Money, again, does not sit still, and cash saved at home is always in danger of being applied to a pressing need. *Chilimba,* in contrast, allows people to accumulate a lump sum that can be used for something that is better than eating. While everyone admitted that on some occasions they had eaten the *chilimba* kitty as soon as they received the money, using it to pay rent or school fees, this was not the preferred way to use the cash. Far better—and not uncommon—were investments in business ventures, such as baby chickens that could be sold at a profit when they were grown or display items like the new "kitchen unit" that my neighbor Bana Kondwani bought with the help of *chilimba* (figure 5). Other informants put their *chilimba* funds in savings accounts or loaned them out informally, earning a high rate of interest in the process. Perhaps the most striking example of the relationship between *chilimba* and moving are groups designed specifically for the purchase of *fipe,* or household goods (see Reece 2015: 144–50 for a similar case from Botswana). In these groups, I was told, members begin by telling everyone else in the *chilimba* what they intended to buy when they collected the kitty. Though I have never observed this, some people in Nsofu told me of groups that enforced these savings plans by accompanying a person to the store to buy the item for which she was saving, perhaps also marking the occasion of the purchase with a party. Here there are several mechanisms built into *chilimba* to guard the money each member has saved and ensure that it goes to a purpose that is better than eating. Even in groups that are not so strictly focused on the purchase of *fipe,* it is clear that for people in Nsofu *chilimba* facilitates moving by helping them acquire items that advance their status position.

From a socioeconomic perspective, *chilimba* relationships are relationships among equals, and there is a strong preference for uniformity among the members of a *chilimba* group—that is, those who participate ought to be drawing on similar resources (also see O'Reilly 1996). People employed in the formal sector, for instance, often form *chilimba* groups with others who work for the same company, who are paid on the same day and earn a similar amount. In the case of Bana Mercy's *chilimba,* the criterion for membership was that everyone be "doing something," whether small-scale business like Bana Annie, or managing rental property like Bana Sinkala, or even occasional trade like Bana

FIGURE 5. Bana Kondwani and her new "kitchen unit," purchased with *chilimba* money.

Mercy. The only time I encountered an obvious disparity among members of a *chilimba* group was in the case of Mrs. Sichone, who had been approached by her housekeeper and asked to join a small *chilimba* group. Everyone who heard about this arrangement found it strange, and Mrs. Sichone herself seemed to acknowledge that it was outside the normal way of doing things, noting that she had only gotten involved with this *chilimba* in order to help her housekeeper. We might therefore think of this particular case as one in which *chilimba* was about dependence, about moving for one party but not necessarily the other.

Similarity among members allows a *chilimba* to run smoothly. However, it is the temporary difference that *chilimba* creates in a group that enables it to run at all. This difference takes the form of economic imbalance, as over the course of the *chilimba* cycle, "members move in turn from being creditors to debtors" (Ardener 1964: 201). In other words, the *chilimba* moves forward as the burden of debt cycles through the group, rolling over until everyone ends up back where they started.[7] As opposed to the stepping stairs of dependence, the image here is of a set of gears that move as the teeth of one cogwheel fill the gaps of the other. Alternating asymmetry creates forward motion, in this case generating sums of cash that one person would find it difficult to amass on her own.

One of the other ways that people on the Copperbelt produce moving is by forming "committees." This word is always used in English, and refers to a group of people who make uniform contributions to a large social event like a wedding or "kitchen party," which is the Copperbelt analogue to a North American bridal shower.[8] Kitchen parties, in particular, are expensive affairs that allow a young couple to outfit their homes. At the various kitchen parties I have attended it is not unusual for a bride to receive an electric stove and refrigerator, even a living room suite, in addition to a large number of pots, pans, plates, and cutlery. The contributions of committee members are used both for food and drinks at the party, as well as for one of the large gifts. Members attend the event in uniforms made specially for the occasion, which set them apart from the rest of those who attend the celebration. Not everyone on the committee is directly connected to the couple getting married; some, for example, may have joined at the invitation of a friend or coworker who is related to the bride.

Part of the motivation for becoming a member of a committee is the fun and camaraderie that come along with a party and its preparations, though there is considerable stress involved in this as well. Beyond the chance to drink and eat and dance, however, membership in a committee also allows a person to build up an expansive network of debt. By helping facilitate the wedding of a workmate's niece to whom she has almost no connection, a committee member ensures that when the time comes for her daughter or son to marry she will have a long list of people she can call on for assistance. This is where committees become a bit like the *chilimba*. A group of people come together on the basis of similarity, albeit a similarity that is somewhat artificially produced as everyone makes the same contribution and dresses alike. At the same time, a committee creates a temporary but longer-term asymmetry by producing a debt that members hope will be repaid in time.

I will have more to say on committees in chapter 7 when we examine a party held for Mrs. Mwanza, but I bring them up here because of their importance in bringing off large social events—events that are responsible for outfitting many Copperbelt homes—by producing temporary debts that facilitate moving. Taken together, asymmetrical relationships of dependence and the alternating asymmetry created through *chilimba* and committees further underscore the importance of economic difference for moving. In all cases, moving is made possible by the transfer of resources above and beyond what is required for day-to-day living, a lump sum that can be insulated from the endless stream of emergencies, exigencies, and expenses that guarantee that most money will be eaten. While these social mechanisms clearly provide a bulwark against economic uncertainty, they are not invulnerable to crisis.

NEGOTIATING ASYMMETRY IN TIMES OF UNCERTAINTY

It took a while for people in Nsofu to realize that Mr. Ntembe had been let go from his position at ZamTel, the national telephone company. Apart from the fact that he was now at home during the week (suddenly, we saw him every Wednesday morning at Higher Calling), by all appearances things were as they had been. Mr. Ntembe dressed immaculately, as did his wife. His children continued at the private school they attended in Nsofu. Their living room was always carefully swept and neatly arranged, with overstuffed green sofas facing a large television set. The enduring markers of social position that Mr. Ntembe had brought into his home were doing their job. As the months passed, however, it became clear that Mr. Ntembe was not simply on leave, as we had initially assumed. Rumors that he had lost his job, and that he had been released without a pension, rang increasingly true. His children did not go back to school when the term ended, but rather played at home all day. The power company disconnected the electricity in their house, and Mrs. Ntembe started cooking on a charcoal brazier while her electric stove sat idle in the kitchen. After Mr. Ntembe had been out of work for more than six months his family moved from Nsofu to an unfinished house on the outskirts of the township, where they rented a few rooms. Blankets and plastic tarps separated the family's quarters from others in the house, and tarps also covered the gaps in the walls that the masons had left for windows. Most of their *fipe* had been sold, but they brought a few items with them, markers of what they had once had—and doubtless hoped to have again.

While the example of the Ntembe family is especially striking, unemployment is not the only thing that can bring about a sudden change in economic status. Here we might consider the experience of Bana Sinkala, whom we have already met in the discussion of *chilimba*. Before her divorce Bana Sinkala and her family lived in a township adjacent to Nsofu, in a row of identical white houses that had once belonged to the mine power company. Occasionally she and I would walk over to this neighborhood to visit some of her old friends. In photos from this time Bana Sinkala is heavier than she was when I first met her, wearing makeup and jewelry, nice clothes and stylish wigs. All of that changed when her marriage ended, leaving her in greatly reduced circumstances, now a dependent on those with whom she had previously been on equal footing.

Beyond these more individualized crises, economic downturn can change the position of a large number of people in a very short space of time. The best example of this from my fieldwork was the *global*, but every drop in the Copperbelt economy, every turn of the boom-and-bust cycle, has a similar effect. Crisis makes moving more difficult. At issue is not just the fact that people in Nsofu have less money to spend as individuals, and that upward mobility is therefore curtailed. Rather, because moving turns on relationships of economic difference, the true impact of crisis is felt in the way it levels the economic playing field, as people lose the gains they have made and the resources they once had. Where stratification provides handholds for forward movement, economic equality offers no such structures. To return to the terms set out above, when the social forms through which people have traditionally made moving happen become less accessible, their capacity to realize this value is limited. While the leveling effects of economic crisis affect everyone, the particular implications of these changes are different for wealthier and poorer people.

As economic conditions worsen, those who have remained in positions of relative prosperity find themselves overwhelmed with dependents. Mr. Zulu, the man we met in the prologue to this book, had a good job at the mine even before his promotion, and as a result of his prosperity he had many dependents. He described his financial responsibilities to me on one of my first visits to his home. Over a meal of hamburger gravy and *impwa,* a locally grown variety of eggplant, Mr. Zulu told me that in his estimation people on the Copperbelt were less able to meet the demands of their extended families than they had been in the past. In the years immediately following independence, Mr. Zulu explained, when the mines were nationalized, one man's wages could support a huge network of kin.[9] Nowadays, however, the number of relatives, friends, and neighbors who came to salaried workers like Mr. Zulu for help often exceeded the resources he had available. As in the fictional remarks in the epigraph to this chapter, the obligation to respond to the needs and demands from kin and neighbors can stretch a person's resources to the breaking point—indeed, they may force him to undo his efforts at moving by parting with important status-marking goods. One day Bana Sam pointed out that the impressive stereo system that had once occupied a prominent place in the Zulu sitting room was gone—sold, she said, so that Mr. Zulu could help a member of his extended family who needed assistance.

As the Zulu family became especially overburdened, some of those who had previously relied on them for material assistance were compelled to appeal to others. One blustery Sunday afternoon, around the same time the Zulus sold their stereo, Bana Daka approached me after church and asked if I could give her K200,000 to help pay her rent.[10] Normally, she explained, she would have asked Mrs. Zulu or Bana Sam, but neither of her regular sources of support was able to help her just then. While Mrs. Zulu had a number of extra expenses, Bana Sam's husband had not received his salary for several months. This example illustrates how the structural changes that accompany economic crisis impact Nsofu's poor. As people like Mr. and Mrs. Zulu are stretched further and further by the demands of others, people like Bana Daka find themselves with fewer sources of assistance.

For those without access to regular income, it can be equally difficult to create temporary asymmetry. When I began asking people in Nsofu if they were part of a *chilimba* group, a number replied that they were not, but that they would like to be. They looked and sounded almost wistful when they said this, and it seemed to me that they recognized the value of *chilimba*, of what it could do for them in their efforts at moving. Seeing their obvious desire, I would ask why it was that they were not involved in a rotating credit group. Their replies were notably similar: they did not dare. As Bana Chanda explained it, she was afraid that she would join a *chilimba* group only to find that she could not keep up with the regular payments. Being the one to break the *chilimba* was a serious offense, one that threatened not only the success of the system but also one's relationships with others in the group. Bana Sinkala told me that her congregation had at one point sponsored a *chilimba* that had fallen apart, and that since then the people responsible for breaking the *chilimba* no longer came to church. Even those who joined a *chilimba* because they were "doing something" sometimes had difficulty meeting its requirements. Bana Mercy once confided that her young daughter had been forced to loan (*ukukongwesha*) her the money she had received for her birthday so that Bana Mercy could make her contribution to the *chilimba*. Like relationships of dependence, then, the alternating asymmetry of the *chilimba* still requires access to regular income, putting it beyond the reach of some and making it difficult for others. Obviously, this is especially true in times of economic crisis, when informal trade or access to wage labor, particularly contract labor, is harder to come by.

It is in this context that we must understand the social lives of Nsofu's Pentecostals. Turning our attention to religion on the Copperbelt, two aspects of the foregoing discussion will be especially important. First is the fact that people on the Copperbelt are always on the lookout for potential patrons or networks through which they might make moving happen, and these have become harder to find because of the leveling effects of economic downturn. While moving is an established part of Copperbelt social life, this does not mean that it must always be realized in the same way, which brings us to the second point to keep in mind going forward. I have already observed that moving is a matter of multiple overlapping metrics of progress, primarily socioeconomic, but also personal and professional. However, as noted in the introduction, there is space here for creativity and expansion, for developing new metrics according to which moving can be realized. As we will see, this is precisely what has happened in Pentecostal groups.

CHAPTER 3

Becoming Pentecostal on the Copperbelt

Before beginning my fieldwork on the Copperbelt, I developed a research program designed to compare the social lives of "Pentecostals and non-Pentecostals." My plan was to examine exchange relationships in households with different religious affiliations in an effort to tease out how Pentecostalism shaped the domestic economy of its adherents. Almost immediately after arriving in Nsofu, however, I realized that this plan would not work, as there was no clear-cut distinction between those who attended Pentecostal churches and those who did not. Most people, regardless of their church affiliation, showed some commitment to Pentecostal ideas like prosperity and deliverance from demons, and engaged in practices like ecstatic prayer and singing. Since I saw very little difference between Pentecostalism and other forms of Christianity, I was curious whether my neighbors in Nsofu had a similar perception, and I made a habit of asking people what made Pentecostalism unique. Several responses to this question appear in the pages that follow, but one in particular is instructive for the argument of this chapter. Mr. Zulu, whom we know quite well by this point, described the difference between Pentecostalism and other forms of Christianity as a difference of social organization. As he saw it, where mainline churches had institutions—committees, dioceses, regional women's organizations—Pentecostal churches were structured around personal relationships.

Mr. Zulu's description of Pentecostalism is an apt one. On the Copperbelt, Pentecostalism is characterized by a network of intersecting social ties that from the perspective of individual believers constitute religious adherence and when observed in the aggregate comprise a religious community, whether a church or fellowship. In this way, Copperbelt Pentecostalism can be productively compared to another Christian context. Writing about a mission hospital on the north coast of Papua New Guinea, Alice Street (2010) observed that patients almost always spoke of their residence in the ward as a time of increased Christian belief. While this is perhaps unsurprising, given both the overt Christian context of the hospital as well as the anxiety associated with illness, Street argues that in this case the increase in religiosity among hospital patients is best explained in terms of what she calls "relational action." Faced with the multiple and often contradictory social obligations of hospital and home, patients cultivated a relationship with God through which these disparate ties were eclipsed and ultimately unified, making recovery possible. A relationship with God, in other words, allowed people to manage their relationships with others in order to bring about a positive change in their lives (see Klaits 2010 for a similar analysis). For Pentecostals in Nsofu, the relational model associated with Christian adherence is identical in focus, though opposite in composition, to the one that Street describes. Believers on the Copperbelt look to relationships with church leaders and with other laypeople to manage their relationship with God—again, in order to bring about a positive change in their lives. The social ties that form in Pentecostal groups, in other words, give believers access to divine transformational power, and it is in their capacity to effect transformation that the value of these relationships is found.

In framing the experience of Copperbelt believers in terms of relational action, my analysis appears to cut against the grain of much anthropological writing on Christianity, which has often highlighted its individualizing effects (e.g., Robbins 2002, 2004a; Errington and Gewertz 1995; Keane 2007; Meyer 1998; also see Bialecki et al. 2008 for a more general survey). Building on a long line of social scientific argument connecting the rise of individualism in the West to the development of Protestantism (e.g., Mauss 1985, Dumont 1986), in these analyses conversion introduces a model of the person that is bounded, agentive, and independent—in short, the individual. By focusing my analysis of Copperbelt Pentecostalism on the social relationships it generates, I do not want to suggest that the well-documented connection between Protestantism and individualism does not apply to Nsofu. Instead, building on an important body of work on Christian personhood in Africa (e.g., Daswani 2011, 2015; Klaits 2011; Haynes 2016;

also see Bialecki and Daswani 2015), I argue that individual and relational modes of personhood are part of a single process through which social ties "literally make someone Pentecostal" (Daswani 2011: 258). On the Copperbelt, this process is primarily concerned with moving by the Spirit. Like moving more generally, moving by the Spirit is realized in individual believers through social relationships, in this case ties to church leaders and to other laypeople. This unique model of moving is central to Pentecostalism's popularity on the Copperbelt and is the primary reason people become believers—a process that requires careful framing.

CAVEAT: CONVERSION VERSUS "ALTERNATION"

Although this chapter explores various aspects of becoming a Pentecostal, I have chosen not to describe this process in terms of religious conversion. For one thing, most of my informants were already Christians when they joined Pentecostal churches. Nearly all of the adult believers that I have encountered on the Copperbelt were raised in mainline Christian denominations; they were Baptists, Anglicans, or Adventists.[1] While some describe their previous church involvement as nominal, a significant number of Pentecostals were very devoted members of their former congregations. Many of today's believers were catechists and Sunday school teachers before they became Pentecostals, and the way they describe their decision to join a Pentecostal church reflects their overarching devotion to Christianity. These believers say that they felt that the members of the churches in which they were raised were not "serious" about their faith—they drank alcohol, for example, something Pentecostals consider incompatible with Christian commitment. In addition, some believers spoke of the increased emphasis on the Bible that they found in Pentecostal circles, which resonated with their own desire to know more about scripture.

This description of the relationship between Pentecostalism and other forms of Christianity is especially applicable to those who became Pentecostals in the early days of Pentecostal expansion—between the late 1980s and late 1990s. Among those who have become Pentecostals more recently, discussions of the lack of seriousness among members of mainline churches still figure. However, these believers are more likely to emphasize the similarities between religious life in Pentecostal groups and the mainline congregations that they have been part of in the past, and may still be part of on a regular or semi-regular basis. In the light of the increasing overlap between Pentecostalism and other forms of Christianity on the Copperbelt in recent years, this makes perfect sense, and it appears that movement from one group to another is no longer the marked transition that it was in the past.

It is because of the continuity of Christian practice in the lives of most believers in Nsofu that I have chosen to avoid the term "conversion" when describing their experience. Instead, I speak of people becoming Pentecostals, joining Pentecostal groups, or beginning Pentecostal adherence. As we will see, these processes are bound up together; people join Pentecostal groups, begin to participate in Pentecostal religious practice, and become Pentecostals in an overlapping process of affiliation that may but does not necessarily involve a shift in religious commitment, let alone religious belief. These subtle changes echo Thomas Kirsch's (2004) discussion of Christianity in southern Zambia in which he, following Travisano (1981), refers to shifts in religious membership not as conversion, but rather as "alternation." The fluid pattern of religious affiliation that Kirsch identifies has clear resonances with the Copperbelt, where church life is structured by a quest for spiritual efficacy, which is in turn connected to a dynamic set of social ties. For many believers, this begins when a display of spiritual power leads to a relationship with a Pentecostal leader.

BECOMING PENTECOSTAL IN NSOFU, PART 1: THE POWER OF A PASTOR

When believers in Nsofu describe their early experiences with Pentecostalism, they often begin with an account of an intractable problem. At times, this is an interpersonal dispute—a conflict with one's relatives over inheritance, for example, or an argument with a coworker. For female Pentecostals, it is frequently the inability to conceive a child. Others describe sickness, physical pain, or strange dreams. Narratives of these afflictions usually include descriptions of the lengths believers went to for relief, which can include anything from trips to the hospital, visits to traditional healers (*bashinjanga*), and consultations with Christian leaders like Catholic priests. Some may even have gone to Pentecostal pastors or prophets for prayer without experiencing any change in circumstances. Then, at some point in this struggle, they heard about a particular Pentecostal leader, usually through reports of a neighbor or relative. It was only after encountering this new leader that the "stubborn situation," as Pentecostals call them, finally began to change.

Recounting these events, believers recall the power of a pastor's prayer, and some of those I talked to spoke of physical responses here, such as crying or relief from tightness in the chest. More important than these visceral markers of power, however, are breakthroughs such as deliverance, resolution of a conflict, or the miraculous provision of a job, a spouse, or a child.

When a pastor's spiritual assistance is able to facilitate a breakthrough and change a stubborn situation, a relationship forms between him or her and the person who has been helped. To a large extent, a believer's relationship to a pastor constitutes her membership in a church, and indeed, it may well constitute her commitment to Pentecostalism more generally. That is, many believers are members of a Pentecostal group, or even consider themselves Pentecostals at all, because of their connection to that group's leader. Some people may not even refer to their church by its name (e.g., Higher Calling, Freedom Bible Church), but will instead simply say that that they attend, for example, "Pastor Ephraim's church." Even believers who would not go that far still regard their connection to a pastor as especially significant. When an older Pentecostal woman heard me talking about a church with nearly a thousand members, she clicked her tongue and tutted in disapproval, "No access to the pastor." The decline in membership at Freedom Bible Church and Higher Calling when popular leaders left provides further evidence for the centrality of the pastor in Pentecostal adherence. Since church participation for many Pentecostals is structured primarily by a congregation's leader, the loss of that leader often means the end of church participation as well.

The central characteristic of the relationship between pastors and laypeople is spiritual asymmetry. Although believers will say that the power to facilitate a breakthrough comes from God and not from church leaders, they will nevertheless attribute the particular work of God in their lives to the special grace that has been given to their pastor. When, for example, people at Key of David witnessed a string of breakthroughs that included jobs for several unemployed church members, Bana Charles explained to me that the congregation was enjoying these blessings because of Pastor Mwanza's divinely given "favor." Her friend, Bana Karen—one of those who had received a breakthrough in the form of employment—agreed. By Bana Karen's account the members of Key of David were prospering because of their spiritual "parent" (*bafyashi*), Pastor Mwanza. She explained to me that leaders like him were able to provide special access to divine power and blessings. As she put it, "All of us have the right to speak directly with God, but those who are his servants are chosen . . . They are our parents, those we draw near to."

Bana Karen's description of Pastor Mwanza as her spiritual parent is not unusual. Pentecostals on the Copperbelt often refer to their pastors as their parents, or "*bafyashi*," in Bemba, and leaders will also sometimes be called "mother" or "father" (see Klaits 2010: 8).[2] In a cultural context where generation is arguably the most salient form of interpersonal hierarchy (e.g., Crehan 1997, Richards 1982), the language of parentage serves as a potent index of the spiritual asymmetry characteristic of the relationship between church leaders and laypeople. Moreover, by referring to their pastors as parents, believers also underscore the responsibility of church leaders to provide for the members of their congregations. Just as relationships across generations are reciprocal ties in which deference and respect on the part of juniors ensure "protection, support, and help" from their elders (Crehan 1997: 100), so too a relationship with one's pastor should produce benefits for laypeople—provided, of course, that they treat their spiritual parents with care and respect, which most believers do.[3]

Becoming a Pentecostal on the Copperbelt, then, means entering into a relationship with a church leader whose unique status as someone chosen by God makes him or her a facilitator of divine breakthrough, a parent who also serves as a conduit of blessing. An account of those who are brought to Pentecostalism after an encounter with a powerful church leader has therefore revealed two important aspects of Pentecostal practice in Nsofu. First, what draws people on the Copperbelt to Pentecostalism is the power available in this religion to bring about change. Writing about Ghanaian Pentecostals, Girish Daswani has similarly observed that believers are primarily interested in "finding a solution to their problems and in eliminating the suffering in their lives" (Daswani 2011: 261), a point that Thomas Kirsch (2004) has made about Christianity in southern Zambia as well.[4] Second, and more importantly for our purposes, if the core of Pentecostal adherence on the Copperbelt is social relationships, the most important of these is unquestionably a believer's tie to her pastor. As central as this connection is, however, it is not the only relationship around which Pentecostal adherence is structured. While many people in Nsofu were brought into Pentecostal churches by a pastor who resolved their stubborn situation, a number of others were attracted by the social connections exemplified in Pentecostalism's unique style of prayer. As an examination of this religious practice reveals, like hierarchical ties between leaders and laypeople, lateral relationships among believers also serve as conduits for the transformative power of God.

BECOMING PENTECOSTAL IN NSOFU, PART 2: THE POWER OF PRAYER

On the Copperbelt, the Bemba verb "to pray" (*ukupepa*) serves as a shorthand term for religious affiliation. So, for example, a person may indicate that he is a Catholic by saying, literally, "I pray at the Catholic Church" (*Ndapepa ku Katolika*). Although this linguistic convention applies to Christians from all backgrounds, there is something unique about prayer in Pentecostal settings. As Pastor Ephraim put it, unlike the members of mainline congregations, Pentecostals pray "one, one"—that is, in Pentecostal groups everyone prays out loud at the same time, a practice that I refer to as "collective-personal prayer" (see Haynes 2016).

In describing what first drew them to Pentecostalism, many believers cite collective-personal prayer as a primary attraction. In order to show what they find so compelling about this practice, I turn to an interview with a woman I call Bana Chanda. Bana Chanda was a Jehovah's Witness who began attending Higher Calling after she was delivered from the spiritual effects of the ritual cleansing she had undergone following her husband's death. These effects were causing physical problems and illness, which disappeared after Bana Mfuwe prayed that the demons responsible for them would be driven away. Once her deliverance was complete, Bana Chanda became a regular participant at Higher Calling, and her observations about collective-personal prayer have much to say about the role of this practice in the religious lives of Copperbelt believers.

> NH: What is the difference between Pentecostal churches and other kinds of churches?
>
> BC: The difference is in prayer . . . with the Pentecostals, there is intercession. But in other churches there is no intercession. There is no one saying, "Let's pray for our families, let's pray for so-and-so"—not at all. At other churches, let's say at our church [*kumyesu*], we have what in the United Church of Zambia is called the reverend. That person is alone in front, and he is the one who prays for you . . . [But with the Pentecostals] each person prays. Alone. So, as a result, with the Pentecostals one learns. You learn how you're going to pray even when you're by yourself . . . In other churches you just sit there—everyone just sits there to pray. They put someone in front, he prays, he prays, he's all by himself and in the room there's just silence. There's no agreeing with one another [*takwaba*

ukusuminishanya], if he prays there's no yelling, "Amen, Amen." There's no support. It's only when the leader says, "Amen" that you can say "Amen" and open your eyes.

By contrasting collective-personal prayer with prayer among the Jehovah's Witnesses or in the United Church of Zambia, Bana Chanda highlights several important elements of this central Pentecostal practice. It is no accident that she begins her discussion of Pentecostal prayer by pointing to what believers call "intercession," the first activity on the agenda at all Pentecostal meetings. During intercession a leader (usually a layperson) calls out broad themes for people to take up in prayer, such as the health of the pastor or the well-being of the children in the group. Individuals then pray along these lines, using collective-personal prayer, for roughly ten or fifteen minutes before the leader calls them to order and moves on to the next prayer topic. As we will see in the next chapter, there are many things happening in intercession that make it an important part of Pentecostal ritual life. For the purposes of our discussion here, however, the key thing to note about intercession is its role as a training ground in which believers develop their ability in prayer. Many believers say that they did not know how to pray—or at least to pray in a way they thought was effective—before they became Pentecostals (Haynes 2016). By attending prayer meetings and joining in during intercession, people develop their ability to pray not only in church but also, as Bana Chanda pointed out, when they are at home by themselves.

Even after they have learned to pray, Pentecostals may still find it difficult to do so. Prayer is hard work. It involves standing and speaking aloud for long stretches of time while doing battle with the powers of darkness. It also requires endurance to stay true to one's convictions even when problems are not resolved. This is why Bana Chanda emphasized the "support" provided by collective-personal prayer, the agreement implied in shouts of "Amen!" Here again, the emphasis is on lay believers doing things for themselves. Pentecostals don't need to wait for a leader to say "Amen," but rather offer encouraging words to one another as they feel they should. In Pentecostal prayer believers are therefore not only given an important space within which to pray by and for themselves, but also to help others as they do the same (see Eriksen 2012). This last point—the spiritual support that comes from collective prayer—merits a bit more discussion.

One Wednesday afternoon, the members of Higher Calling met as usual for prayer. The community center where they had been gathering since leaving the Ntembe home was cool and dark, illuminated only by the slanting afternoon sunlight that filtered through the open door. On this particular day the task of leading intercession fell to Clementine, a young single mother who had been a close follower of Bana Mfuwe. Pacing back and forth across the front of the room, Clementine listed off topics and requests, which the dozen or so women gathered for the meeting picked up eagerly in collective-personal prayer. As the intercession time drew to a close, one or two members of the group did not stop praying along with everyone else, but continued weeping and praying in tongues and other languages well after the rest of the group had fallen silent. This sometimes happens at Pentecostal gatherings, and I will take up some of the implications of such situations in more detail in the following chapter. For now, this example is helpful because of what it teaches us about how the collective efforts of a group shape the prayers of individual believers.

On the day after this Higher Calling meeting I paid a visit to Bana Chanda, who had also been present at the gathering. Sitting in the shade of her yard we chatted about new developments in the fellowship. Bana Chanda reported that the weekly prayer and fasting meeting had been moved to Bana Chilomba's house, effective the coming Saturday. In her opinion, this change was a positive one, as it would hopefully encourage more people to come to the meeting. Fasting was difficult when the group was too small, Bana Chanda went on, as under these circumstances it was hard for the Holy Spirit to work, and one could easily get bored. In contrast, a large group made this challenging religious task easier. To illustrate her point, Bana Chanda referred to the Higher Calling meeting that both of us had attended the day before. The reason that a few people had such powerful experiences with the Holy Spirit, she explained, was because there had been a good crowd; with so many there, one of the young women even spoke in tongues.[5] As a result, Bana Chanda concluded, everyone at the meeting was encouraged.

While Bana Chanda's remarks are directed specifically at the difficulty of fasting alongside prayer, rather than at prayer by itself, her comments nevertheless provide us with an important insight into the "support" provided by other participants at a Pentecostal meeting. According to Bana Chanda, the power of Pentecostal prayer follows not from its aggregate weight—not, in other words, from a sense that the combined efforts of many believers make for something that is more effective than any individual prayer might be on its own. Rather, the great strength of collective-personal prayer is that it empowers each person to more effectively pray "one, one." The relationship between the group and the individual in Pentecostal prayer therefore presents an interesting partial inversion of Durkheim's theory of religion, in which the collective ritual energy of the group overwhelms the individual (cf. Csordas 1997: 110); in contrast, in Pentecostal prayer the individual is strengthened in her individuality as the "support" of the group enables her to more effectively bring her unique requests before God.

The effects of collective-personal prayer on individual believers can extend beyond their initial context, as the experience of another woman at Higher Calling demonstrates. When leaders asked church members to share testimonies during prayer meeting one Wednesday morning, Bana Leonard marched quickly to the front of the chapel. Standing before the group she was radiant, her voice full of feeling as she related what had happened to her following the church retreat the week before. Returning home after days of prayer with others from Higher Calling, Bana Leonard said, she walked in her front door and began to pray that all of the rooms in her house would be fruitful. That very evening her husband came home bearing bags of wonderful foods, including meat and Cremora, a nondairy coffee creamer manufactured by Nestlé that is a high-status product in Nsofu. The next day, Bana Leonard continued excitedly, her husband pulled up to the house in a taxi loaded with yet more food. Perhaps even more miraculously, he got out of the car and called to her using the nickname "Ssweetie," a detail that elicited special whoops of approval from members of the congregation and that, by suggesting an improvement in marital relations, also represents what was likely another answer to prayer for Bana Leonard.

Testimonies like that offered by Bana Leonard, linking specific instances of divine provision and breakthrough to participation in group prayer, as well as testimonies connecting regular attendance at prayer meetings to positive change more generally, are common in Nsofu. In these testimonies Pentecostal prayer emerges as a ritual practice that transforms stubborn situations in an individual's life by mobilizing the power of a particular relational network. In contrast to the dyadic, spiritually asymmetrical relationships that form between church leaders and laypeople, collective-personal prayer produces a web of lateral ties in which each member retains a high degree of independence and through which each member stands to benefit. Pentecostal prayer creates a rolling tide of ritual energy that propels everyone forward and that, as testimonies like Bana Leonard's make clear, help to bring about a breakthrough.[6]

Taken together, the examples of those who are drawn to Pentecostalism by the power of a pastor and those who are drawn by the power of collective-personal prayer represent the experiences of the vast majority of those who join Pentecostal churches on the Copperbelt. These models are in no way mutually exclusive, nor are they characteristic only of new Pentecostals. Most believers continually rely on both the mediatory efforts of church leaders and the prayer support of their friends, turning to these different sources of assistance under different circumstances. Bana Ezra, who at various points attended both Freedom Bible Church and Key of David, explained to me that when she was facing a problem she would invite women from the church to come to her house and help her in prayer, just as her friends would come to her when facing difficulties. However, she added, when she felt that a problem confronted by a friend was especially difficult, she would advise that person to seek the help of Mrs. Mwanza in prayer. Prayer was Mrs. Mwanza's job, Bana Ezra explained, and she was better equipped than a layperson to deal with tricky situations. What emerges in Bana Ezra's account is almost a religious division of labor—or at least a clear instance of religious specialization—that allows believers to make use of different types of relationships in different circumstances, always working toward the common goal of a breakthrough.

MOVING BY THE SPIRIT

It is not difficult to see similarities between the relationships that form in Pentecostal churches and those we explored in the previous chapter. Pentecostal congregations, like other Copperbelt social domains, are organized by ties of dependence, as well as lateral networks that propel their individual members forward. While there are obvious points of overlap between the relational patterns of Copperbelt congregations and those found outside the church, however, the examples presented in this chapter also point to a model of moving that differs in some important respects from the one we have employed up to now. This is what I mean by moving "by the Spirit." Like the general model of moving outlined in chapter 2, moving by the Spirit is a value. More specifically, it is a value made up of two ranked but interrelated subvalues that I refer to as prosperity and charisma.

For Pentecostals on the Copperbelt, prosperity typically comes about as a result of a breakthrough and is realized in things like a healed body or newfound employment, as well as new or renewed social relationships—

a husband who calls his wife "Sweetie," for instance. In the theological framework of Pentecostalism these blessings find their expression in the prosperity gospel, which holds that "Christians enjoy unassailable claims to certain blessings as well as to right relationships with God, other humans, and nature" (Attanasi 2012: 5).[7] The prosperity gospel turns on the notion that God has constructed the universe in such a way that his people ought to prosper; put differently, God has created a system in which he must bless believers, so long as they know how to enter into that system effectively. In part, this is a question of personal righteousness, as many of the promises of blessing recorded in the Bible connect divine favor to holiness. Beyond a person's behavior, however, the key to activating and receiving the blessings that God has already granted a believer is found in demonstrations of faith (see Coleman 2004: 433). The primary way that followers of the prosperity gospel express their faith is by giving "seed offerings," monetary gifts that carry the expectation of a divinely increased return. The influence of the prosperity gospel, at least in its most vulgar, "give-to-get" form, has waned on the Copperbelt in the last decade. This is the result of, among other things, stories of con artists posing as pastors in order to swindle believers out of their money. Nevertheless, Pentecostals remain committed to the notion that God wants his people to prosper—that is, that he wants them to enjoy the sorts of blessings I have just described. Believers see these things as their God-given right, not least because a new baby or smart suit serves as an important Pentecostal apologetic (Haynes 2012: 134–35). As we will see in chapter 6, they also continue to give seed offerings and to "claim" their blessings through the performative speech acts that Pentecostals call "positive confessions" (Coleman 2006a).

While prosperity, the first element at work in moving by the Spirit, largely follows the contours of moving as we have already defined it, charisma serves to focus moving by the Spirit on new forms of realization. I am using the term "charisma" in more of a Pentecostal-theological than a Weberian sense, though as we will see there are situations in which the latter model is appropriate. In general, though, charisma as I am employing it here refers simply to the development of religious skills. In believers' accounts of what attracted them to Pentecostalism, this theme is prominent—more prominent than prosperity, in fact. In Pentecostal churches people learned to read and study the Bible for themselves, and as a result grew in their knowledge and understanding of scripture. Even more importantly, they learned to pray effectively. As noted above, many believers say that they did not know how to pray before they became Pentecostals, but that over time they developed their skill in this practice. The same holds for disciplines like fasting. Progress in these areas is a central component of what it means to move by the Spirit. This aspect of Pentecostal moving, like prosperity, is realized in display, as others recognize one's charisma in a loud and long prayer, a well-articulated testimony, or a worship chorus sung with particular feeling (see Csordas 1997).[8]

The way that charisma is realized as a component of moving by the Spirit is well illustrated in the experience of Moses, a young man who also lived in the Mwanza home during my doctoral fieldwork. Moses was quiet and shy, a contract worker for Barclays Bank who was more comfortable in English or the Nyanja of his native Lusaka than he was in Bemba. Despite his timid nature, Moses occupied an important role in the ritual life of Key of David. Moses was a prophet, and during Sunday services or prayer meetings he would sometimes go to the front of the sanctuary to deliver a word from God. During these ecstatic speeches Moses was transformed, his shyness replaced with boldness, the stutter that so often inhibited his speech overwhelmed by the passion of his proclamations.

Although I was aware that there had been some tension between Moses and the Mwanzas while I was living in their house, I was surprised to learn that not long after I left the field Moses stopped attending Key of David. Before leaving the church he had married Rita, a young woman who was part of the Key of David music team. When I returned to the field in 2013 I found the couple and their baby daughter living in a house on the edge of Nsofu that had once belonged to Bana Sam and her family, who had since moved to Lusaka. Hoping to find out what had prompted Moses and Rita to leave a church in which they had been so invested, I asked if I could interview them. They agreed, and on a cool June evening I arrived at their home just as they were finishing dinner. I settled into one of the plastic garden chairs lined up neatly in the living room and waited until Rita had cleared the dishes and Moses had washed his hands before beginning our conversation.

The first half of the interview focused on a series of conflicts surrounding Moses and Rita's wedding. Listening to their grievances, it seemed to me that the couple had left the church largely because of interpersonal issues. I was therefore caught off guard when Moses paused for a moment to note that even in the absence of these difficulties they would still have left Key of David—in fact, Moses added, by the time of his departure he had been contemplating a move for some time. The reason for this was that he felt "limited" by the environment at Key of David. While Moses was supposed to be in charge of intercession for the church, he did not feel he had free rein to develop the prayer ministry in the way that he would like. Moreover, he wanted to grow and gain experience in other religious skills, such as preaching and teaching. In Moses's view, advancement along these lines should not have required him to put himself forward; rather, he believed that it was the responsibility of the person leading the church to create such opportunities for members of the congregation. About six months after their wedding the couple approached Pastor Mpezeni, whose church the Zulus were already attending. Pastor Mpezeni knew Moses well and had often invited him to lead intercession during overnight prayer meetings at his church. As soon as they joined his congregation, Pastor Mpezeni put Moses in charge of intercession and allowed him to make his own programs. Moses had also been leading Bible study and occasionally taking the pulpit when Pastor Mpezeni was out of town. For her part, Rita was singing on the praise team, as she had at Key of David, assisting with the Sunday school, and serving on the hospitality team welcoming new visitors to the church.

While there is no doubt that the strained relationships and miscommunications surrounding their wedding had a great deal to do with Moses and Rita's decision to leave the church—Rita referred to these events as a "catalyst" for their departure—in Moses's telling, the primary reason they stopped attending Key of David was that there were not enough opportunities for him to develop his religious skills—that is, to move with regard to charisma. More specifically, Moses felt that Pastor Mwanza did not facilitate his progress in this way, did not pull him up as Moses felt he ought to. Moses's frustrations with what he felt to be a lack of opportunity at Key of David highlight the role of church leaders in helping laypeople like Moses realize charisma as part of moving by the Spirit. Like the relationships of dependence that are key to social life on the Copperbelt more generally, ties between pastors and laypeople are expected to facilitate spiritual development. As Moses put it, movement in Pentecostal groups ought not to be a matter of individual ambition, but rather of a relationship through which one is entrusted with ever-greater responsibility and thereby allowed to progress. Here again, moving is not about getting ahead, but rather about being pulled up.

The possibility that moving by the Spirit involves increased responsibility in church turns our attention from the ways that laypeople realize charisma to the ways that charisma is realized by pastors. The difference here is less a difference of kind than it is a difference of degree, as the particular religious capacities that believers cultivate while moving by the Spirit are the same as those cultivated by pastors. What separates church leaders from laypeople is first the fact that they demonstrate these capacities in greater measure, and second—and more importantly—that they exercise these capacities on behalf of others, for example by praying for someone to be healed. Pastors have access to the power of the Holy Spirit that ordinary believers do not (and in this regard they brush up against Weber's definition of charisma [Weber 1946: 245–64]). This extraordinary power is, as we have seen, the basis for the relationships of dependence that are so central to Copperbelt Pentecostal social life.

The fact that charisma is a metric of moving common to both leaders and laypeople sheds light on a puzzle that I encountered in the field. I always found it odd that some Pentecostals believed that prominent lay leaders—people like Mr. Chibale, an elder at Key of David, or Mr. Moyo, who served a similar role at Freedom Bible Church—would eventually become pastors. Since both of these men were employed in high-paying jobs, it seemed ridiculous to me that they would ever leave those positions for the comparative penury of the pastorate. In the light of the role that charisma plays in moving by the Spirit, however, these assumptions are not strange at all. Since pastors are simply those who have moved the farthest in their congregations with regard to the spiritual skills that all Pentecostals are cultivating (and since most pastors were first active as lay leaders before they entered formal Pentecostal ministry), the expectation that charismatic laypeople might eventually lead churches of their own makes perfect sense. Here I should point out that the movement associated with charisma does not culminate in the pastorate. Among Zambian Pentecostals there are those who use the title of "bishop," which is occasionally bestowed by a denomination, but which is more commonly used to refer simply to someone who has planted more than one church, as was the case for Pastor Ephraim. In this usage "bishops" are people who oversee multiple congregations. Some Pentecostal groups have developed still-higher ranks of church office, including "apostle," a title that sits above bishop. In the light of the importance that believers attach to charismatic progress, which Pentecostals expect to be worked out in formal titles and hierarchies, it seems possible that in time more and more ranks will develop, pushing the horizon of charismatic achievement out even further.[9]

CRISIS AND CREATIVITY

To sum up my discussion thus far, moving by the Spirit is a unique form of moving made up of two subvalues: charisma and prosperity. Moving by the Spirit is realized as each of these values is realized—as people become symbols of prosperity (with heavy bodies, nice clothes, and so on) and of charisma (praying loud and long, taking on an official position in a church, or displaying the power of God by praying for someone to be healed). This value is realized in individual believers through the social relationships that form in churches, whether ties of spiritual dependence that form between pastors and laypeople or the lateral ties of collective-personal prayer, which we have seen also have the power to facilitate a breakthrough and to inculcate spiritual skill. These ties are fundamental to Pentecostal adherence—indeed, it is impossible to be a believer outside of such relationships. It is because of the capacity of Pentecostalism to help believers realize moving by the Spirit that this form of Christianity has witnessed such rapid growth throughout Zambia. In particular, by presenting an extant value in a new form, Pentecostalism offers a social domain that responds both to recent economic circumstances and to established cultural frameworks.

Although the unique form of moving found in Pentecostal churches would probably always be compelling to people in Nsofu, given its obvious resonance with local models of the good, moving by the Spirit has become especially important in the wake of economic changes and crises, whether structural adjustment or the *global*. When traditional patrons become fewer and harder to find, alternative models of dependence, such as the relationships that form between church leaders and laypeople, take on new importance. The same is true of new kinds of lateral networks, such as those found in collective-personal prayer. Finally, when other avenues of achievement are closed off by economic collapse, advancement in a church hierarchy—becoming an elder or the head of women's ministry—represents one of a very few available means of getting ahead. In short, as traditional forms of moving have become harder to realize, moving by the Spirit has emerged as an especially attractive option. It is not just that Pentecostal relational life mirrors the relational life of the Copperbelt, then, but also that Pentecostalism has become a site for moving that is comparatively insulated from economic crisis.

That said, it would be a mistake to view the popularity of Pentecostal moving as only the result of unpredictable economic circumstances. Young Zambian men like Moses have always been on the lookout for new ways to make moving happen, independent of what was happening in the Zambian economy. This is partly because markers of moving like foreign commodities did not historically retain their symbolic power from one generation to the next. It was therefore necessary for each cohort of young people, men in particular, to search for new avenues of achievement—that is, to look for new ways of moving (see Pritchett 2001: 243–46). In this vein, leadership in a Pentecostal congregation represents an "innovative [strategy] in the process of becoming 'someone' in society" (Lauterbach 2010: 260) in the same way that labor migration, trade, or entrepreneurship have done for generations of Zambians.[10] While new frameworks for moving have become especially important in times of economic crisis, then, we must not reduce moving by the Spirit to simple pragmatism or treat it as a second-order framework of advancement that is only attractive when other avenues have been closed off. On the contrary, moving by the Spirit is part of an overarching Copperbelt social project in which novel metrics of moving are always developing.

The picture I have painted of Copperbelt Pentecostalism in this chapter is a rather rosy one. However, there is more to moving by the Spirit, and especially to balancing prosperity and charisma, than I have shown thus far. As we turn our attention to Pentecostalism's ritual high point, the Sunday morning service, my aim will be to complicate the model I have developed here, to introduce some contrast into this overexposed image. While Pentecostal ritual is a key site of social reproduction, it also contains the seeds of social breakdown—the tools that believers use to dismantle the very relationships that I have argued constitute their religious lives and make Pentecostalism so compelling. An analysis of Pentecostal ritual therefore reveals the fault lines that cut across Nsofu's many congregations, and the problems presented by moving by the Spirit.

CHAPTER 4

Ritual and the (Un)making of the Pentecostal Relational World

And afterward,
I will pour out my Spirit on all people.
Your sons and daughters will prophesy,
your old men will dream dreams,
your young men will see visions.
Even on my servants, both men and women,
I will pour out my Spirit in those days.
—Joel 2: 28–29

The wind blows wherever it pleases.
You hear its sound, but you cannot tell where it comes from
or where it is going.
So it is with everyone born of the Spirit.
—John 3: 8

One Sunday afternoon I returned to the Mwanza home after spending the morning at Freedom Bible Church. I found Pastor and Mrs. Mwanza relaxing in the sitting room after a simple lunch of *nshima* and beans. Settling in on the green checked sofa, part of a matching set that ringed the room, I inquired about the church service at Key of David that morning. Pastor Mwanza responded that they had faced some serious spiritual warfare during the meeting, as the devil had caused some of the strongest members of the church to fall asleep during his sermon. After the service, Pastor Mwanza made a point to speak to those who had nodded off, letting them know that they had almost certainly been targeted because of their status as church leaders, and presumably adding that they ought to be more vigilant during Sunday morning meetings. All Pentecostals know that the devil likes to disrupt church, and stories of satanic hindrances to Pentecostal worship were common in Nsofu. Believers told me that demons might convince someone that she needed to wash clothes on Sunday morning or bring an unexpected guest just as someone was getting ready to leave for church. The expectation that Satan would target Pentecostal worship indexes its importance in the social lives of believers, and my aim in this chapter is to show how formal ritual life both reinforces and challenges the relationships that structure Pentecostal adherence.

Like most anthropological discussions of ritual (see Stasch 2011), previous studies of Pentecostal worship have primarily been concerned with social life, and more specifically with the kinds of relationships and institutions that follow from Pentecostal practice. Here we find two key models of social organization at play, which we can broadly characterize as horizontal and vertical. Analyses focused on horizontal relationships often emphasize what Victor Turner called "communitas" (see Turner 1969), demonstrating how shared ritual practice—praying and singing together, for example—generates social ties and creates a sense of belonging. In such situations, "a direct, egalitarian encounter, a fellowship between people as people, frequently occurs," and this makes Pentecostal ritual an important site of "community building" (Albrecht 1999: 212; also see Luhrmann 2012: 279). In contrast to the horizontal ties that ritual creates among believers, studies that emphasize the vertical aspects of Pentecostal ritual have focused on the relationship between laypeople and church leaders. Key here is Paul Gifford's work in Ghana, which demonstrates that practices like prophecy and deliverance make pastors into "famous figures" known for their charisma (Gifford 2004: 108). Similarly, Thomas Kirsch, writing about an African Independent Church that shares many characteristics with Pentecostal groups, connects the power of religious leaders to ritual practice. In particular, preaching and reading from the Bible create a connection between the authority of scripture and that of the preacher, who mediates the power of the text by bringing it to life through speech (Kirsch 2008: 153).

Taken together, these analyses suggest that Pentecostal ritual life creates democratic, open-ended, and largely egalitarian religious communities, while at the same time producing differentiated, asymmetrical relationships between leaders and laypeople.[1] These relational axes mirror those that emerged in the last chapter. As we have seen, the process of becoming a Pentecostal on the Copperbelt is one through which people are drawn into relationships that take two primary forms: vertical ties to church leaders that reflect the overarching paradigm of dependence, and horizontal ties to other believers that, as networks of religious practice, also have the potential to facilitate moving by the Spirit. Not only do the horizontal and vertical aspects of Pentecostalism reflect important elements of Copperbelt social life, they also point to a key theological tension at the heart of this form of Christianity (see Meyer 2010: 122). By this I am referring to the often-strained relationship between charismatic authority and democratic access to the power of the Holy Spirit. It is this tension that I wish to focus on in my discussion of Pentecostal ritual. More specifically, I want to argue that both the vertical and horizontal poles of Pentecostalism are critical to the relational lives of Copperbelt believers as I have described them so far, and that this is true not in spite of the fact that from a social structural perspective they work against each other, but rather precisely because this is the case. In order to make this argument, I must first describe in a bit more detail the theology and practice behind Pentecostalism's two relational poles.

Because Pentecostalism turns on the biblical promise that God will pour the Holy Spirit out on "all flesh" regardless of age, status, or sex, believers understand the gifts of the Holy Spirit—prophecy, speaking in tongues, and so forth—to be available to everyone.[2] Here is Pentecostal egalitarianism at its most basic: in principle, at least, the Holy Spirit is no respecter of persons (Robbins 2004b: 120). One corollary to the idea that everyone has equal access to the Holy Spirit is that positions of religious leadership are also open to all believers (Kärkkäinen 2010: 228; also see van Dijk 1992), a fact that turns our attention to the processes through which a fundamentally egalitarian religion develops a religious hierarchy. When a certain person appears to be particularly adept in exercising spiritual gifts, perhaps by giving accurate prophecies or successfully casting a demon out of a fellow believer, he or she will often very quickly rise to a position of leadership in a congregation. As we saw in the last chapter, pastors and church leaders are those who have a unique anointing from the Holy Spirit that enables them to exercise with special skill and efficacy the spiritual gifts that are available to everyone—and in particular to exercise them on the behalf of others. This charismatic difference structures the asymmetrical ties that form in Pentecostal churches.

If the process of spiritual differentiation that I have just outlined happens in an established group, it may simply result in the emerging leader being incorporated into the existing church hierarchy. However, it may also give rise to a schism. When a believer on the Copperbelt begins to demonstrate his spiritual distinction, others soon start referring to him as "pastor," and from there it is a short step to him organizing a prayer meeting or fellowship of his own, usually with an eye to eventually establishing a church. The possibility of schism—of a new religious hierarchy—therefore follows directly from Pentecostalism's egalitarianism, as at any moment a different person might receive the power of the Holy Spirit, which, like the wind, "blows wherever it pleases."[3] As Birgit Meyer puts it, "As every believer, in principle, can be filled with the Holy Spirit and assume spiritual authority, there is room . . . for endless fission and the opening of new churches" (2010: 122). In short, the horizontal and vertical poles of Pentecostalism coexist in dynamic tension, which sometimes bubbles over into conflict. In the potentially endless cycle of schisms, religious authority develops out of the egalitarian space of Pentecostal worship, and a new church or fellowship is formed. In turn, this new religious community may be challenged from within as worship gives rise to still other emerging leaders that may threaten the established structure.

Having traced the broad contours of how both egalitarianism and hierarchy emerge from Pentecostal theology and practice, we are now in a position to explore in greater detail how these relational poles are expressed and produced in Pentecostal worship. In the analysis that follows I take as my focus the most important of Pentecostal meetings, the Sunday morning service. This gathering serves as something of an urtext for Pentecostal religious practice, providing the liturgical map for most Pentecostal meetings, including overnight prayer services, midweek fellowships, and even the family devotionals that were sometimes part of life in the Mwanza household. The prayers, songs, and messages that believers encounter on Sunday morning therefore inform their religious practice in both formal and informal contexts, and a close reading of a Sunday service therefore sheds light on Pentecostal ritual life across the board.

THE PENTECOSTAL WORSHIP SERVICE IN BRIEF

Pentecostal services almost always begin with intercession. At some meetings this is scheduled before the start of the main service, while at others it is simply the first activity on the agenda. Intercession is rather sparsely attended, and those who show up for this portion of the service are usually the most dedicated and zealous members of the congregation (or ethnographers who have not yet figured out that Pentecostal meetings do not really get going until well after their scheduled start time). The discussion of Pentecostal prayer in the last chapter has already given us a sense of what this activity looks like. Intercession is facilitated by a leader who is typically a layperson and never the senior pastor; indeed, members of the pastoral staff rarely attend this part of the service. The intercession leader instructs the group to pray for a series of specific topics ranging in scope from the nation of Zambia to individual "burdens" (*fisendo*) known only to a believer him- or herself.

Once a theme has been announced, believers address it in prayer for anywhere from five to fifteen minutes before moving on to another topic. Petitions are made through collective-personal prayer, and even the small number of people who attend intercession can generate quite a bit of noise. During intercession, prayers offered in English, Bemba, and occasionally glossolalia ricochet off cement floors and out open windows. For some believers, collective-personal prayer gives rise to ecstatic experiences as, caught up in the weight of their petitions and the power of the Holy Spirit, they prostrate themselves while weeping aloud or work up a sweat denouncing the power of the devil. Despite the din created by collective-personal prayer, however, the leader remains in control. When she feels that a topic has been sufficiently addressed, she will indicate that everyone should be quiet, either with a loud "Amen!" or the staccato clapping of her hands. At this signal everyone falls silent, and the leader then proceeds to announce the next prayer item on the agenda.

Intercession is followed by what is called, in English, "praise and worship," which amounts to thirty to forty-five minutes of call-and-response singing. It is during praise and worship that most people come to the service. This includes the pastor, who is never the first to arrive and usually waits until the meeting is in full swing before entering the room. The music moves from upbeat songs accompanied by dancing to more contemplative pieces, which in turn move believers into a second period of collective-personal prayer. This time, there is no one choosing a topic, and participants are instead free to pray, weep, and sing in whatever way they—and the Holy Spirit—choose. While in this respect the collective-personal prayer that follows praise and worship is unstructured, the same mechanism used for bringing everyone together during intercession is again employed to signal the end of these prayers, as a church leader will stand up and either offer a loud prayer that gets everyone's attention or simply say, "Amen." When this happens, believers return to their seats and wait for the next part of the service, the sermon.

Sermons in Pentecostal churches last for anywhere from thirty minutes to over an hour, depending in part on whether or not the pastor has

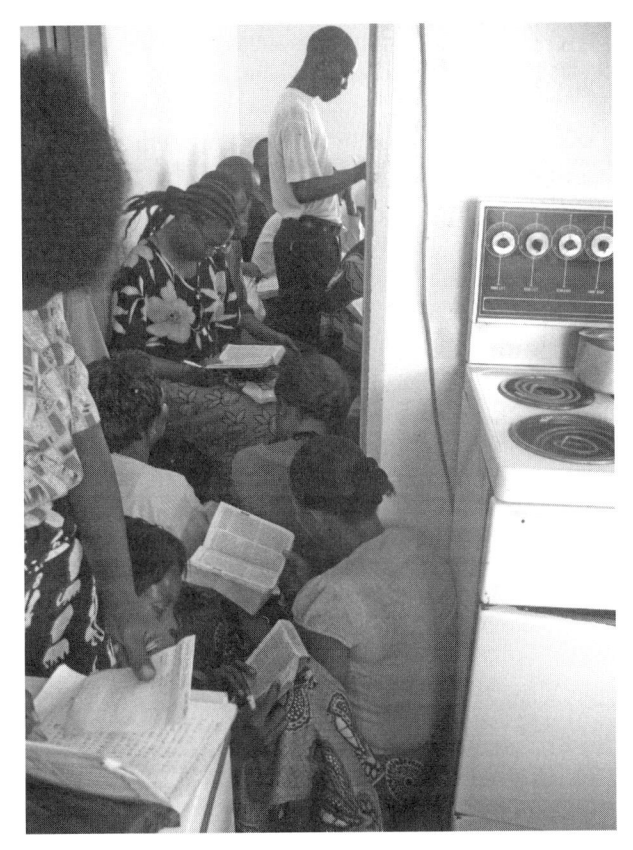

FIGURE 6. Believers crammed into a house for a meeting, spilling into the kitchen, as well as into bedrooms and out the front door.

chosen to make use of an interpreter.[4] During the sermon believers sit quietly in the plastic garden chairs or school desks that have been provided for them if they are lucky, on the floor if they are not (figure 6). Some doze, but most pay at least enough attention to write down the scripture references mentioned in the sermon or follow along in their Bibles if they have them. And, particularly if the preacher is skilled and the topic exciting, many are not only dutiful note-takers but also keen participants. While preaching, pastors use several rhetorical devices to keep believers' attention, including asking them to "turn to their neighbor" and repeat a phrase such as, "Get ready!" or "Are you listening?," a practice common on Pentecostal television. Pastors will also say the first part of a word and wait for their audience to finish it, a technique used in traditional storytelling throughout Zambia.

The final component of a Pentecostal meeting is prayer ministry, presided over by the pastor and possibly other church leaders as well, though this is less common. This takes one of two forms. Sometimes a pastor will conclude his sermon by asking people who want to be prayed for to come to the front of the room, where he will lay hands on them and pray for them, sometimes causing them to fall to the ground. Alternately, the meeting may end without the pastor offering prayer only to have believers seek him out once everyone has gone outside. After the service a popular pastor will find himself with a queue of people waiting to see him, and he will either meet with them individually at that moment or schedule another time to attend to them later in the week.

Regardless of whether prayer ministry has been incorporated into the formal service or develops afterward, Pentecostal meetings always end with a receiving line, with the pastor and leaders in front and the remaining members of the congregation joining as they work their way down, so that everyone greets everyone else with a handshake (figure 7). After this, the meeting breaks up in stages. Some people head home right away, while many others linger to visit with friends, or perhaps to have a quick meeting of one of the many smaller groups attached to the congregation, such as the women's ministry or the choir.

Among different churches there are a few small variations to the outline I have provided here, particularly with regard to the point in the service at which the monetary offering is taken up and whether people are given time to share testimonies. Nevertheless, what I have presented here is a standard structure of Pentecostal worship, one that is remarkably uniform across the Copperbelt. Readers familiar with other kinds of Christian practice will likely recognize the order of worship that I have just outlined as typical of more conservative Protestants, with the meeting oriented around the exposition of the biblical text through a sermon, rather than the Eucharist, as in a Catholic or Anglican mass.[5] It is certainly true that the structure of Pentecostal worship on the Copperbelt is informed by Protestant practice more generally. Since most believers were part of missionary-established denominations before they became Pentecostals, this is not surprising. However, while Nsofu believers have doubtless taken a leaf from the Protestant prayer book, so to speak, there is more to how Pentecostal services are organized than just their adoption of available Christian forms. This is because of the way that this order structures the relationship between vertical and horizontal elements. As we make a second pass through the Pentecostal worship

FIGURE 7. Receiving line at Key of David with Pastor and Mrs. Mwanza at the front of the line.

service, what we will be watching for this time is how these elements are expressed in the various stages of a church service.

FROM EGALITARIANISM TO HIERARCHY IN PENTECOSTAL WORSHIP

Let us begin at the beginning with intercession, the first step of a Pentecostal service and one of the most egalitarian components of Pentecostal worship. That this is the case is most immediately obvious in the fact that intercession takes place before the pastor has arrived. More importantly, we have seen that while engaged in collective-personal prayer believers are extremely independent. The noise generated by collective-personal prayer means that this is a chance for everyone to have God's ear more or less privately and to voice not only the concerns of the church but also their own personal requests. This last element, the individual "burdens" included among the list of petitions a leader offers for intercession, is of special importance to many believers. Indeed, after one of the rare occasions where a leader failed to create space for individual requests during intercession, Bana Sinkala told me that she felt as though she "had not really prayed." Here again we see how Pentecostal prayer, despite its collective nature, serves primarily to infuse the individual with religious power.

Notwithstanding all of these individualized, egalitarian aspects, however, it is clear that intercession is not a completely personal affair in which each believer may do exactly as she pleases, but is rather governed by the leader, who chooses the topics and tells people when to start and stop praying. Intercession leaders like Moses were sometimes skeptical as to whether people actually followed their directions, but for the most part believers emphasized the need to stay together (*ca pamo*) in intercession, to be one (*umo*) with the group, though they also felt there should be space to pray for individual burdens. Intercession is therefore marked by a tension between individual religious expression and the authority of lay leadership. This tension is also evident during praise and worship, with its call-and-response singing, and comes to a head when the music gives way to another round of collective-personal prayer, this time involving the entire congregation.

The second period of collective-personal prayer is the most critical moment in the service. For one thing, it is the point where the most people are present, as many will have arrived late and at least a few will leave early. More importantly, this time of collective-personal prayer represents the service's ritual climax, a moment of "intense and absorbing intimacy with a perceived divine presence" (Lindhardt 2011: 23), and a space within which individual believers have direct access to the power of the Holy Spirit. In contrast to prayer in mainline congregations, when believers could only pray quietly "in their hearts," collective-personal prayer actively involves everyone in a religious practice in which individual experiences with the Holy Spirit are especially pronounced (Haynes 2016). All of this means that in this moment of collective-personal prayer believers are most clearly confronted with Pentecostalism's democratic character; as promised in the Bible, the Spirit is poured out on "all flesh." Little wonder then that during collective-personal prayer the tension between Pentecostal egalitarianism and the authority of church leaders sometimes develops into a conflict.

Occasionally, when a leader calls the people to order at the end of collective-personal prayer, one or more believers will not respond. If someone appears to be having an especially moving experience with the Holy Spirit—is on the floor weeping uncontrollably, for example—he or she

Ritual and the (Un)making of the Pentecostal Relational World | 83

may continue to pray or cry even though everyone else has quieted down. The first few moments of this are very uncomfortable. The private space created by the noise of so many voices has dropped away, and everyone gathered is suddenly privy to the earnest prayers of one or two believers. In such moments it is difficult to avoid the sense that these prayers might cause the whole meeting to fall apart, and indeed, such situations do contain elements that might upend the structure of a Pentecostal church. Like the young Malaysian workers who are possessed by spirits on the factory floor (Ong 1987), believers who are overcome by the power of the Holy Spirit and continue to pray after they have been told to stop are effectively contesting established frameworks of power. While I do not think that the believers who have such experiences would describe them in these terms, it is clear that this is how church leaders perceive these moments. In such situations, a pastor can make one of two moves.

The first possible response to someone who will not stop praying is to treat that person as a religious bellwether. If a believer is having a particularly powerful experience with the Holy Spirit, as evidenced by her inability to stop praying when she is told to do so, her behavior can be regarded as a sign that God wants everyone to continue in collective-personal prayer. The easiest way for a pastor to signal this is to simply allow the person to keep praying, perhaps by singing a song or beginning to pray himself. In the uncomfortable tension that surrounds these moments, such a response serves as sufficient—albeit tacit—approval for another round of collective-personal prayer. After a few more minutes of everyone praying, leaders may make another bid to bring the group back together, and this second bid is usually successful. Markers of divine approval are not always so indirect, however. One Sunday at Key of David, for example, collective-personal prayer resulted in a handful of people, including one or two members of the music team, weeping on the floor after everyone else had quieted down. A few moments passed before Moses came forward, picked up a microphone, and offered a prophecy. Using the first person, as he was speaking God's words, Moses explained to the congregation that God had placed several members of the church "on the operating table," removing sin from their lives to make them more like him. By the time Moses's prophecy was over everyone was silent, and those who had been on the floor had begun to stand up. Ushers quickly moved to the front of the room to receive the offering and the service proceeded without interruption.

The other possible response to someone who will not stop praying is to reject her bid for control and force her to be quiet. This may be as simple as shouting another "Amen," more sternly than before, perhaps with an addition that requires a more obvious response—for instance, "Amen, you people of God?" (*Mwe bantu ba kwa Lesa*).[6] I have seen pastors approach someone praying on the floor and touch her on the shoulder, perhaps with the addition of a quick prayer, a gentle but clear sign that she needs to quiet down. In more serious cases, stronger measures will be taken to keep a person under control. The most extreme example of this that I saw was the response of Higher Calling to a woman named Gwen. Gwen would frequently continue praying after the rest of the group had stopped, and she was loud and sometimes frightening in her petitions, so much so that Bana Chanda's young son Tim refused to sit near her during prayer meetings (see Haynes 2016). Eventually, a member of the church leadership was assigned to sit with Gwen during the service in order, believers said, to keep her prayers from getting out of control.

Bana Chanda did not feel this measure was sufficient, and she told me that she thought Gwen should be banned from Higher Calling, an opinion that at least some other church members shared. Several people at Higher Calling thought Gwen was a nuisance at best and, while they never made this accusation outright, my impression was that some thought that the situation was much worse—namely, that she was under the influence of demons. It is not difficult to see why people would draw this conclusion. Just as allowing prayer to continue is effectively to acknowledge that the Holy Spirit is at work, so forcibly stopping it suggests that the influence may not be divine, but rather demonic (Lynn 2013). As some believers explained it to me, the Holy Spirit inside the person hears when a pastor says "Amen," and the Holy Spirit will obey these directions because the same Spirit is working in the pastor. In contrast, a demon will not obey the man of God, but will instead sow "confusion" in the congregation by causing someone to be disruptive. This latter accusation is a strong one, as the English loanword "confusion" connotes the devil's desire to overthrow or undermine the work of the church. In contrast to the disorder that comes from Satan, Pentecostals on the Copperbelt regularly insist that "Lesa wa order"—God is a God of order (see Bialecki 2011).

These two potential responses obviously take opposite tacks, one smoothing over the disruption by ruling that God is behind it, the other stopping it in its tracks by, in the most extreme case, suggesting that it is the work of the devil. I have seen church leaders gently force people to be quiet far more frequently than I have seen them allow prayer to continue after they have called for order. While this latter option is probably easier, its implications are more dangerous, as the choice to keep praying suggests that the Holy Spirit is doing something that the pastor did not know about. Since this moment represents the point in the service when believers are most visibly confronted with the unpredictable movement of the Holy Spirit, an indication of a spiritual shortcoming on the part of a pastor would be especially damaging.

If the praise and worship time culminates in a moment at which egalitarianism presents its strongest opposition to established religious hierarchies, the sermon represents a clear move in favor of pastoral authority. Up to this point the service has emphasized the outpouring of the Holy Spirit on everyone, but during the sermon there are numerous indicators that the Holy Spirit's power has been concentrated in the particular person of the preacher. Indeed, several aspects of the church service have indexed his spiritual superiority even before the sermon begins. As the pastor approaches the pulpit, a junior pastor or lay leader will usually carry his Bible for him, sometimes dusting off the pulpit with a handkerchief before setting the book down. The spatial arrangement of a Pentecostal meeting, whether it is held in a church building, a home, or a classroom, also points to the authority of a pastor. Church leaders always sit at the front of the room, sometimes on a dais. While laypeople may be on the floor or at school desks, pastors sit comfortably on plastic garden chairs or a sofa. In some groups they are provided with bottled mineral water, soft drinks, cookies, and sweets, though no one else at the meeting is given any refreshment. Even before a pastor begins to preach, then, his authority has been communicated in a number of ways.

Pentecostal sermons on the Copperbelt are characterized by two complementary approaches. The first of these is what believers sometimes refer to as "scolding" (*ukukalipila*), or even "punishment" (*ukupanika*). When scolding, pastors reprimand their congregations for their failure to conform to the standards of Pentecostal adherence—for not giving enough, praying enough, or fasting enough, for instance. While people feel somber after such messages, they will usually speak of them in positive terms, saying that these are the sorts of things they need to hear so that they can become better Pentecostals.[7] In addition to scolding, the other approach pastors take in their sermons is encouragement (*ukukoselesha*). If scolding is about reprimanding believers for not doing the things that they should, encouragement is about spurring them on to do those very things. Encouragement is typically framed in terms of promises that faithful Pentecostal adherence will result in blessings, and sermons that take this approach understandably evoke the most positive responses. Often, preachers will move back and forth between scolding and encouragement in the same sermon. Through these different elements of preaching pastors actualize their roles as parents. Like a parent, a pastor instructs his followers about what they ought to do and reprimands them when they fail to do what he says. Pastors are able to offer this type of guidance because of their position of religious superiority, and that position is therefore both indexed and reinforced as believers listen to sermons each week.

After the authority of the pastor has been established through the sermon, the service concludes with a final demonstration of his special spiritual power. Simply put, prayer ministry happens because pastors have a unique anointing from the Holy Spirit that makes their prayers especially effective. They are, to return to Bana Karen's words, "chosen" by God, closer to him than other believers, and this is why Pentecostals go to church leaders for prayer. In so doing they both underscore a pastor's special spiritual status and reproduce the religious distinction between church leaders and themselves. In other words, whether a pastor offers prayer ministry in the context of the service or it develops organically afterward as believers wait to meet with him, his spiritual power is visibly confirmed as others come to him for prayer.

Over the course of a Pentecostal church service, then, the egalitarian elements of Pentecostalism, which emphasize the outpouring of the Holy Spirit on all believers, give way to a religious asymmetry in which certain people stand out as having special skill with regard to spiritual gifts. Here it is worth pointing out that as the service progresses, ritual work is increasingly accomplished by church leaders acting alone. During intercession the pastor is not present, and the role of the lay leader is minor, as the work of prayer is carried out primarily by other lay participants. Praise and worship and, to a lesser extent, the sermon, are likewise dependent on the participation of ordinary believers as they join in the call-and-response singing and respond to the rhetorical cues of the pastor. In contrast, prayer ministry is unidirectional, as the work of prayer in this case is carried out by church leaders acting without the assistance of laypeople—indeed, in prayer ministry pastors are acting *on* ordinary believers, or at least on their behalf.

In these observations we are given an important clue about how the various social ties that form in Pentecostal congregations sit in relationship to each other. While both egalitarian and hierarchical relationships have a part to play in Pentecostal worship, the progression of the church service is one in which asymmetrical ties are ultimately emphasized. In other words, hierarchy encompasses egalitarianism every time believers come together for worship. This arrangement suggests that in the network of social ties that sits at the heart of Pentecostal adherence, connections to church leaders are the ones that matter most. It is not difficult to see why. Although breakthroughs can come about through collective-personal prayer as surely as they can through the mediation of a pastor, just as moving can happen through both savings associations and patronage, there is something special about the tie between a pastor and a layperson—perhaps a bit of extra efficacy, or at least a bit of extra efficiency. If pastors are closer to God than ordinary people are, it stands to reason that their intervention carries more weight than that of a layperson, even if that layperson can also draw on the spiritual energies of other believers to build her own prayers. In the political economy of moving by the Spirit, a relationship with a powerful pastor is an especially valuable thing to have.

While an analysis of Pentecostal worship has pointed to the particular importance of ties between pastors and laypeople, we have also seen that for all the gains that hierarchy makes over the course of a church service, egalitarianism is nevertheless present in nearly every part of the ritual. Even prayer ministry, which we have identified as the most asymmetrical part of a Pentecostal meeting, is either preceded or followed by a receiving line that includes everyone. From a social structural perspective, this egalitarianism runs contrary to the hierarchical ties I have emphasized so far, as it spreads access to the Holy Spirit democratically through the congregation, rather than concentrating it in a few individuals. The egalitarian moments in Pentecostal worship are moments in which any believer might receive a special anointing from God, which may take away from the authority of the pastor and even result in a schism. While on the one hand Pentecostal ritual therefore reproduces and reinforces spiritual distinction, on the other it leaves room for the possibility that existing frameworks of authority might be dismantled. This potential for "endless fission," while obviously destructive to the charismatic asymmetry that I have argued is central to Pentecostalism's appeal, is in fact a key component of this religion's long-term social productivity.

UNDOING HIERARCHY, OR WHY EGALITARIANISM MATTERS

While relationships to pastors are especially significant to Pentecostal laypeople, these ties are also extremely vulnerable. For most believers in

Nsofu, particularly those with fewer financial resources, the greatest threat to Pentecostal relational life is the possibility that access to their pastor will be dictated by individual economic status. What they are afraid of here is the possibility that their pastor will spend more time and devote more spiritual attention to those who make greater financial contributions to the church. If this happens, the pastor is no longer acting like a good parent, treating all of his spiritual children equally. Instead he is, as they put it, "choosing" (*ukusala*), giving preferential treatment to some members of his congregation. Bana Chanda described it to me this way:

> Naomi, here in Zambia this is the way things are: if someone has money, lives very well, then pastors—you'll see—a pastor will be very close to you. In every little thing. You might have a request or a prayer or simply say that you are not feeling well, you're sick, and they might pray for you for one whole hour. But someone who doesn't have money might say, "I'm sick" and they pray twenty, twenty-five minutes.

The reason that this possibility is especially worrisome to poorer Pentecostals is obvious: a pastor who chooses is a pastor to whom they may not always have access, a pastor whose spiritual resources can help them move by the Spirit will be doled out in such a way as to leave them wanting.

These fears are not unreasonable. Small independent churches like the ones I studied do not usually have the financial means to support a pastor's family. Even though Key of David had a higher number of professionals—that is, people who were able to contribute more money—than any of the other churches I followed, the Mwanzas were often stretched thin. The congregation covered the family's rent, and Mrs. Mwanza worked as a teacher, which helped a bit, as did contributions from Moses and me. But there were still times when we had to wait for everyone to come home so that we could put together enough money for the evening meal, or when the electricity meter ran out before we could pay it. Because I lived in the Mwanza home, I am most familiar with their circumstances, but I know that other pastors also struggled to make ends meet.[8] A number were involved in business ventures alongside their ministries, or had spouses who were employed, and this made a difference. But by itself the money raised in the congregation was hardly enough to keep up with the church's expenses, to pay the rent on a classroom for worship, much less to raise money for a new keyboard or to register the church with the city council, the first step in securing a plot of land for a building. By the time these needs were met, there was often precious little left to support a pastor and his family.

Under these circumstances, it was a great temptation for pastors to focus their energies on those who were able to help them out financially. Every pastor I spoke to said that he would pray for anyone who came to him for help, regardless of his or her circumstances. However, when pressed, most would also admit that if they had to make a choice between traveling to the home of someone they knew would give them money "for transport," as the local euphemism has it, and someone who could not provide them with any such gift, they would choose the former. That such decisions are far from what any pastor would consider the ideal does not change the fact that choosing sometimes happens. Believers are incredibly sensitive to this possibility, readily indignant at any hint of choosing on a pastor's part.

Although the primary reason for believers' resistance to choosing is surely that they feel they are in danger of being excluded from a relationship with their pastor, there are other problems that choosing creates for the Pentecostal social world as we have defined it. First, by seeking the support of those who can help him financially, a pastor effectively reverses the central, structuring asymmetry in his congregation. By receiving resources from someone who is his spiritual son or daughter a pastor is, at best, entering into a sort of alternating asymmetry similar to that of *chilimba*, in which contributions of money and spiritual services move back and forth in roughly equal amounts. At worst, this asymmetry is completely reversed, as the pastor is now dependent on his spiritual child, rather than the other way around. This in turn undermines the spiritual difference that makes moving by the Spirit possible.

Second, when pastors seek the support of wealthier laypeople, Pentecostalism loses some of its uniqueness as a framework for moving. If a central component of this religion's attraction lies in the alternative mechanisms for and metric of moving that it makes possible, then the introduction of overtly financial modes of dependence into Pentecostal social life collapses the distinction between relationships that form inside and outside the church. Not only does this undermine the potential of Pentecostalism to provide a new avenue of moving, but it also introduces new vulnerabilities into Pentecostal social relationships. Relationships of dependence that are structured by economic difference are, as we have seen, unreliable in times of economic uncertainty. Any change that represents a move toward these types of relationships therefore threatens the comparatively secure social framework of Pentecostalism.

It is in the light of the vulnerability of ties to church leaders to what Bana Chanda once described to me as "corruption" that we can return to the egalitarian features of the Pentecostal service. Over the course of a Pentecostal meeting, ritual practice not only moves from egalitarianism to hierarchy but also allows the former at least one moment of unbridled expression. Although we have identified egalitarian elements throughout the course of a Pentecostal service, the moment of collective-personal prayer that follows praise and worship represents not only the ritual high point of the service but also the moment when the egalitarian aspects of Pentecostal theology—the promises that the Spirit will be poured out on all flesh and that it goes wherever it pleases—are most pronounced. Consequently, this is also the point when established Pentecostal hierarchies are most clearly threatened. While it is unlikely that new leadership will emerge from within the congregation at such a moment, the unpredictable movements of the Holy Spirit during collective-personal prayer serve as a reminder to everyone that special spiritual power might appear anywhere at any time. As Weber reminds us, charismatic authority is by definition unstable, and established spiritual hierarchies are easily broken down and replaced with new ones. Understood in these terms, democratic forms of religious practice, especially collective-personal prayer, represent both a counterpart and a potential corrective to Pentecostal asymmetry that has been corrupted.

All of this means that what is at stake when collective-personal prayer goes on after a leader has told people to stop is not just the control of that particular meeting, but rather a pastor's position. It makes sense therefore that the only way pastors are able to regain control in these moments is through a tacit appeal to supernatural forces, whether good or evil. The implication of both responses is that leaders still have the superior power of the Holy Spirit, either to cast out demons or to discern that God wishes collective-personal prayer to continue. In both cases the pastor's response is clearly aimed at something much larger than the people who will not stop praying. By taking control of these situations, church leaders communicate to the members of their congregations that their charismatic power remains intact, that the Holy Spirit's anointing still rests on them. At bottom, then, these moments are a commentary on religious authority, and on the very real possibility that it might change hands. Given the potential for corruption in Pentecostal relationships, this notion is comforting for some, cautionary for others.

Although the egalitarian aspects of Pentecostal worship are especially important for their potential to give rise to new leadership, I should be careful to point out that situations when collective-personal prayer threatens to get out of hand are relatively rare in Nsofu. Typically, worship reaches a fevered pitch only to quickly and effectively be brought back under control. As believers insist, *Lesa wa order.* I think this arrangement reflects the thing they want most from their religious lives: an established charismatic hierarchy that structures relationships of religious dependence that in turn make it possible to move by the Spirit. That Pentecostal ritual has the potential to effect this desired result is quite clear, and this is reflected in the structure of the Sunday service, as it moves toward increasingly hierarchical forms of religious practice. At the same time, egalitarianism is never far behind, and for all that Pentecostal worship underscores the capacity of this religion to create hierarchical ties, it also contains within itself the tools to replace existing relationships with new ones as necessary.

What we take from our discussion of Pentecostal ritual are therefore two key points. First, of the different social relationships through which believers realize moving by the Spirit, the one that they consider most important is the mediatory skill of church leaders. Second, relationships to church leaders, while immensely valuable, are fragile and easily corrupted. The vulnerability of Pentecostal social ties to choosing is central to the way that Pentecostalism is practiced in Nsofu. In the next three chapters, I explore how the need to protect these relationships shapes Copperbelt Pentecostalism, with regard to both gender dynamics and the internal economy of individual congregations. As we will see, this is primarily a matter of negotiating the relationship between the two sub-values that make up moving by the Spirit: charisma and prosperity.

CHAPTER 5

Prosperity, Charisma, and the Problem of Gender

Pentecostal churches on the Copperbelt sponsor numerous activities for women. In addition to regular "ladies" meetings, which bring together the female members of a congregation, there is a steady parade of larger women's events, including the popular "Women of Influence" conference held each year in the Kitwe city center. There is an extent to which these gatherings seem superfluous. Demographically, the difference between a women's meeting and an ordinary Pentecostal service is often minimal. All Pentecostal churches in Nsofu have more women than men, and many of the smaller independent congregations are overwhelmingly female in composition, at least as far as laypeople are concerned. In this regard, the township is no different from other parts of the world. Globally, most Pentecostals are women (e.g., Martin 2001: 56; Hunt 2002: 159–60). The result of this simple demographic fact has been a steady stream of social scientific research into the effects of Pentecostal adherence on gender relations. Does Pentecostalism, with its notably egalitarian theology, promote gender equality?

In contrast to research on seniority, which has shown Pentecostalism to challenge existing hierarchies (van Dijk 1992, Lauterbach 2010), the impact of this religion on gender is more difficult to parse. On the one hand, it is clear that Pentecostalism opens up new opportunities that can be "deeply empowering" for women (Brusco 2010: 81; also see Pfeiffer et al. 2007), from leadership in the church (Gill 1990, Lorentzen and Mira 2005) to entrepreneurship (Frahm-Arp 2010, van de Kamp

2010). On the other, there can be no doubt that Pentecostalism reinforces patriarchy. Female believers are subordinated to male leadership first and foremost in the home, but often also in the church as well (Mate 2002, Soothill 2007, Ajibade 2012). This latter observation certainly applies to the Copperbelt. Although the majority of believers are female, there are very few women in charge of Pentecostal groups, and fewer still who have achieved positions of significant influence.[1] In general, the female leaders that are found on the Copperbelt oversee Pentecostal fellowships rather than churches, a fact that further demonstrates their marginalization, since on the whole these groups are less influential, less visible to the general public.[2]

In this chapter I explore the reasons for Pentecostalism's curious gender disparity as it relates to church leadership.[3] Why, in a religion that promises equal access to the spiritual powers necessary for ministry, are there so few female pastors and bishops? At first glance, the answer to this question seems obvious. In a cultural context like that of Zambia, where women are subordinate to men in most domains (see, e.g., Crehan 1997; cf. Evans 2014), it comes as no surprise that established gender hierarchies are reflected in the church. Indeed, as Jane Soothill (2007, following von Doepp 2002) has argued for Ghana, Pentecostalism is perhaps especially likely to replicate existing patterns of gender discrimination. Unlike other forms of Christianity, which may bar women from the pastorate while still reserving other spaces, such as women's groups, for female control, the open-ended leadership structures of Pentecostalism reproduce dominant models of gender hierarchy with particular ease.

While I do not wish to dispute the claim that gender hierarchy in Pentecostal churches reflects broader cultural patterns, I do want to suggest that in the case of the Copperbelt there is more at stake in the subordination of female leadership than the reproduction of the status quo. Rather, the (pre)dominance of men in the Pentecostal pastorate reflects one of the core tensions of this religion, namely that between charisma and prosperity, which we have identified as the two primary elements that together make up moving by the Spirit. To be a bit more specific, it is in the context of gender relations that we begin to understand how prosperity and charisma relate to each other as subvalues under the overarching value of moving by the Spirit. This arrangement protects the ties that form in Pentecostal groups from corruption, which we have seen is the primary threat to Pentecostal social life. An analysis of how gendered authority is negotiated in Copperbelt congregations therefore serves to move us beyond the binary categories of egalitarianism and patriarchy that have characterized so much writing on Pentecostal gender dynamics. More importantly, my discussion in this chapter also expands our understanding of the framework of value that undergirds structures Pentecostal social life.

In the analysis that follows, I focus my attention on the few women who have managed to secure leadership positions in Copperbelt Pentecostal groups. These women represent important exceptions that will help us prove the rules of Pentecostal gender hierarchy as expressions of the relationship between charisma and prosperity. Before going on to examine the lives and ministries of female church leaders, however, I must first clarify the analytical role that gender plays in my discussion.

GENDER IN SOCIAL AND STRUCTURAL PERSPECTIVE

Although my discussion in this chapter focuses on specific women and men, and on practices that might be considered by people on the Copperbelt to be (stereo)typically male or female, my argument turns on an understanding of gender that extends beyond bodies or persons. To wit, in what follows I treat gender as "a social and structural category" (Eriksen 2009: 89). By referring to gender as a social category, I mean that different kinds of social action are gendered. As Marilyn Strathern puts it in her now-classic treatment of gender and exchange in Melanesia, "Gender demarcates different types of agency. Persons differently impinge upon one another, and imagining 'male' or 'female' ranges of efficacy becomes a way of eliciting these diverse types" (1988: 93). Gender in this definition serves as a way of marking different social orientations or relational modalities, which are not the exclusive province of men or women, but are nevertheless gendered male or female. Indeed, in Strathern's framework these relational models are not only gendered but gendering—that is, through male or female ways of "[impinging] upon" others a person emerges, at least in a given relational instance, as gendered. Put yet another way, persons are not by themselves male or female (in Strathern's treatment they are androgynous), but rather appear as such through and in different relationships. This means, of course, that a person with a male body might be male in some relationships, female in others, and that the same is true for someone with a female body.[4] It is this definition of gender as relational practice that I am drawing on when I refer to gender as a social (rather than simply sociological) category. To illustrate what I mean by gender as a structural category, I turn to Annelin Eriksen's work on Christianity on Ambrym Island, Vanuatu.

Although Eriksen draws on Strathern, at least insofar as she also approaches gender in relational terms, gender in her analysis is also a mechanism for differentiation and ranking, and as such a framework of value. In her work male and female forms of social action gain or lose importance—emerge as more or less valued—with changes in Ambrym's religious landscape (Eriksen 2009, 2012). Eriksen's model of value is informed by Dumont, particularly his notions of "encompassment" and "levels," which in Eriksen's analysis become tools for understanding how gender is operationalized in Ambrym Pentecostalism (Eriksen 2014). As noted in the introduction, hierarchy for Dumont is defined by encompassment. As he describes it, the relationship of encompassment is the relation "between a whole (or a set) and an element of this whole (or set): the element belongs to the set and is in this sense consubstantial or identical with it." At the same time, the element is distinct from the set and therefore also "stands in opposition to it" (Dumont 1980: 240). According to Dumont, this relationship is sometimes reversed: the lower-ranked or encompassed value can become the more highly ranked or encompassing value (see Dumont 1986: 252–53). However, this is only true on less important "levels" of a given society. One of Dumont's classic examples here is the relationship between an Indian priest and king. While at the highest level—the encompassing whole that Dumont identifies in religion—the priest is superior to the king, in matters of state, which represent an inferior level, the king is superior to the priest.

In addition to her structural analysis, which I return to in the conclusion to this chapter, Eriksen's work also provides us with a second point that is helpful in exploring how gender shapes Copperbelt Pentecostalism. In many ways, churches on Ambrym resemble their counterparts on the Copperbelt, at least insofar as they are marked by a similar tension between pastoral authority and the democratic outpouring of the Holy Spirit, a tension that often gives rise to schism (Eriksen 2012). In Eriksen's treatment, this familiar Pentecostal dynamic is gendered. Eriksen argues that the concentration of hierarchical authority in the charismatic individual of the pastor is a male way of mobilizing religious power, while the dispersed collective power of the Holy Spirit in prayer is a female way of mobilizing religious power. These gendered models in turn reflect traditional frameworks of masculinity and femininity on Ambrym, with the former realized most fully in the context of the secret men's cult that dominated ritual life on the island prior to the arrival of Christianity.

On the Copperbelt, while traditional gender relations certainly differ from those found in Vanuatu, when it comes to Pentecostalism a similar dynamic to that which Eriksen has described on Ambrym obtains. Following Eriksen, I argue that the female Pentecostal mode of establishing relationships relies heavily on certain egalitarian practices that are not found in the male Pentecostal mode of establishing relationships. As we will see, the social orientation that I treat below as female requires church leaders to personally identify with laypeople. This process of identification is grounded in collective prayer alongside ordinary believers, although it also relies on other rhetorical practices.[5] In contrast, identification of this sort is not part of the male social orientation, which is based on differentiation and hierarchical distinction as seen in practices like preaching, prophecy, and deliverance. Nevertheless—and here my analysis departs from Eriksen's—the ultimate difference between these two modes of sociality is not one of egalitarianism or hierarchy; as we will see, the spiritual asymmetry that we have identified as central to the tie between church leaders and laypeople is found in both kinds of relationships. What is different, however, is the process through which the social tie is established, and, more importantly, the axis along which spiritual asymmetry is measured, whether an axis of prosperity or charisma. With this understanding of gender in place, we can now turn our attention to the ministry of Nsofu's most successful female Pentecostal leader.

"THAT WOMAN REALLY PRAYS"

Bana Mfuwe's was a name that I began to hear almost immediately upon my arrival in Nsofu, and even after she left for South Africa people spoke of her often. While believers had a number of good things to say about Bana Mfuwe, the remark I heard most frequently was simply, "That woman really prays" (*Balapepesha*). In part, what believers meant by this was that Bana Mfuwe was faithful in Pentecostal practice, since, again, "praying" often serves as a shorthand term for religious adherence. However, they also meant just what they said, namely, that Bana Mfuwe prayed seriously and frequently. What is interesting about this statement is that it is the sort of remark that is usually used to describe an especially dedicated layperson, rather than a church leader. Indeed, there were several ways in which Bana Mfuwe could be identified with laypeople. For one thing, her sermons often highlighted her experiences of struggle, including her failure to finish school, early problems in her marriage, and her husband's initial lack of support for her Pentecostal commitment—challenges with which many members of her congregation were personally familiar. In addition, while a great deal of time was devoted to prayer at Higher Calling, it was rare to see prayer ministry of the type that typically concludes Pentecostal services. Although Bana Mfuwe did meet with people one-on-one for prayer, this usually happened in private meetings rather than in public displays of power. In contrast to prayer ministry at the hands of a few church leaders, prayer at Higher Calling was largely collective, and Bana Mfuwe was often in the thick of it, mixing her petitions with everyone else's. At the end of long prayer and fasting retreats her voice would be hoarse from hours of intercession. She was, as people said, someone who really prayed.

If we take Bana Mfuwe as representative of female Pentecostal leaders on the Copperbelt, which I think we can, this brief discussion suggests that the reason there are so few women in leadership is that they do not effectively mobilize the markers of charismatic asymmetry that I have shown to be central to the Pentecostal pastorate. Rather than reinforce their spiritual superiority, women relate their own experiences of struggle; rather than demonstrate their charismatic power through public prayer ministry, they pray alongside church members until their voices are finished (see Eriksen 2012). While there is certainly a difference in how female Pentecostal leaders present themselves in public, it would be a mistake to assume that the spiritual asymmetry that we have identified as central to Pentecostal social life is not found among female leaders. On the contrary, there were clear signs that people thought of Bana Mfuwe as religiously superior. Believers at Higher Calling referred to Bana Mfuwe as their spiritual parent or mother, for instance, which we have seen is a clear marker of special religious status. What makes Bana Mfuwe different from people like Pastor Mwanza is therefore not a lack of spiritual asymmetry as such. Rather, what is unique about this female Pentecostal leader and others like her is first the axis along which spiritual asymmetry is measured and second the ritual mechanisms through which it is produced. In the discussion that follows, I treat each of these in turn.

Despite Bana Mfuwe's regular appeals to her past struggles, it was abundantly clear that these were largely a thing of the past. Since the group met in a chapel behind Bana Mfuwe's house, and since she often prayed for people in her well-furnished sitting room, the material blessings that her family enjoyed were visible to everyone who came through Higher Calling. Bana Mfuwe's physical appearance was further proof in this regard: fashionable clothing, powdered skin, a plump figure. During prayer meetings Bana Mfuwe would sometimes balance her youngest child on her hip; unlike many women at Higher Calling, she did not need to pray for a baby. Although her husband was generally not present at Higher Calling meetings, his tacit approval was evident in everything that happened, as he presumably did not mind that his house had been taken over by Pentecostals or that his wife spent so much time in ministry. Here again was an answered prayer, the supportive marriage that eludes so many believers. Taken together, these visible blessings set Bana Mfuwe apart from the members of her fellowship and made her into a symbol of prosperity as it is locally defined. Her life was proof that God could make marriages happy, could provide money for nice clothes and children's private school fees.

That Bana Mfuwe's prosperity was a key element of her spiritual distinction was made especially clear to me when I accompanied her to a midweek home group (*citente*) held in a shanty compound near Nsofu. On the day of the meeting I arrived at Bana Mfuwe's house to find her smartly dressed in a gray suit, her hair swept up in a stylish wig. Rather than walking or taking the bus, as I had done when I had accompanied other laypeople to this fellowship, at Bana Mfuwe's insistence we traveled in a taxi, which left us at the end of a dirt road on the edge of the compound. As we drew close to the brick house where the meeting was being held we could hear the sound of singing floating down the street. Inside we found more than a dozen women crowded into a tiny sitting room, barefoot beneath their *citente* wrap skirts, many with babies tied to their backs. The singing continued as we joined the meeting, and I slipped into a corner as Bana Mfuwe went to the front of the room and led the group in her signature call-and-response chant:

> *Ine ukucula, cula? Awe!*
> *Ndi mwana wa ba Lesa!*
> *Ine ukulomba, lomba? Awe!*
> *Ndi mwana wa ba Lesa!*
>
> Will I suffer? No!
> I am a child of God!
> Will I beg? No!
> I am a child of God

The women chanted along until they were breathless. When they had finished, they sank into chairs or found seats on the floor and looked expectantly to the visiting preacher.

Bana Mfuwe did not disappoint. By way of a sermon she related her personal testimony of struggle. When she first became a believer, her husband had disapproved of her participation in Pentecostal services, forbidding her to attend prayer meetings and even throwing her out of the house at one point. Bana Mfuwe had persevered despite these difficulties, she explained, and had ultimately experienced a breakthrough. The women listened attentively as she spoke of how her husband had welcomed her back into the home and no longer stood in the way of her religious practice, but instead allowed her to host meetings at their house. And not only that; he also gave her money for household expenses, bought her gifts, and—notably—called her "Sweetie." The crowning point in Bana Mfuwe's testimony came as she described her family's plans to move to South Africa. For people on the Copperbelt, South Africa represents the most proximate point of access to the West and the sure promise of a better life. In the eyes of those who heard Bana Mfuwe's message, then, it appeared that this woman who had already received so much was on her way to enjoying an even greater blessing. As Bana Mfuwe related her family's plans, she began to tremble, a sign of the presence of the Holy Spirit that underscored the spiritual power of her testimony.

Bana Mfuwe's visit to this cell meeting illustrates a second aspect of her relationship with the members of her fellowship, namely the religious and rhetorical process through which spiritual asymmetry was produced. What is most striking in this example is how identification—in this case, accounts of familiar struggles, rather than the shared work of prayer—opened the way for a particularly powerful mode of spiritual distinction. The gap between Bana Mfuwe's circumstances and those of the women at the *citente* was evident the moment she arrived, well dressed and unsullied by the journey thanks to the comfort of the taxi, an expense many there would have found prohibitive. Despite the clear differences between her and her audience, however, Bana Mfuwe was still able to collapse the distance between them. As believers repeated her declarations in the opening chant they stepped into the discursive space she embodied before them, a space in which they would not struggle or beg, as it was evident that Bana Mfuwe did not. All participants in the chant spoke in the first person, which meant that everyone made the same proclamations that Bana Mfuwe did in the same terms. Just as the chant served to bring the congregation closer to her, so the first part of Bana Mfuwe's testimony served to bring her closer to them. Like many of the women at the meeting, she too had faced hardships in her marriage and home, and her experience was therefore further likened to theirs.

It was only after these exercises in identification that Bana Mfuwe opened the gap between her and her audience again by testifying that she had received the sort of breakthroughs that many of them were waiting for. While this move served to set Bana Mfuwe apart as someone who had attained a superior level of divine favor, it did not sever the connection that Bana Mfuwe had established with her audience earlier in the meeting. This is because the distance between them was temporal rather than physical. Just as her past had been like their present, so her present represented a model of their future. In time they might move from where they were to where she was, even if over the same period she moved further still. While in her difference Bana Mfuwe became a symbol of unique prosperity, then, in the connection she had forged with her audience by identifying with their experiences Bana Mfuwe also came to represent the possibility that faithful Pentecostal adherence could have similar results for anyone.

In the example of Bana Mfuwe we therefore have a model of Pentecostal relationality that, while ultimately structured by religious distinction, nevertheless depends on an ongoing process of identification, on the ability to collapse the all-important difference between leaders and laypeople. Here, a brief example from another female Pentecostal leader provides an additional case in point. In September of 2014 I interviewed Pastor Janice, whose name I had long heard mentioned in Pentecostal circles and whose fellowship meetings I had once attended in a township adjacent to Nsofu. By the time of our interview Pastor Janice had moved her meetings to Nsofu proper. Although at that point she was only leading a women's fellowship, she had her sights set on starting a church and was happy to report that she was on her way to achieving that goal, having recently acquired a plot of land not far from Key of David. During our conversation Pastor Janice spoke of the role of testimony in her ministry, of the care she took to communicate to others that the good things she had—a new Toyota 4x4, fashionable clothes, successful children and grandchildren—had come to her only by the grace of God.

Inspired by her emphasis on testimony, I decided to test my theory about female Pentecostal leadership on Pastor Janice. Did she think that she served as an example of what the members of her fellowship were hoping to receive? Her response is instructive:

> You know, there's always the other side, the negative and the positive side of a person . . . People have seen my negatives like people saw how Sarah [the wife of the biblical patriarch Abraham] suffered before Sarah had a baby . . . Hannah suffered before [she] had Samuel. So I'm a person who people have seen in my suffering and people have seen in my blessings. Definitely they've

come to me to ask, "How has it happened?" and I've opened up to say, "This has come because of the Lord Jesus Christ. I'm now saved, I'm now born-again." In the past—I've been a drunkard before. People who drank with me can remember how I was, [but] now I'm praying. Even people can see . . . we used to be in the bar together, but today [I'm] preaching the gospel. How did it happen?

Pastor Janice's comments outline the identification and distinction that we have already seen employed by Bana Mfuwe. By highlighting the distance she had covered in her own life, from drunkard to minister of the gospel, Pastor Janice both placed herself in the position of the sinners she was trying to speak to about Jesus and suggested that they too could close the gap between where they were and where she was.[6] Here again we see a Pentecostal leader move from identification to distinction in a process that reinforces her position as an example. As Pastor Janice put it, she is someone who aroused curiosity; people look at her life and ask, "How has it happened?" In responding to their questions, Pastor Janice was careful to point to God as the source of her transformation. Earlier in our conversation, she took similar care to identify God as the source of the good things she had received. In demonstrating prosperity to those around her, then, Pastor Janice was not only an example of what others hoped to attain, but also proof that God could intervene even in very difficult situations.

PROSPERITY AND CHARISMA AS PENTECOSTAL SOCIAL ORIENTATIONS

In contrast to the model of religious distinction that we have developed in our discussion of Bana Mfuwe and Pastor Janice, a model that is structured by differences in prosperity, most religious distinction on the Copperbelt is, as we have seen, structured by differences in charismatic power. The mechanism through which this distinction is produced is also very different from what we have just explored, primarily because there is very little identification involved. Where Bana Mfuwe was known as someone who "really prayed," people like Pastor Ephraim, who serves as a paradigmatic example here, were known as prophets, preachers, and skilled exorcists. Each of these practices is vertical rather than horizontal in orientation—acting on, rather than acting alongside, a believer. So too, while the sermons of those set apart by charisma may include references to past hardships, these messages are, in my observation, much more likely to speak of spiritual exploits—of the people who have been delivered by a preacher's prayers or of the long nights he has spent fasting. Far from being inclusive, then, charismatic distinction is exclusive. Indeed, as we saw in the last chapter, it is threatened by the possibility of inclusion. Leaders like Pastor Ephraim are sought out not because they are like the members of their churches, but precisely because they are different. They are chosen and anointed, can help bring about breakthroughs with their prayers or, for those gifted in prophecy, provide revelations for those facing problems that they do not understand.

This subtle distinction between the power *to effect* answered prayer and the power *of* answered prayer further illuminates the difference between the gendered social orientations of Copperbelt Pentecostal leaders. In teasing this difference apart, I have found it helpful to draw on two categories developed by David Graeber, which he calls "action" and "reflection" (Graeber 2001: 91–116). In Graeber's analysis, "action" refers to the power—often hidden or undefined power—to act in the world, as seen, for example, in the power of money. Action is future-oriented and therefore mysterious, because it denotes potential activity that might take any number of forms. In contrast, reflection, as Graeber defines it, looks to the past. As in the case of an heirloom, the power of reflection follows from what has already taken place—from the fame of the person who made an object, for instance, or from what others have done to try to acquire it. Where action is hidden, reflection invites display. As Graeber puts it, action is "the power to act directly on others (a potential that can only be realized in the future)" while reflection is "the power to move others to action by displaying evidence of how one's self has been treated in the past" (Graeber 2001: 114). In describing action and reflection Graeber variously identifies these qualities in different kinds of Malagasy charms and the *wampum* beads used as currency in colonial northeast North America. He also draws on discussions of gender, particularly dress in the eighteenth century, which saw men adopt the more uniform outfits that eventually became the modern suit, while women continued to pursue individualized and elaborate clothing. This sartorial distinction is, Graeber argues, one of action (hidden, undefined male potential) and reflection (women as particular objects of display that inspire action in others).

The connection between Graeber's categories and the social orientations we have just identified with Pastor Ephraim and Bana Mfuwe is not difficult to see. Pastor Ephraim's power, the power of charisma, is all action because it is all potential, all possibility. Like the power of money, this power is undifferentiated and general, only becoming specific in the future when it is realized in a miracle. It may produce an exorcism for one person, a divine healing for another, and a breakthrough in the form of employment for a third. In contrast, Bana Mfuwe's power, which we have identified with reflection, displayed divine blessing for all to see. Her fashionable clothes, happy marriage, and heavyset body demonstrated that Bana Mfuwe was someone to whom God had given many good things. These various aspects of Bana Mfuwe's prosperity indicate that her power was one of reflection, a demonstration of God's past work in her life, as Pastor Janice's testimony illustrates further. Bana Mfuwe therefore attracted a following not so much because believers hoped that she would be able to influence God on their behalf, but because she offered proof that God could intervene in situations like their own.

In the examples of Bana Mfuwe and Pastor Janice, then, prosperity emerges as a social orientation, one in which religious distinction is produced through a process of identification and measured primarily according to visible markers of blessing. In the example of Pastor Ephraim, the social orientation at work is one of charisma, in which differentiation is emphasized across the board and spiritual asymmetry is structured by superior facility with the power of the Holy Spirit. While I have shown how both prosperity and charisma structure social relationships in Pentecostal groups, I have not yet demonstrated how this analysis relates to the broader understanding of gender that I introduced above. Can we say that charisma and prosperity, as I have described them here, are gendered? Simply citing men and women as paradigmatic examples is not sufficient in this regard. Likewise, while Graeber's discussion clearly indicates that action and reflection have gendered qualities, and while he argues that this pair is present in numerous cultural and historical contexts, we should be wary of uncritically applying it to a case like the Copperbelt, far removed from any of the examples that Graeber provides. The true test of whether or not we can think of charisma and prosperity as gendered modes of social actions is their capacity to transform those who mobilize them into women or men. To demonstrate that charisma and prosperity fit this definition, I turn my attention to a female Pentecostal leader who is perhaps more exceptional than any other.

"IT IS AS THOUGH SHE RECEIVED HER HUSBAND'S GIFT"

In July of 2013 I traveled to Ndola, the provincial capital of the Copperbelt, to interview Nelly Chikwanda, the first female Pentecostal bishop in Zambia and, by her reckoning at least, one of only two Pentecostal women to ever hold the title on her own (she could not recall the other's name).[7] Nelly Chikwanda, whose name I have not changed here, oversees a large network of thirty Pentecostal churches. Her office is located in a converted house in one of Ndola's "low-density" neighborhoods. The lawn is tidy, dotted with large shade trees and bougainvillea; a faded metal sign near the road announces that this is the headquarters of New Life Ministries International. Bishop Nelly was expecting me, and I was ushered into her office soon after I arrived. I perched on a red sofa wedged in alongside her massive desk, while Bishop Nelly settled into an office chair that seemed too big for her short frame. Her hair was elaborately worked into thick braids that coiled around her head, and she wore a burgundy suit with a straight skirt. Amid the collection of files and bibles arranged around the room were several photos of Bishop Nelly, including a very large portrait balanced on a filing cabinet above a tea tray. On her desk was a small magenta towel trimmed with lace, a feminine version of the washcloths and handkerchiefs that Pentecostal preachers use to mop their brows in the middle of a sermon.

Bishop Nelly is something of a Pentecostal celebrity in Zambia. I had once seen her preach at a large women's rally in Kitwe and had heard her name in television advertisements for major Pentecostal events in Lusaka. Despite her prominence, Bishop Nelly said that she considered herself an unlikely choice for leadership. She became involved in Pentecostal ministry through her husband, the late Bishop Matthews Chikwanda, who had been part of an important cohort of early Zambian Pentecostal leaders. Bishop Nelly said that while her husband was still alive she saw herself primarily in a support role, working behind the man of God, as she put it, raising her children and helping at the church. All of this changed, however, with her husband's unexpected death in the year 2000. When Bishop Matthews Chikwanda died—or, as Bishop Nelly put it, "graduated"—he was in charge of three churches. Initially, she had no thought of taking over the ministry, but began to change her mind when several of her late husband's spiritual "children" suggested that she was the best person for the job. As they pointed out to her, no one knew her husband's heart like she did, and as his wife she was their one surviving spiritual parent. No one was better positioned to lead them. Eventually, these claims were persuasive and Nelly Chikwanda assumed the title of bishop.

Despite claims that she preferred a support role, it was also clear to me that Bishop Nelly had an enduring passion for ministry. When she first became a Pentecostal she was still at school and attending a Baptist church. She was full of evangelistic zeal and recognized that the gifts of the Holy Spirit were powerful tools in this regard, an observation that drew her away from her more traditional denomination and toward Pentecostalism. Through her early experience in the Pentecostal student movement she discovered that she was what she called a "channel of blessing," a phrase she used to describe herself throughout our conversation. This role in ministry was, as she put it, "formalized" once she married a pastor and developed further when, after working outside the home for a while to support her family, she joined him in full-time ministry. "I am a pastor at heart," she said, and serving alongside her husband allowed her to operate in that capacity. Little wonder, then, that when her husband died the pastors who had worked under him asked her to "carry the mantle" of his ministry, as she put it.

What is important about Bishop Nelly's example for our purposes is that she is a woman who has taken on charisma as her primary social orientation. While her account suggests that this was not always her approach to ministry—that she may at one time have been more a symbol of prosperity, reflecting divine blessing in her marriage and children—in taking over her husband's position she appears to have inherited more than just his title. In her description the late Bishop Matthews Chikwanda was a powerful "general" in God's army. It is therefore worth mentioning a conversation I had with Bana Charles before I went to meet with Bishop Nelly. When she heard that I planned to interview this well-known woman, Bana Charles, a Pentecostal who had at one point attended Key of David, asked if I had ever heard Bishop Nelly preach. Forgetting about the conference where I had once seen her, I replied that I had not. My lapse of memory proved beneficial, as it prompted Bana Charles to offer her own description. Bishop Nelly, she said, preached "like a man." Puzzled, I asked what she meant by this. Bana Charles replied that when Bishop Nelly preached she preached "with power" (*amaka*, a word that also translates to "strength"). "It is as though she received [*ukupokelela*] her husband's gift [*bupe*]," said Bana Charles. While Bishop Nelly is obviously a woman, Bana Charles's remarks suggest that in terms of her role in Pentecostal ministry and the way she relates to those under her she is male—preaching with a strength that indexes her spiritual authority, her ability to mediate divine power as a "channel of blessing."

It is in the light of Bishop Nelly's example that I argue that the social orientations of charisma and prosperity are gendered—that is, that they are gendering. As in the case of women who occasionally took part in the men's cult on Ambrym (see Eriksen 2009: 99–100), Bishop Nelly

Chikwanda is engaged in what we have identified as a male way of creating relationships, and doing so becomes, at least in the context of these relationships, male. Ideally, I would also include in this section a male Pentecostal leader who has adopted prosperity as his primary social orientation and become female as a result. However, I cannot include such an example because I do not have one. While I have heard people mention male leaders who, based on their remarks, may have structured their relationships by prosperity, I have never personally encountered such a person. This observation is itself important to my argument, and I return to it below. For now we will have to rely on the example of Bishop Nelly to show that charisma and prosperity are gendered.

Having laid out how gender figures in this analysis as a social category, I now explore it in structural terms. As we will see in the final section, approaching gender in this way provides two related insights. First, a closer examination of how gender structures the relationship between charisma and prosperity helps us to respond to the question of why there are so few female Pentecostal leaders on the Copperbelt. Second, and more importantly, this discussion highlights a key tension in Pentecostal religious life by revealing how charisma and prosperity operate not only as social orientations, but also as subvalues.

PROSPERITY IN ITS PROPER PLACE

So far I have demonstrated that prosperity and charisma represent ways of relating through which church leaders function as male or female in a given set of social ties. This is gender as a social category. Approaching gender as a structural category allows us to build on this discussion in order to explore how gender operates as a framework for value, a system of differentiation and ranking. My goal in the structural analysis of gender is to get at the process of valuation that operates in moving by the Spirit, which hinges on the relationship between charisma and prosperity. What the gender dynamics of Pentecostal leadership on the Copperbelt reveal is that prosperity is not as valued as charisma and usually occupies a subordinate position. While prosperity dominates social life in some Pentecostal groups, in the vast majority of Pentecostal churches it is charismatic distinction that structures the all-important relationship between church leaders and laypeople.

We have already had glimpses of the superior position of charisma in believers' understanding of moving by the Spirit. It is evident in the greater importance they attach to spiritual development compared to material gain. Similarly, the preference for hierarchical ties to church leaders as a mechanism for moving by the Spirit has highlighted the particular efficacy of charisma when it comes to making moving happen. Finally, charisma outranks prosperity in the hierarchy of values that make up moving by the Spirit because of believers' fears of favoritism, or choosing, in their congregations. In relationships structured by charisma, all that matters is the spiritual superiority of church leaders. This means that charisma leaves no room for choosing, as the members of a congregation are all equally in need of the religious services of their pastor, the parent who cares for and offers spiritual services to them all. Charisma is therefore both the most efficient and the safest way to organize Pentecostal social life so as to move by the Spirit. Since values are ordered by their capacity to realize still-higher values (Robbins 2013b: 104–5), charisma must rank more highly than prosperity within the overarching framework of moving by the Spirit.

Expressed in Dumont's terms, the relationship between charisma and prosperity is one of hierarchical encompassment, in which the former is simultaneously identified with and distinct from the latter. From the perspective of the encompassing whole that is moving by the Spirit, charisma and prosperity are identified with one another, both indexes of this overarching value. Here, both values are markers of divinely ordered progress, both signs of a breakthrough. When it comes to relationships with church leaders, however, these values can work against each other, and are therefore contrary to one another. Dumont's framework also allows for the possibility of "reversal," for lower-ranked values—in this case prosperity—to encompass their opposites, but only at less important "levels" of social life. To take another of his examples, which is especially appropriate here, while a woman may be subordinated in most social domains by virtue of her sex, in the context of her own household where she is a wife and mother, she dominates all relationships (Dumont 1980: 241). In the case of the Copperbelt, we have seen that there are Pentecostal communities in which prosperity represents a dominant value, thanks to a leader who forms relationships this basis, rather than on the basis of charisma. However, these groups are small fellowships that are relatively marginal, and therefore represent less-valued "levels" of Copperbelt society.

This analysis sheds new light on the marginalization of female church leaders on the Copperbelt. Pentecostalism is always at some level about the democratic access of believers to the power of the Holy Spirit, and insofar as this is the case there is a strong pull for gender equality. Seen from this angle, all that should matter in the process of becoming a pastor is a believer's connection to God, not his or her sex. The problem for Pentecostals on the Copperbelt, however, is that elevating the female social orientation, which we have identified with prosperity, above the male social orientation, which we have identified with charisma, means changing the relationship between the two subvalues that make up moving by the Spirit. The continued relegation of women to the sidelines of church leadership is therefore not simply an extension of existing gender hierarchies but also a reflection of the relationship between charisma and prosperity.

Of course, as we have seen in the case of Bishop Nelly, it is not necessary for female leaders to adopt the female social orientation, to establish relationships with laypeople that are structured by differences of prosperity rather than charisma. However, the fact of the matter is that the women who enter Pentecostal ministry almost always find themselves in relationships organized by prosperity. One possible reason for this is that women participate more easily in the processes of identification that are so central to prosperity as a metric of spiritual distinction. Whether or not this is the case I am not prepared to say definitively, though I will note that most female Pentecostal leaders are, like Bana Mfuwe, known for their capacity in prayer rather than prophecy or preaching, and that this suggests some affinity or at least association between women and collective prayer, a central mechanism of identification.

More important to the marginalization of female leaders, however, are some very practical concerns. Doing full-time Pentecostal work demands significant material and social support. For women, this usually takes the form of a husband who earns enough money to free his wife from having to work or do business outside the home, giving her time for ministry. Also important is a husband's good will, as Pentecostal leadership requires a woman to often be away from home, or perhaps to pray for strangers in her sitting room. These considerations mean that in order for a woman to be in Pentecostal ministry, she must possess key financial and social markers of blessing. In other words, women who lead Pentecostal groups are by definition prosperous, and therefore more likely to form relationships with their followers on this basis. The very small number of women in the Pentecostal pastorate is therefore closely bound up with the practical considerations of entering full-time ministry, which keep many women out of church leadership and ensure that the few who buck this trend will establish relationships on the basis of prosperity, confining them to a form of Pentecostal sociality that is not as highly valued.

These observations may also explain why I have never met a male leader who had prosperity as his primary social orientation. Here again, practical considerations have a part to play. While the women who have time to devote to Pentecostal ministry are necessarily prosperous, the men who start new churches or fellowships are very often not. Indeed, their availability for ministry is in part a function of youth, singleness, and often unemployment, a freedom from the obligations of work and family that would otherwise limit a man's ability to devote many hours to ministry. But even established male pastors who are married and more financially secure still structure their relationships with lay believers around charisma. Here one possible explanation is that just as women may engage more easily in the identification that shapes prosperity, so men may find it easier to operate according to the distinction that defines charisma. This is perhaps especially true in churches where the vast majority of laypeople are women, as the historic separation of women from men in both social (e.g., Epstein 1981: 106) and domestic (e.g., Hansen 1992: 275) contexts may persist in the church. Perhaps the simplest explanation for the predominance of charisma among male Pentecostal leaders, however, is its capacity to attract a following. As we have seen, a pastor who gains a reputation as a powerful man of God, able to work a variety of miracles, will quickly fill a house or classroom with those who want to see him. It is therefore no surprise that those who can organize their churches on the basis of charisma understandably choose to do so, and these individuals are most often men.

In addition to explaining why gender hierarchy persists among church leaders despite Pentecostalism's egalitarianism, an analysis of gender has signaled the paradoxical position that the prosperity gospel has for Copperbelt believers. Recall here that the primary reason prosperity is compelling as a metric of moving by the Spirit is because of the impact that the prosperity gospel has had on Christian practice throughout Zambia. Despite the widespread acceptance of its basic teachings, however, the prosperity gospel also presents serious challenges for believers. As we will see in the next two chapters, the prosperity gospel, more than any other element of Pentecostal teaching or practice, opens the door to choosing, to the possibility that relationships between church leaders and laypeople might be structured by believers' capacity to give to the work of God. While our discussion of gender has shown that among Pentecostals prosperity must usually be subordinate to charisma, it is not always easy for believers to keep prosperity in its proper place.

CHAPTER 6

On the Potential and Problems of Pentecostal Exchange

But the servant replied,
"Look, in this town there is a man of God;
he is highly respected, and everything he says comes true.
Let's go there now. Perhaps he will tell us what way to take."
Saul said to his servant,
"If we go, what can we give the man? The food in our sacks is
    gone.
We have no gift to take to the man of God. What do we
    have?"
The servant answered him again.
"Look," he said, "I have a quarter of a shekel of silver.
I will give it to the man of God so that he will tell us what
    way to take."
(Formerly in Israel, if a man went to inquire of God, he
    would say,
"Come let us go to the seer,"
because the prophet of today used to be called a seer.)
"Good," Saul said to his servant.
"Come, let's go."
So they set out for the town where the man of God was.

—1 Samuel 9: 6–10

As 2008 drew to a close, Pentecostal congregations in Nsofu organized prayer meetings and periods of fasting to prepare for the New Year and to reflect on the one that was ending. In this spirit, believers at Key of David planned a thanksgiving service, something many Copperbelt congregations do on an annual basis. The event was scheduled for the last Sunday in December, and leaders at Key of David began announcing it

FIGURE 8. A church member gives his contribution during the Key of David thanksgiving service.

weeks beforehand in order to give everyone in the congregation time to prepare. Preparation was necessary because thanksgiving services are chiefly about giving special offerings, and believers needed time to save up for the event. On the appointed Sunday, seemingly everyone came to Key of David with gifts in hand. Since the congregation was hoping to plaster the church building, several people brought sacks of cement, which they dragged to the front of the church when it came time to give their contributions. Others brought clothes or household items wrapped in plastic shopping bags. Still others had envelopes that presumably contained cash. Rather than simply putting these contributions into a bucket or basket, as usually happened when the offering was collected on Sunday mornings, during the thanksgiving service church members gave their gifts directly to Pastor and Mrs. Mwanza, who shook hands with everyone who contributed before depositing the gifts either on the floor or in a large cardboard box covered with green cloth (figure 8).

This display of giving was the culmination of the church service, and all of the ritual activity leading up to it, from songs to the sermon, had been focused on this point. Unlike most Copperbelt Pentecostal churches,

Key of David began its Sunday morning meetings with Bible study, a more didactic and interactive activity than a sermon. On the day of the thanksgiving service Mr. Chibale was in charge of the Bible study. He used the lesson to encourage people to "invest" in heaven, where, he said, each person had an account. Heavenly investments were more secure than their earthly counterparts, Mr. Chibale explained, as they were not subject to market whims or currency devaluations. While descriptions of Pentecostal giving that frame it in market terms pop up rather regularly on the Copperbelt, they may have been especially compelling at the end of 2008, as the effects of the *global* were making themselves felt. Having outlined the virtues of investing in heaven, Mr. Chibale emphasized that the goal of church leaders in hosting a thanksgiving service was not to "manipulate" people into giving—a word that Pastor Mwanza also used in his sermon that morning—but rather to provide the congregation with an opportunity to prosper.

The principles of giving that structured the Key of David thanksgiving service were clearly derived from the prosperity gospel. Gifts to the church were not only expressions of gratitude for what God had done in the preceding year, not only acts of "thanksgiving," but also investments in the future, deposits in a heavenly bank (Hasu 2006) that were guaranteed to yield good results. Despite the joyous atmosphere that surrounded the event, the care that Mr. Chibale took to communicate to the congregation that the church's intention was not to manipulate anyone suggests that the thanksgiving service was also quite fraught. Our discussion in the previous chapters has given us some indication of why this was the case. Prosperity, especially the prosperity gospel practice of giving material offerings, threatens the democratic access to church leaders that makes it possible for believers to move by the Spirit. That being said, it should be clear from my discussion up to this point that in spite of the dangers it presents to Pentecostal social life, prosperity has not ceased to shape the religious practice of Copperbelt believers.

We might well ask why the prosperity gospel remains so important to Pentecostal practice, given the problems it presents. Here, the Key of David thanksgiving service provides us with a clue. During this event believers did not simply leave their gifts at the front of the church or slip them anonymously into an offering basket, but instead handed them directly to their pastors. The position that Pastor and Mrs. Mwanza occupied as recipients of believers' offerings is significant. As we will see in this chapter, giving offerings to church leaders both produces and strengthens the ties of religious dependence that we have identified as central to moving by the Spirit. If the gifts presented during the Key of David thanksgiving service point to the reason for the prosperity gospel's ongoing popularity, however, the work that Mr. Chibale put into framing the event tells us something equally important about this ritual. Even though gifts were presented to Pastor and Mrs. Mwanza, throughout the thanksgiving service these offerings were described as gifts to God. This emphasis on the divine recipient of seed offerings was crucial in managing the risks created as believers placed their gifts in the hands of their pastors. On the Copperbelt, then, the potential and problems of the prosperity gospel are worked out through a dual definition of contributions like money or bags of cement as "gifts to God and gifts to men" (Gregory 1980), or what I will be calling sacrificial offerings and socially productive gifts.

In the discussion that follows, I describe the distinction between Pentecostal gifts to God and gifts to men as one of different "registers" (Agha 2001). In linguistic anthropology, registers refer to linguistic practices that mark diverse social domains, whether those associated with group boundaries (e.g., youth slang) or particular kinds of activity (e.g., prayer). Although no one can claim mastery over all the registers available in his or her society, most people are comfortable in several registers, and the ability to deploy the right one at the right time is a key element of cultural competence. Importantly, the notion of registers is also connected to value—to judgments about what kind of language is superior in general, as in classed or standardized speech, or what kind of language is appropriate to a particular circumstance, as in ritual or technical contexts. Taken together, the ideas that multiple registers operate simultaneously in a shared social space, that people move in and out of a given register depending on the context, and especially that it is possible to understand them as structured by an underlying framework of value, make registers a productive way to think about the different models of exchange in play in Copperbelt Pentecostal practice. In referring to the human and divine axes of Pentecostal exchange as different registers, then, I want to highlight first their simultaneity and second their variability, as people draw on different registers to accomplish different goals. My primary motivation for taking up the language of registers here, however, is to further explore the process of valuation that undergirds Pentecostal life on the Copperbelt, and more specifically the relationship between charisma and prosperity that we began to address in the previous chapter. The first step in this analysis requires us to examine how the prosperity gospel operates as a form of nonmarket exchange.

THE ECONOMICS OF PENTECOSTAL PROSPERITY

It is not difficult to interpret the prosperity gospel according to a capitalist framework. Here, Mr. Chibale's comments reflect a larger tendency among adherents and analysts alike toward the language of the market; seed offerings are often described as "investments" (Ukah 2005: 263), the promised blessings as "dividends" and "miraculous [returns]" (Comaroff and Comaroff 2000: 315). Despite the prevalence of these interpretations, however, some of the most productive treatments of the prosperity gospel have approached it not according to capitalist logic but rather in terms of a gift economy. Drawing on Mauss's (1954) classic discussion, the "charismatic gift" (Coleman 2004) is here one that compels a return. The reason for this is, famously, because the gift is inalienable, retaining a part of the giver even after it leaves her hand. Once this part of her self begins to circulate in a larger economy of exchange, it must eventually come back, and Pentecostals expect that this return will be greater than the initial contribution. After all, the Bible promises that those who give will receive in return "a good measure, pressed down, shaken together, and running over."[1] This anticipated increase is linked to the inalienability of the charismatic gift at two points. First, as it circulates a seed offering not only remains connected to the original giver but also comes into contact with other figures in the Pentecostal community, particularly charismatic leaders. For example, followers of the prosperity gospel in Uppsala, Sweden, expect that seed offerings will produce a return gift because these contributions are incorporated into a religious economy that includes well-known pastors (Coleman 2004, 2006a). The power of these famous figures in turn enlivens the gifts of ordinary believers, and it is in part because of this power that they expect that their contributions will eventually produce a divinely increased harvest.[2]

Although in this framework religious leaders have a role to play in facilitating a believer's return gift, it is clear in Coleman's analysis that the responsibility for this blessing ultimately falls on God. Here is the second aspect of the gift's inalienability: it initiates a divine transaction as believers "lay claims to the power of God by indebting God to them" (Wiegele 2005:9); seed offerings, in other words, are efforts to "bind [God] by a contract" (Hubert and Mauss 1964:66). By invoking Henri

Hubert and Marcel Mauss's classic work on sacrifice here, I not only want to gesture toward important treatments of the prosperity gospel as a "sacrificial economy" (see Coleman 2011) but also to further flesh out our understanding of the role of church leaders as recipients of gifts to God.[3] As adherents to the prosperity gospel point out, such gifts must always be made through other people. These are typically ritual specialists who, like the "sacrifier" in Hubert and Mauss's essay, accept the gift on God's behalf, just as Pastor and Mrs. Mwanza did during the Key of David thanksgiving service. Importantly, although it is church leaders who act as recipients of these gifts, because seed offerings are ultimately gifts to God they do not result in an obligation on the part of a pastor to make a return to the giver. In the spirit of Saint Paul, who was careful to remind those who contributed to his ministry that their expected return would come from God (Peterman 1997), the responsibility of the return for seed offerings falls on God as well—though again, as with the initial sacrifice, this gift must come through human agents, who are often airbrushed out of testimonies of divine returns after the fact (Coleman 2004: 432). It is in the light of this expectation that a return will come from God and God alone that Martin Lindhardt, writing about Pentecostals in Tanzania, states that "donations [to the church] do not create bonds between individuals or indebtedness of the ministry to donors" (Lindhardt 2009: 52).

Despite his statement that Pentecostal gifts neither create debts in those who receive them on God's behalf nor by extension produce social relationships in the way that we would expect of a gift given from one person to another, Lindhardt notes elsewhere in the same article that in the congregations he studied contributions to the church did in fact have effects that appear to contradict his statement. Those who gave large amounts or loaned their cars for church business were given literal positions of prominence in the church, seated in the front and treated with special honor, whether or not they held positions in the congregational hierarchy (Lindhardt 2009: 56). In other words, generous donors were receiving a return gift from the church in the form of increased status, a gift that indexed some form of social relationship, or at least social obligation. This ethnographic detail at first suggests that Lindhardt has simply got it wrong—that in simultaneously reporting that seed offerings do and do not create social ties in Pentecostal congregations he is mistaken on one or both accounts. However, I do not think that this is the case. Rather, Lindhardt is hitting on a central and productive tension found in prosperity gospel practice more generally.[4] At the very least, this tension is evident on the Copperbelt, where seed offerings are both sacrifices to God that do not generate human debts and gifts to men that result in socially productive indebtedness. It is these two aspects of the Pentecostal gift that represent the different registers of exchange—namely, that of gifts to God, or sacrificial offerings, and gifts to men, or what I am calling socially productive gifts. Having outlined the contours of these registers here, we are now in a position to turn our attention to how they are expressed in Copperbelt Pentecostalism.

SOWING IN GOOD SOIL

For Pentecostal congregations meeting in classrooms, one of the first signs that the congregation is doing well—an early marker of corporate moving by the Spirit—is the purchase of furnishings that allow them to transform the space they have rented so that it feels less like a school. Although usually they cannot do anything about the fact that believers are sitting at desks, they can at least cover the blackboard with a curtain and perhaps bring in nice chairs for the pastor and his wife. When I first began to visit Freedom Bible Church, the congregation had not been able to do much in this regard. This changed, however, one Sunday in August of 2008. That morning I arrived to find a sheet of green, checkered linoleum spread across the floor at the front of the room where the music team would soon start singing. The chalkboard was covered with a matching green curtain. On the opposite wall of the classroom hung a new clock, positioned so that whoever occupied the wooden pulpit would be able to see the time.

After the usual prayers and songs, as well as a few testimonies, Pastor Kabre made his way to the front of the room to preach. He began his sermon by stating that Christians ought to be what he called "problem solvers," rather than people who were constantly mired in difficulty. If, he continued, those in the congregation repeatedly found themselves in trouble, it might be because they were not demonstrating their faith in the way that they should—that is, by giving. Having appealed to this familiar prosperity gospel principle, Pastor Kabre used most of the rest of the sermon to describe the different ways that people could give to God. Among these were gifts to the poor, to one's kin, or to orphans and widows. The topic to which Pastor Kabre devoted most of his time, however, was giving to "Levites," a term he said referred to those full-time Christian workers whose ministry obligations left them unable to pursue other forms of employment. In this sermon, church leaders emerged as the most important recipients of seed offerings, as people who were among the best equipped to accept these contributions on God's behalf.

The main point of Pastor Kabre's message was that gifts to God must be given to other people, but not to just anyone. When Pentecostals described the process through which they determined who ought to receive their seed offerings, they sometimes continued the agricultural metaphor by emphasizing the need to "sow in good soil." My neighbor Bana Ilunga explained to me that there were several criteria through which she would determine whether or not someone fit into this category. Bana Ilunga was a pastor, one of the first women to be ordained by the Pentecostal Assemblies of God Zambia. When I asked her how she could tell if someone was "good soil," Bana Ilunga first told me that one could discern this simply based on whether or not a blessing followed the gift of a seed offering to a particular person. If time passed and she had not received anything, Bana Ilunga might first solicit the help of others in praying that any satanic powers that stood in the way of her blessing would be removed. Should the blessing fail to materialize after these spiritual interventions, she would know that the person who had received her gift was not good soil.

Bana Ilunga then explained that one of the primary signs that someone was not good soil was if he or she failed to live by Christian moral standards. Here she drew on her own experience of having given a seed offering to a Congolese pastor who, by the time I arrived in Nsofu, had developed quite an infamous reputation. Soon after he came to the township this pastor was facilitating well-attended meetings in Bana Samson's comfortable home. A number of people reported having given him seed offerings, including large sums of money. Bana Samson had even bought him a television set. Perhaps especially because so many Pentecostals had given to this pastor, a scandal erupted when it was revealed that he had proposed marriage to a woman in Nsofu despite having a wife and family in Congo.[5] His former followers threatened to turn him over to the police with accusations of fraud, and the man promptly left town. For Bana Ilunga, the scandal came as no great surprise. The seed offering she had giving to him had not produced any kind of harvest, she explained, and this had suggested to her that his character was flawed even before the scandal confirmed her suspicions.

Beyond the need to give to a pastor with high moral standards, Bana Ilunga added that she preferred to give her seed offerings to those who were materially poor. When an offering went to someone who was already comfortable, she explained, it would make little difference in the life of the recipient, and that person would soon forget both the gift and the giver. In contrast, when the same gift went to someone who really needed it, its impact would be much more profound. A jug of cooking oil or bit of cash matters a great deal more to those living hand-to-mouth than it does to those who have no trouble making ends meet. A poorer recipient would therefore be more likely to remember the gift and in turn to pray for the one who had given it. Because of the increased prayers they would offer on her behalf, Bana Ilunga felt that the poorer members of her community were more likely to be good soil than their wealthier neighbors. While the responsibility for making a seed offering fruitful was God's, in Bana Ilunga's telling extra prayers toward this end would help guarantee that the seed would produce a good harvest.

Through these conversations, Bana Ilunga foregrounded the role that those who receive seed offerings play as religious intermediaries. Insofar as this role is filled by church leaders—which it usually is—it is familiar: pastors have special access to divine power; they are, as Bana Chanda once put it, "keys" that unlock spiritual blessings. It is because of their position as intermediaries that recipients of seed offerings must be righteous people (*balungami*). Here, as in Bana Ilunga's discussion of good soil, pastors' capacity as ritual specialists is indexed in the need for them to be upright individuals, in their having cultivated an appropriate spiritual state before receiving Pentecostal offerings on God's behalf (see Hubert and Mauss 1964: 20–23). In the light of their role as religious intermediaries, the emphasis that Pastor Kabre placed on giving seed offerings to church leaders emerges as more than mere fund-raising (Harding 2000: 109)—though he was certainly acting in the financial interests of his fellow pastors. By focusing on righteous church leaders as recipients of seed offerings, Pastor Kabre and Bana Ilunga connected the notion of pastors as good soil to the religious asymmetry that plays such a central role in Pentecostal social life, as the very act of receiving a seed offering marks a pastor or church leader as someone who is spiritually superior. Seed offerings do more for the relationship between church leaders and laypeople than just index a pastor's charisma, however. These gifts also serve to build and strengthen this tie. This is true because seed offerings are not only gifts to God but also gifts to men, as the remainder of Pastor Kabre's sermon makes clear.

"WHAT CAN WE GIVE THE MAN?"

As he had done when describing the other ways that believers could give to God, Pastor Kabre drew on the biblical text to demonstrate the importance of giving to church leaders. He chose the episode in the life of King Saul that serves as the epigraph for this chapter. In this story, the king and one of his servants prepare to inquire of a prophet. Before setting off, King Saul anxiously asks, "If we go, what can we give the man? The food in our sacks is gone." His servant replies that he has a bit of silver, which will suffice as an offering. Only after they have secured an appropriate gift do they proceed to the home of the "man of God." After one of the church elders read this passage aloud, Pastor Kabre began to discuss the relationship between giving to preachers and prosperity:

> So, let's you and me learn about visiting . . . the man of God. Let's not go empty handed [*fye na iminwe*], because sometimes you go to the man of God, you get there and he prays for you quite all right. But you may find that he's dying of hunger [*bali na ukufwa ulushile*]. A pastor in Lusaka once told me, "Look, in church there is no partiality, but sometimes you might not be able to make it [*kuti wafilwa ifyakucita*]." You're sitting at home and then someone comes with a problem . . . That person comes with rice, she has maize meal or something. Then someone else comes empty handed. You will pray for that person quite all right and the first one quite all right. But there is a difference in that when you go into the kitchen you will find maize meal, and you will remember the person who brought it . . . you will look over here and see some cooking oil and remember and go and kneel down and pray . . . You look at this curtain, you remember, you look at the floor . . . right now I'm praying as I'm looking at that clock.

The pattern that emerges from Pastor Kabre's sermon was one I often heard articulated in Nsofu, and its basic contours have already been laid out in Bana Ilunga's discussion of good soil. One of the main reasons that believers felt they could count on their seed offerings to yield a harvest of prosperity was because these gifts stood in the homes of those who received them as inalienable reminders of their givers. Contributions of money or food would therefore continually call people, most often pastors and church leaders, to pray that the one who made that offering would receive what she asked for. The ongoing prayers of a charismatic leader would in turn increase the likelihood that a believer's request would be granted. The message implicit in the remainder of Pastor Kabre's sermon was therefore that by giving seed offerings and other contributions to Pentecostal pastors, believers would produce a

2014 (A SEASON OF BLESSING AND ENLARGEMENT : 1 CHR 4:9-10) TITHE RECORD

MONTH	Wk 1	Sign	Wk 2	Sign	Wk 3	Sign	Wk 4	Sign	Wk 5	Sign
Jan										
Feb										
Mar										
Apr										
May										
Jun										
Jul										
Aug										
Sep										
Oct										
Nov										
Dec										

FIGURE 9. The inside of a Key of David tithing envelope, complete with 2014 theme of "Blessing and Enlargement."

longer-term religious obligation in their human recipients—first and foremost an obligation for prayer, but often also to some social commitment, especially a visit to a believer's home.[6] Seed offerings are therefore gifts that directly produce social ties.

The Pentecostal pastors I knew in Nsofu took the obligation to pray for those who gave to them quite seriously. One morning Mrs. Mwanza and I took advantage of a day off from her job to linger together in the sitting room in our *citenge* wrap skirts, sipping instant coffee and chatting. When I asked her about the gifts that laypeople brought to Key of David, Mrs. Mwanza told me that she and her husband kept a careful record of these contributions and encouraged the members of their church to help them in this task by giving their offerings in special envelopes labeled with each person's name (figure 9).[7] Mrs. Mwanza explained that she used this record as a guide for prayer and specifically that she made sure to pray that those who gave regularly would receive the blessings for which they were hoping.

Pentecostal leaders in Nsofu would sometimes even render spiritual services in response to a gift that was not made with religious intentions. For example, after concluding a round of household consumption surveys I wanted to show my appreciation to the participants by giving each of them a bottle of cooking oil and a bag of sugar. One of the people who received these items was Bana Ilunga. I did not realize the spiritual implications of my contribution until a conversation I had with her a few weeks after she had received the gift. Seated together on the low stoop of her house, Bana Ilunga explained to me that every time she used a bit of the sugar or oil I had given her she made a point to pray for me. Even though I had not asked her for spiritual help, it was clear in the eyes of this Pentecostal pastor that the appropriate response to a gift was prayer for the giver.

So, while Pentecostal contributions are undoubtedly offerings made to God through religious intermediaries, it is clear that they are also gifts that create an obligation in church leaders even as they compel God to act. As such, they represent a key aspect of Pentecostalism's social productivity. By giving to their pastors, believers work to build and strengthen the spiritually asymmetrical social ties that we have seen are constitutive of many people's religious membership. As Bana Junior explained to me during a conversation about Pastor Kabre's sermon, eponymous contributions brought directly to the pastor at home or after a meeting were—unlike gifts placed in an offering basket, which might be from anyone—the paradigmatic example of productive seeds that would yield a harvest.[8] Again, these gifts index charismatic hierarchy and provoke religious obligation, and in so doing produce the return gift in the form of social relationships through which believers realize moving by the Spirit.

At this point in the discussion we might very well ask why seed offerings are made to serve as gifts to God at all. Since contributions to church leaders strengthen the highly valued asymmetrical ties that form in Pentecostal churches, and since these relationships are one of the things that make this form of Christianity so attractive, why don't believers simply pursue human exchanges and eschew what I have been calling the sacrificial aspect of their seed offerings? Responding to this question requires us to return to the perennial problem of choosing, to the troubling possibility that pastors may focus their attentions on those church members who are most able to support them financially. Because they represent an opportunity for a believer to display her wealth and to establish a relationship with her pastor on that basis, the gifts I have been describing can easily stir up fears about favoritism, thereby threatening the very relationships they create. It is in the light of this problem that the dual logic of Pentecostal giving becomes important, as the notion that seed offerings are gifts to God protects the social bonds that they produce as gifts to men. In order to demonstrate how this is the case, it is helpful to examine gifts made in a religious context far removed from the Copperbelt.

THE POISON IN THE (PENTECOSTAL) GIFT

In trying to understand Pentecostal seed offerings, I have found it helpful to turn to ethnographic studies of the South Asian *dan*, the so-called "Indian gift" that transmits impurity from the giver because it bears with it a part of her person (Parry 1986, Raheja 1988). The particular danger of the *dan* varies with the actors who receive it. Jain renouncers, for instance (see Laidlaw 1995, 2000), are threatened by the corrupting potential of the food they receive from lay Jain families. Renouncers are famed ascetics who strive to purify themselves as much as possible from the negative effects of karma. This makes eating very dangerous. Even if the food given to them as alms—that is, the *dan*—has been meticulously prepared according to the rigorous requirements of Jainism, the violence of cooking is enough to make a renouncer impure. What's more, the dependence implied in these donations presents a further risk to the Jain ideal of unencumbered asceticism.

In the light of the danger of the *dan*, certain elements of this exchange take on particular importance. Key here is a carefully ritualized conversation in which renouncers adamantly refuse the daily alms lay families offer them, while the latter simultaneously insist that renouncers accept these offerings. Not only do renouncers ceremonially reject what they are offered, but they also take care to ensure that the food they receive was not prepared especially for them and, as an added precaution, mix it together with what has been given to others in their community before it is consumed. This last measure both removes any enjoyment that might come for the food's particular flavor and serves to further distance individual renouncers from those who have prepared and given it. Through these various measures, the dangerous gift of food is rendered safe for those who receive it; in other words, the *dan* becomes the theoretically illusive free gift that "makes no friends" (Laidlaw 2000; also see Derrida 1992).

However, despite the distancing effects of renouncers' repeated refusal, as far as Jain laypeople are concerned the *dan* is *not* a free gift but is instead part of a reciprocal exchange through which they receive religious instruction and karmic merit. More importantly, this gift may even produce an enduring bond with a particular renouncer (Laidlaw 1995: 324–29). In this example, then, ritual exchange is worked out in two different registers, one that denies a social tie and another in which a social tie is developed.[9] As James Laidlaw (1995: 319) puts it, "While from one perspective there is only one thing which changes hands in the transaction, this thing constitutes two quite different kinds of object of consumption for the two participants." These parallel spheres of interpretation enable ritual specialists to remain free of the taint of social relationships even as social relationships form.

In contrast to Jain renouncers, who are at least officially outside of the relational entanglements of everyday life, the danger of the *dan* for Brahmin priests in the pilgrimage city of Benares lies primarily in the fact that although they are solidly embedded in the relational life of their communities, the gifts they receive go unreciprocated (Parry 1989). While the whole point of the *dan* is to offer a meritorious gift without an expectation of a return, Jonathan Parry notes that this soteriological function is worked out in a wider social context in which a return is required. The tension between these two modes of exchange is what gives this gift its "moral ambiguity" (Parry 1989: 77). It is also, therefore, the source of the layers of ritual process surrounding *dan*. As in the Jain case, then, ritual reflects the difficulties involved when one gift serves two contradictory ends, here a religiously motivated soteriology and a socially motivated reciprocity.

On the Copperbelt, as we have seen, seed offerings, like the alms given to Jain renouncers, can be interpreted according to one register as socially productive gifts to men; seed offerings produce religious obligations. However, introducing material exchanges into the relationship between leaders and laypeople can be extremely dangerous. Gifts of money or maize meal could easily give certain church members greater access than others to their spiritual parent. Let me be clear here that the danger does not lie in the presence of material contributions as such. Pentecostals have no qualms about giving to church leaders that they believe to be morally upright, and indeed, they know that if they want to give seed offerings to God, they must give them to other people. As good spiritual children, they also want to honor their pastors by giving them gifts. What makes members of Pentecostal congregations nervous is therefore not that certain people are giving to their pastors, but rather the possibility that leaders might be organizing their relationships around distinctions of material wealth, rather than charismatic authority. As we saw in chapter 4, the risk of choosing is augmented by the fact that pastors are often financially dependent on the people they serve, a point that Pastor Kabre's sermon emphasizes. By describing the church leader in his hypothetical example as "dying of hunger," Pastor Kabre used a bit of hyperbole to foreground the very real difficulty many Pentecostal leaders have in making ends meet. It is in the light of these circumstances that he spoke so frankly to his congregation, stating that although officially there was no "partiality" in church, in point of fact preferential treatment was often given to those who provided the pastor with material assistance.

Like the *dan*, then, seed offerings are marked by moral ambiguity. The similarity between these two gifts does not end there, however. Just as Parry connects the danger of the *dan* to the layers of ritual that surround it, so too the ritual aspects—and more specifically the sacrificial aspects—of Copperbelt seed offerings provide protection for leaders and laypeople alike. In the Jain case, the ritualized conversation between renouncers and laypeople is part of a larger matrix of precautions that, from the perspective of renouncers, render the *dan* unrecognizable as a gift that would create an obligation. Seen from this angle, the Jain *dan* is more like a gift to God than a gift to men, as from the renouncers' perspective these layers of ritual practice remove the obligation of the gift, resulting in "the alienation of the inalienable" (Gregory 1980: 645, emphasis removed). We could make a similar argument about seed offerings by suggesting that the dangerous aspects of these gifts are "symbolically [destroyed]" (Gregory 1980: 647) when they are brought into the realm of divine exchange. This is because the status of a seed offering as a gift to God foregrounds the spiritual status of the pastor who receives a gift on God's behalf.

As we have seen, a Pentecostal chooses to bring her seed offering to a particular pastor because she believes him to be good soil, a spiritually pure intermediary capable of receiving the gift on God's behalf and interceding effectively on hers. Pastors are able to fill this role because of their spiritual superiority—their moral standing and capacity in prayer. All of this means that in the context of seed offerings, the sacrificial register obscures the obligation of the socially productive gift by foregrounding the spiritual authority of the pastor rather than the material wealth of the giver. Indeed, the very act of receiving these gifts serves to produce and reinforce a pastor's charismatic power (see Coleman 2004: 436). In the sacrificial register there is no doubt that the relationship between a pastor and a layperson is occasioned and structured by the religious skill of a spiritual parent, rather than the economic resources of an individual believer. Material wealth may figure here, of course, but it is not the framework around which social ties develop. Through sacrifice the danger of the gift to men is therefore overcome. In turn, the lack of human obligation in sacrifice makes the human obligation of the socially productive gift possible by hiding one inside the other; charisma encompasses prosperity as the gift is hidden (perhaps even smuggled) by the sacrifice. We can therefore apply Laidlaw's conclusion about the Jain case to that of seed offerings as well: "The fact that the free gift does not create obligations or personal connections is precisely where its social importance lies" (Laidlaw 2000: 618).

The two registers of Pentecostal exchange make it possible for believers to create and reinforce relationships through material gifts—the same way that relationships are created and reinforced across the Copperbelt—without allowing those relationships to be defined by material distinction. In this dual character, seed offerings can hardly be said to be unique. Gifts to men are very often something else besides (Rio 2007). What is interesting about the Copperbelt Pentecostal case is therefore not the simultaneous presence of multiple registers of exchange as such, but rather how the distance between these registers expands and contracts in service of social relationships (Bloch and Parry 1989). This observation allows us to incorporate gifts to men and gifts to God into the process of Pentecostal valuation that we have developed so far. While prosperity is central to moving by the Spirit on the Copperbelt, it also presents a threat to Pentecostal social life and therefore needs to be controlled. In seed offerings charisma is made to encompass prosperity, which is only allowed to develop insofar as it does not threaten charisma's position in Pentecostal social life.

What an examination of charisma and prosperity in the context of exchange has shown is that the tension between these subvalues gives Pentecostalism not only its structure, as our analysis of gender revealed, but also its internal momentum. In the interaction and interdependence of gifts to God and gifts to men, social life is propelled forward as charisma encompasses prosperity over and over again. Building on this observation, we can argue that it is the process of valuation, and especially the ongoing domestication of dangerous or ambivalent values like prosperity, which makes a social world dynamic. Value therefore animates social life at two points. By themselves values shape social action, orienting and informing relationships and institutions by structuring local notions of the good. But in their interaction and juxtaposition in an ongoing process of valuation, values like charisma and prosperity also generate movement, which reveals itself again in the fabric of social life—in the case of Copperbelt Pentecostalism, in the rules, rituals, and relationships that work to keep prosperity in its proper place. As a process, value therefore shapes human social life by informing what people are trying to create as well as what they are trying to control.

Values are also reflected in particular social practices, and indeed, it is in social practice that people represent values back to themselves. This last observation turns our attention to another aspect of Copperbelt Pentecostal exchange, that which is aimed at caring for one's spiritual parents.

CHAPTER 7

Mending Mother's Kitchen

Mayo mpapa, naine nkakupapa.
(Mother carry me, and I will carry you.)

—Bemba proverb

The cool dry months of the southern hemisphere winter are a popular time for weddings on the Copperbelt. On Saturday afternoons in June or July it is common to see a group of bridesmaids in matching *citenge* outfits, the bride in a white dress, posing for photographs on one of Kitwe's carefully manicured traffic roundabouts. In the neighborhoods immediately adjacent to the city center—"low-density" areas where houses sit in the middle of expansive lawns—women dressed in their finest clothes flock to "kitchen parties," another feature of the wedding season. Copperbelt kitchen parties are like North American bridal showers, but on a larger scale (or at least, a larger scale than any bridal shower I have ever attended). At a kitchen party a bride will receive mountains of gifts, including dishes, pots and pans, and small appliances such as electric kettles. Young women also rely on their kitchen parties for the purchase of some of the bigger items for their homes, such as stoves and deep freezers. As Thera Rasing (2002) has pointed out in her discussion of Copperbelt kitchen parties, these events are all about display and conspicuous consumption, to which I would add that as such they are pivotal points in the process of moving. They are also a significant source of stress. Weddings and kitchen parties cost a great deal of money, and even when the expenses are shared by a number of people they represent a considerable burden. In addition to these financial concerns, which are shared by everyone charged with planning a wedding or a kitchen party, for Pentecostals these events can present an added challenge when they overlap with the tricky work of giving to their pastors.

In this chapter I continue my discussion of the role that exchange plays in moving by the Spirit by examining gifts that, unlike seed offerings, are made exclusively to church leaders. These gifts do not have the resources of the sacrificial register to protect them, which means that although they are socially productive, they are also especially dangerous. My analysis in this chapter focuses on the role of lay leaders, individuals who occupy a complicated position in their congregations. On the one hand, prominent laypeople are important signs of a pastor's power, as well as key contributors to the practical needs of a church. On the other, their role in the church is incredibly fraught, and they bear much of the scrutiny that follows from fears about choosing. As a result, it often falls to them to do the difficult social work of keeping prosperity in its proper place so that everyone can move by the Spirit. By examining the efforts of laypeople toward this end, we not only gain a more fully developed picture of the social world of Nsofu Pentecostals but also add another layer to our understanding of how that social world is animated by values. To wit, the work of prominent lay believers involves turning their leaders into icons of value, and more specifically into icons of moving by the Spirit. This work is done in service of an entire congregation, as it orients the social actions of leaders and laypeople alike, structuring and enlivening their understanding of a good social world.

This chapter takes a slightly different form from those that precede it, as my analysis is framed in terms one long ethnographic example, a kitchen "mending" party given for Mrs. Mwanza. While this event does not represent an everyday occurrence, its extraordinary scale is particularly effective in throwing the internal social tensions of Nsofu Pentecostalism into relief. The relational dynamics and practical concerns that shaped the kitchen mending reflect a more common pattern in Copperbelt churches, which means that the conclusions drawn from a close reading of Mrs. Mwanza's party have important things to say about Pentecostal social life more generally.

A PARTY FOR THE PASTOR'S WIFE

Early in 2009 several of the women at Key of David decided that the church would throw a "kitchen mending" for Mrs. Mwanza. A kitchen mending is similar to a kitchen party in that its goal is to fill a woman's home with status-marking items. The "mending" element of the event

> *The Women of Key of David Worship Centre Invite*
> *Miss/Mrs.* _____ *to:*
>
> *Kitchen Mending*
> *for: Mrs. Mwanza*
>
> **Date:** 27 June 2009
> **Time:** 13:00 to 17:00
> **Venue:** Key of David Worship Centre
> **Guest of Honor:** Pastor Lily Nyrenda
>
> **Color Scheme:** Black, white, and silver
> Strictly no plastics, please!
>
> **RSVP:** Mrs. Chibale 0967-427944
> Miss Haynes 0966-035447
> Mrs. Kufuna 0978-541982
>
> *"The wise woman builds her house"* (Prov. 14: 1)

FIGURE 10. Template for the invitation card for Mrs. Mwanza's kitchen party (with pseudonyms).

referred to Mrs. Mwanza's status as a married woman whose kitchen was in need of an update; dishes bought at the time of her wedding had chipped or broken; pots were dented and darkened after cooking hundreds of meals. Roughly a hundred women were invited, and each of them was expected to bring a gift to "mend" Mrs. Mwanza's kitchen. The party was scheduled for the coming June (figure 10), a choice in timing that was strategic on several fronts. In addition to the cool weather that marks Copperbelt wedding season, June was a safe distance from the period when people would have made their rental payments and paid their children's second-term school fees.[1] This meant that in June people were more likely to have money. Indeed, financial concerns like these shaped the timing of the event down to the day; the kitchen mending was scheduled for the last weekend of the month, set to coordinate with the payday cycles of those who worked in the formal sector. In these ways, the women organizing the kitchen mending hoped to be able to make the most of the financial resources of their church community.

For events like Mrs. Mwanza's kitchen mending, expenses fall into two categories. First, there is the cost of the party itself. Smaller presents and even some of the bigger items come from guests, who in return for their gifts expect to be feted and fed, plied with dancing and drinks (alcohol at non-Pentecostal events, endless soft drinks at their Pentecostal counterparts). Although this exchange is normally kept in the background, if the party is not to people's liking it can quickly come to the fore, and I have heard stories of guests who took back their presents because they felt that the food and drink offered were not sufficient. A successful kitchen party or kitchen mending therefore requires enough money to ensure that those invited enjoy themselves. In addition, party organizers are responsible for the purchase of one large gift. In the case of Mrs. Mwanza's kitchen mending, the thing she wanted most was an "upright" refrigerator. Many people on the Copperbelt have freezer chests, but refrigerators, which are a great deal more expensive, are far less common. A refrigerator is therefore not just a source of convenience, but also a marker of status.

Faced with the looming expenses of the kitchen mending, the women of Key of David did what everyone on the Copperbelt does on such occasions: they formed a committee. I discussed the structure and function of committees in chapter 2, and so will only briefly revisit these characteristics here. Copperbelt committees are common forms of collective fundraising, ways for people to pool large amounts of money for special events, primarily weddings and kitchen parties. One of the most important things about committees for the purposes of this analysis is that participation in these groups requires nothing more than a contribution of the required amount of money, and that amount is the same for all members. Committees are therefore organized on the basis of symmetry within and asymmetry without—that is, symmetry among committee members and asymmetry between them and those who are not on the committee.

In the case of Mrs. Mwanza's kitchen mending, committee members were each required to contribute K250,000 toward the party and the refrigerator.[2] The committee was comprised of roughly half a dozen women from Key of David, myself included, as well as two or three others from outside the congregation. The women at Key of David who did not join the committee were not exempt from contributing, but were each required to give K100,000, a more significant amount of money for some than it was for others.[3] The mandate covered a large number of women, some of whom had at best a tenuous connection to Key of David. Finally, in an effort to cast as wide a net as possible, the committee also solicited the help of people like Moses, who might not otherwise have contributed to the kitchen mending, as he was unmarried and therefore would presumably not be helping a woman pay for committee membership or the required minimum donation. While the kitchen mending was overwhelmingly a female concern, then, it drew on the resources of the entire congregation.

For several months leading up to the kitchen mending the committee met almost weekly. We used some of our time together to plan the party, discussing how to decorate the church and what we would wear (this detail was very important: committee members always wear a uniform chosen especially for the occasion, which can be anything from shirts and trousers in the same color scheme to special attire made for the big day; our committee, determined to make the event as grand as possible, chose the latter route). The task that took up the greatest portion of our time, however, was making and continually revising the budget. At each meeting we carefully went over the itemized list of expenses, making small adjustments from week to week. I was usually responsible for the group's record keeping, as I had a notebook with me anyway, and my fieldnotes from the weeks leading up to the kitchen mending include detailed budgets with the numbers crossed out again and again, as well as quotes for the price of ice and the required deposit for several dozen crates of Coca-Cola. Some changes to the anticipated cost were the result of fluctuations in the price of food, the primary expense associated with the kitchen mending. However, the main source of uncertainty in the budget was other people in the church, as no one was sure whether those women who were not on the committee would make the donations they had been asked to.

The woman in charge of the committee was Bana Chibale, whose husband had led the Bible study on divine investments during the thanksgiving service. Although she had been careful to schedule the kitchen mending at a time of year when people were more likely to have money, Bana Chibale and the rest of the committee members did not rely on timing alone to ensure that women from the church made their contributions. In an effort to secure payment, Bana Chibale enlisted the efforts of Mrs. Zulu, whose tactics rivaled those of any debt-collection agency. Mrs. Zulu hounded the members of Key of David every chance she got, calling them on the phone and stopping by their houses unannounced to ask for whatever money they might have at the moment. She was especially concerned to intercept working church members near enough to payday to ensure that they contributed to the kitchen mending before the rest of their salaries were eaten in the form of groceries, school fees, and electricity bills. Once, while she and I were together in town, we tracked down Bana Karen at work, walked with her to the bank, and stood over her shoulder while she withdrew some cash from her account and begrudgingly handed it over to the triumphant Mrs. Zulu.

If Mrs. Zulu had been brought in to play the heavy, so to speak, Bana Chibale took a different tack in her efforts to bring in funds for the kitchen mending. Where Mrs. Zulu secured donations largely by attrition, Bana Chibale preferred to appeal to people's consciences. These appeals took several forms. For one, Bana Chibale was careful to point out that it would not look good if those who had been invited to the party arrived to find that the food was inadequate or, worse yet, that the group had not been able to buy Mrs. Mwanza the longed-for upright refrigerator. If that happened, Bana Chibale said, they would all be embarrassed and ashamed (*asebanya*), and the reputation of the church, of Pentecostalism—even of God—would be tarnished. At other points Bana Chibale appealed to the promise of an eventual social return on an investment in the kitchen mending. One day, she would point out, their daughters would need kitchen parties and their own kitchens would need to be updated. By giving to Mrs. Mwanza's kitchen mending, the women of the church would ensure that when the time came for them to solicit the help of others it would be forthcoming. Similarly, contributions to the party were occasionally described in the familiar Pentecostal language of seeds. Just as money given to the kitchen mending carried the promise of reciprocity within the larger Nsofu social world, it was also said to provoke heavenly return gifts. Beyond appeals to reputation or reciprocity, however, Bana Chibale frequently reminded the churchwomen that contributions toward Mrs. Mwanza's kitchen mending were part of their relationship with their spiritual mother—a status Mrs. Mwanza held both as the wife of a church leader and as the leader of the women's ministry and a pastor in her own right.

Bana Chibale had used the argument that the kitchen mending was Mrs. Mwanza's due as a spiritual parent throughout the fund-raising period, and as time ran out she took this as her primary mode of persuasion. One afternoon less than a week before the kitchen mending, all of the women at Key of David gathered in the empty church building to learn the dance steps we would perform at the party. When we had finished rehearsing we moved to a corner of the room for a final meeting. Bana Chibale was visibly strained. Before the dance rehearsal I had seen her doubled over in prayer, loudly petitioning God to spare the kitchen mending from failure. Seeing so many of the churchwomen grouped around her, Bana Chibale gave one final request for help. Surely, she cried, they would never allow their "real" mothers (that is, their mothers by biological kinship) to hold a kitchen mending with insufficient funds! In the same way, she implored, it would be wrong of them to leave Mrs. Mwanza, their spiritual mother, alone in her hour of need.[4]

The meeting broke up quickly after Bana Chibale's impassioned plea. A number of women were upset by what she had said. Some of them knew that there was simply no way they would be able to produce the cash they were supposed to contribute before the rapidly approaching event, by then just days away. Among these women was Bana Daka, whose husband had been laid off at the mine a few months before. Feeling the pressure to give and knowing she could not make the required payment, Bana Daka said that she did not plan to attend the kitchen mending. It would be unfair for her to come and eat food toward which she had not been able to contribute, she reasoned, and she therefore planned to stay away.

If the reaction of those had not been able to give what was asked of them was one of anger or embarrassment, those who had already given were equally upset. Members of the committee, in particular, were very worried that despite their best efforts they would not be able to give Mrs. Mwanza all that she wanted—indeed, all that they had effectively promised her. Even if they were able to throw a successful party, with enough food and soft drinks for everyone, two days before the kitchen mending there was still not enough money to buy Mrs. Mwanza the coveted upright refrigerator. When Mrs. Mwanza got wind of this news, she was visibly crestfallen. The main reason she had wanted to have a kitchen mending in the first place, she confessed to me, was to get an upright refrigerator, and while she was sure to receive other small gifts, she felt that on their own these would not make the event worthwhile. As far as I know, this is the first serious indication that Mrs. Mwanza had of just how difficult it had been for the committee to come up with the necessary funds for the kitchen mending. She was not usually present on those occasions when a committee member exhorted the rest of the women to give their required contributions. Nor was she generally welcome at committee meetings—indeed, she was only invited to attend when the agenda included questions of who to invite or how to decorate, and as soon as these had been discussed, the committee shooed her away.

The day before the kitchen mending I returned from my morning run to hear Mrs. Mwanza's voice echoing down the corridor of our house. She was speaking loudly on the telephone, trying to make herself heard over a bad connection. Although the day before she had been despondent at the possibility that the kitchen party might not result in a refrigerator, in this conversation her mood had audibly lifted. Mrs. Mwanza was laughing out loud and singing a modified version of a Pentecostal chorus, which usually goes, "Something good in my life, Oh Lord." In Mrs. Mwanza's version, the "something good" she expected was "something good in my kitchen." Although everyone in the house had been privy to Mrs. Mwanza's phone call, it was technically a private conversation, and I therefore had to wait until later that day to find out what it was about. The phone call was from a Zimbabwean man who had spent months stranded in Nsofu after he was the victim of an employment scam. He was calling from across the border in the Democratic Republic of Congo, where he had recently found a job. During his time in Nsofu this man had been accommodated by members of Key of David, whose care for him represented what anyone would recognize as an act of exceptional charity. He had been very involved in the church before going to Congo, and I assumed that he felt a great debt of gratitude to the congregation that had given him so much. He had already contributed to the kitchen mending by sending six and a half yards of high-quality Congolese *citenge* material for Mrs. Mwanza, which she had given to a tailor to make an elaborate outfit for the party. Now, it appeared, he had taken it upon himself to further ensure that the event would be a success, as he had wired K500,000 as a loan to help with the party. These funds, along with a few extra last-minute donations, including gifts from Mrs. Phiri and Bana Chibale that doubled their committee contributions, meant that even though several Key of David women were unable to contribute toward the kitchen mending, the committee would still be able to buy a refrigerator for Mrs. Mwanza.

The next morning dawned dry-season clear and cold enough for me to see my breath when I stepped outside. After months without rain a thick layer of dust had muted the colors of the landscape. I left the house just after 6:00, taking the narrow footpath that served as a shortcut to Bana Chibale's house, where I was soon joined by several other committee members. Together we spent the morning frying chicken, chopping cabbage for salad, peeling potatoes, and boiling rice over charcoal braziers set up in Bana Chibale's back yard. Hours later the sun had warmed the day and we had finally finished. After changing out of our cooking clothes and into our matching committee outfits, we made our way to the church. Other women from the congregation had been at work while we cooked, and we found the Key of David sanctuary transformed, filled with chairs we had hired for the occasion and decorated with most of the furnishings from Mrs. Phiri's sitting room.

FIGURE 11. "African print" outfits worn by kitchen mending committee members.

All of the women from the church were smartly attired, and although the committee's outfits were distinct, the other women had dressed to coordinate. The committee uniform was black trousers and a long tunic made from the very fashionable material that people on the Copperbelt called, in English, "African print," which in this case meant a motif of spears and calabashes (figure 11). The other women from the church were also wearing black trousers, and some had similar tunics made of black and white fabric, although the pattern was different and the material of lower quality. Those who did not get new clothes for the event wore black trousers and the white Key of David polo shirts that we had made for a special women's Sunday service the year before. The effect was to set the members of Key of David apart from the other guests, all of whom came in their best clothes—smart suits or *citenge* dresses. When Mrs. Mwanza arrived she outshone them all in her new Congolese *citenge* attire, and some women jokingly called her "*banabwinga*," a bride.

The party went off without a hitch. In addition to Mrs. Mwanza's visiting relatives, who came all the way from Lusaka, a number of her workmates and neighbors were also present, as were members of some of Nsofu's other Pentecostal churches. The guests had either each brought small gifts or in some cases pooled their money to purchase larger items, including a dinette set. The committee and churchwomen, anthropologist included, successfully performed the dances we had choreographed. When it came time for us to formally present our gift, the committee left the room and danced back in to lead Mrs. Mwanza to the upright refrigerator. She wiped her eyes as Bana Chibale opened the refrigerator's doors to show off the present, and wrapped several of the committee members in emotional embraces while all around her the dancing continued. During the party, none of the resentment or worry that had marked the weeks leading up to the kitchen mending was evident. Instead, people ate, drank, and listened attentively to Bana Nyrenda, a popular Pentecostal preacher who had been invited as the guest of honor. Bana Nyrenda preached a brief sermon and also took time to pray for Mrs. Mwanza, who knelt before her while the senior preacher laid hands on her forehead.

Although unity prevailed among the Key of David women during the few hours of the kitchen mending, as soon as Mrs. Mwanza and the other guests had gone home the divisions evident since the party was first announced quickly resurfaced. The food that was served had been carefully rationed by the committee, which meant that there was quite a bit left over. As they began to clean the sanctuary for the next day's church service, the women of Key of David pulled plastic containers and bags from their purses and headed toward the committee to ask for more food to take home to their families. Even though they had taken care to leave a cache of prepared food back at Bana Chibale's house, committee members were forceful in their efforts to reserve most of the leftovers for themselves and others who had given particularly large contributions to the kitchen mending. These actions prompted sharp complaints from the other women, who felt entitled to a share of the leftovers. While some acknowledged that they had not contributed as much money as they had been asked to, they pointed out that all of them had supplied labor in the days leading up to the event—cooking as well as cleaning and decorating the church.

At length much of the remaining food was distributed and we committee members made our way back to Bana Chibale's house, lugging crates of leftover soft drinks between us as we picked our way through the rutted streets in the dark. When we arrived at the Chibale home we filed into the back bedroom, where we had left pots of chicken, rice, and potatoes, as well as several crates of soft drinks. Although everyone was tired—my main memory of this moment is of fighting to pay attention through a haze of exhaustion—the committee was exacting when it came to food distribution. Pieces of chicken and bottles of Coke were painstakingly divided among committee members or set aside for people like Moses. Individual drumsticks or potatoes moved from one container to another as people argued about the proper proportions. This went on for a long time, but finally everyone was satisfied, and I went home, delivered a bowl of party food to Moses in exchange for his contribution, and went straight to bed.

The next morning I watched as Mrs. Mwanza sorted through the heap of gifts she had received. In addition to the coveted refrigerator and the dining table and chairs, she had been given a large assortment of kitchenware, including dishes, pots, and pans. Wrapped in her usual *citenge,* her hair still tightly braided into the wig bought for her special day, Mrs. Mwanza looked tired but satisfied. As she explained it to me, she was happy not only because she had received the gifts she was hoping for but also because she believed that the kitchen mending had been spiritually significant, that those who came had been encouraged in soul as well as fed in body. Indeed, she also felt it would make a good impression on those who did not attend the event, but merely heard about it. As I prepared to leave the field a few weeks later, Mrs. Mwanza asked me which aspects of my time in Nsofu I planned to write about. When in response I mentioned the kitchen mending, she was very pleased. At least, she said, you will go back to your country with a testimony: "This woman used to live one way and now lives differently." Clearly, as far as Mrs. Mwanza was concerned, the kitchen mending was a successful Pentecostal event—that is, an event shaped by moving by the Spirit.

EXAMINING THE KITCHEN MENDING: THE PROBLEM OF SUPER-MEMBERS

It should be clear from my description that the kitchen mending caused a great deal of social strain and emotional distress for the women at Key of David. While there are several axes along which problems crystalized, the most prominent of these was the role played by wealthy church members like Bana Chibale. This woman and her husband, as well as Mr. and Mrs. Phiri, represent a larger category of Pentecostal laity that I came to think of during my fieldwork as "super-members." Super-members are fixtures in every Copperbelt Pentecostal congregation, easily identifiable by a few key characteristics. During Sunday services or prayer meetings they sit at the front of the church, smartly dressed and carrying large Bibles. Super-members are visibly dedicated believers; they pray loudly and long during intercession, sing enthusiastically during praise and worship, and follow along in their Bibles during the sermon. Many also take part in the formal aspects of Pentecostal worship, as Mr. Chibale did during the Key of David thanksgiving service. For his part, Mr. Phiri helped collect the offering. In addition to their visible religious commitment, super-members are almost always the most financially prosperous members of a congregation. Mr. Chibale had a well-paying job as a medical officer at the mine, and his wife also made a good salary as a government employee; Mr. Phiri worked for Barclays Bank. When I first began to attend Key of David, Mr. Chibale and Mr. Phiri were the only people who drove to church, though over time the number of cars outside Key of David on Sunday mornings increased, a point that I return to in a moment.

Super-members play a central role in the running of their congregations. They are among the most reliable attendees at Pentecostal meetings, often arriving early to help set up or staying late for extra meetings. They also contribute a disproportionate amount of money to the church. For example, in one Pentecostal congregation in the Copperbelt city of Chingola, a prominent laywoman, a successful tailor who was also a deaconess, singlehandedly paid the monthly rent on the classroom the church used for worship. Perhaps even more important than the financial contributions they make to a church, however, is the role that super-members play in bringing honor to its leaders. The number of visibly successful people in a congregation indexes a pastor's power in two complementary ways. First, it shows that the pastor is able to attract "big" people (*bakalamba*, a word that also refers to elders and older siblings), an observation that calls to mind classic arguments about "wealth in people" in sub-Saharan Africa, and perhaps especially Jane Guyer and Samuel Belinga's more recent emphasis on wealth in *certain kinds* of people whose skills, loyalty, and services are especially valuable (Guyer and Belinga 1995). Second, a critical mass of successful men and women in a church suggests that at least part of the reason for their status is their attachment to a particular man of God who is able to facilitate moving by the Spirit for people in his church. Seated in the front of the sanctuary in a nicely tailored suit, the keys to his Citroën sedan resting on top of a large Bible, Mr. Chibale offered proof that God could pour out the kind of blessings that for Copperbelt believers are typically mediated by a pastor. I always found it strange that people in Nsofu would drive to church even if they lived very nearby, until I realized that parking their vehicles in front of the church building every Sunday was a way of bringing honor to their pastor, demonstrating his ability to both attract successful people and make people successful.

This dynamic was certainly in play at Key of David, and increasingly so over the course of my research. When I returned to the field in 2013, for example, I found that the church had grown, and in the process drawn an even larger number of professionals. Where once only Mr. Chibale and Mr. Phiri drove to church, now there were more than half a dozen cars parked at Key of David on Sunday mornings.[5] The church building's prominent position on the main road ensured that this development did not go unnoticed, and several informants who were not part of Key of David but knew that I lived with the Mwanza family commented on the number of cars there each week. God was blessing the congregation, they said, an observation suggesting both that God was bringing people—and presumably big people, people who drove—and that God was making the people who were already in the church into big (or even bigger) people. Again, each of these aspects of blessing is a reflection on Pastor and Mrs. Mwanza, who acted as mediators of divine gifts for lay believers.

While super-members are therefore essential to the existence and growth of a church in large part because of their wealth, their material success also makes these figures very controversial. As prominent lay leaders, super-members have the attention of their pastors in ways that most other laypeople do not. Because of their many congregational responsibilities, super-members spend a great deal of time with their pastors, and because they are involved in the process of church decision making, they may be his confidants as well. I got used to seeing Mr. Chibale in the sitting room of the Mwanza's house, where several times a week he and Pastor Mwanza would meet to discuss church business over tea or nshima. In addition, as individuals with access to greater resources, super-members are also in a position to provide special assistance to the pastor, for example, by driving him places if he does not have a car of his own. In these ways, super-members easily stir up perennial Pentecostal concerns about choosing.

Faced with accusations of favoritism, pastors will not deny that they are closer to super-members than they are to others in their churches. However, they will also be quick to point out that the reason for this closeness is the spiritual status of people like Mr. Chibale. According to church leaders, it is on the basis of their religious merits, and not their relative wealth, that super-members enjoy a special relationship with their pastors. It is certainly possible to situate these explanations within a Pentecostal social framework structured by charisma. In this case, the spiritual commitment and maturity of super-members reduces the distance between them and their pastors, and their privileged intimacy with church leaders is therefore the result of the fact that they are more like pastors than other laypeople are—indeed, as we have seen, they are often perceived as being on a path toward the pastorate. In this framework, whatever special closeness exists is warranted, the result of super-members' proximity to a pastor on the gradient that matters most, namely that of charisma.

While some laypeople have no difficulty in accepting this explanation, others are left with niggling doubts, particularly when they look at members of the congregation who appear to be as devout as super-members but who are not given positions of leadership. Might the reason that such people are excluded from the church hierarchy be that they do not have as much money? These doubts are well expressed by a cartoon published in the *Post*, Zambia's main independent newspaper. The *Post* has a running "Agony" cartoon, which always features the same picture, a man with a look of embarrassment on his face under the heading, "Agony is . . ." These cartoons often portray the anxieties of Zambians with middle-class aspirations, as in: "Agony is . . . wearing your best clothes to dinner, only to find that your maid has been wearing the same outfit." In a similar vein, a recently published cartoon read, "Agony is . . . your rich neighbor getting a chorus of 'Amens' at every pause, yet you got none in an earlier prayer." The fact that this cartoon was published in one of the most popular papers in Zambia suggests that anxieties that spiritual status—in this case, in the form of "Amens" that affirm the power of someone's prayer—is accorded to some people simply on the basis of their wealth are widespread. This anxiety lingers just below the surface in Copperbelt Pentecostal congregations, animating many of the social tensions in these groups.

In the light of the worries that super-members generate, it is not surprising that it is around these particular believers that controversy often crystalizes. Here the kitchen mending was simply one example of a larger pattern in which the practical aspects of running a congregation make it difficult for super-members to communicate that their special access to the pastor comes from their spiritual strength and skill, rather than their wealth. Pentecostal groups are always raising money for something, whether a trip to a convention, a wedding, or a new building, and contributions toward these efforts are meant to be made over and above the weekly offering. Part of the problem with all of this fundraising, of course, is that it puts pressure on poorer members of congregations to make contributions that they often feel they cannot afford.[6] By the same token, pledge drives and other ways of raising money regularly present opportunities for super-members to distinguish themselves on the basis of their wealth. By setting themselves apart in this way, super-members make it difficult for others in their churches to believe that their relationship with the pastor is the same as everyone else's.

While the position of super-members is difficult to navigate, leaders like Bana Chibale are not left without spiritual and social resources for keeping prosperity in its proper place. We have already seen that Pentecostals in Nsofu employ two parallel registers of exchange when giving seed offerings, and that by carefully maneuvring between these registers they are able to reinforce the position of charisma as the primary ordering force behind the relationships formed in their congregations. Similarly, it is possible to identify two contrasting interpretive registers in the kitchen mending. By skillfully deploying these registers, super-members were able to preserve the hierarchy of subvalues that makes up moving by the Spirit.

OFFICIAL AND UNOFFICIAL INTERPRETATIONS

The first interpretive register evident in the kitchen mending was available to everyone involved in the event: guests from outside the church, laypeople from Key of David, the committee members, and Mrs. Mwanza. I call this register the "official" register because it was characterized by the ideals of spiritual asymmetry and dependence. The central relational motif of this register was that of parentage, seen most clearly in Bana Chibale's appeals to the women to give their spiritual mother the same kind of respect and support they would give to their "real" mothers. In using this language, Bana Chibale was drawing on a wider set of cultural models in which parents are worthy not only of respect and care but also of their children's material support. This is evident in the proverb quoted in the epigraph of this chapter, as well as in the gifts children are expected to give their parents as they grow. Many people in Nsofu said that a person's first paycheck should go in full or in large part to his parents, as his mother and father had been responsible for preparing him for gainful employment. Bridewealth serves as another example here, as payments to a young woman's parents are in many respects a response to the care they have given her, a way of honoring their position and acknowledging their efforts in raising and educating their daughter. Giving is therefore implied in and serves as an index of the parental relationship on which the tie between Pentecostal leaders and laypeople is modeled. Here we can reiterate that the language of parentage exerts an equalizing force on lay believers. As Pentecostals often pointed out, parents are supposed to love all of their children equally. In the official register of pastoral parentage, then, the only social distinction in play was that between Mrs. Mwanza and her spiritual children. All of the Key of David laywomen, in other words, were included in the same social category.

While in this official register all believers at Key of David were equally involved in the honor given their spiritual mother, it is not difficult to see another register at play in the kitchen mending. In this register there are more status distinctions than just those of spiritual parentage. Most obvious here was the difference between the committee members and the rest of the congregation, a difference that was first and foremost one of economic status. By its very nature the committee reinforced divisions between wealthier and poorer members of the church, as the only qualification for membership in the committee was the ability to pay the required sum of money (and here my involvement serves as a case in point). To be sure, not everyone on the committee had the same amount of influence as those at its helm, Bana Chibale in particular. Nevertheless, making the donation required for committee membership positioned people in a more powerful group. In this register of interpretation we can therefore identify social fault lines running across a group that is officially unified in their status as laypeople, and it is in this register that we can situate all the conflict and tension that went on in the months leading up to Mrs. Mwanza's party.

Guests at the kitchen mending from outside the congregation were privy only to the official register of the event. When these visitors arrived they saw the women from the congregation all clad in black and white—a sartorial choice that obscured the divisions among them. While we in the committee had our special outfits, we did not stand out sharply from among the remaining laypeople in the way that a committee often does at these events. Instead, the image we presented was overwhelmingly one of unity, a unity that was further emphasized in our dancing. After the guests had taken their seats all of the women from Key of David entered together in a choreographed step, which further demonstrated that the women in the church were operating as one in their efforts to honor their spiritual parent. From the perspective of the guests who came from outside the church, the divisions that had marked the weeks leading up to the kitchen mending were concealed by these public displays of harmony among the laypeople.

Guests from outside the church were not the only ones who had access only to the official register of the event, however. From the earliest stages of preparation right through to the kitchen mending itself the committee focused much of its energy on confining Mrs. Mwanza to this register as well. This is clear in the decision to exclude her from most of the planning process, and especially from those parts of committee meetings that revolved around the budget. During these conversations individual members of the congregation were regularly mentioned by name, along with a report as to their progress toward payment, and these conversations therefore revealed the lack of unified support among the laywomen. Similarly, Mrs. Mwanza was also shielded from the fact that a few members of the committee made up the shortfall in the budget by adding to the large contributions they had already made, closing the gap that prevented them from buying Mrs. Mwanza the gift that she wanted so badly. Although several of us knew that Mrs. Phiri and Bana Chibale had furnished the extra money necessary for this gift (and many others could probably guess that this was the case), their contribution was officially treated as a secret. This meant, again, that Mrs. Mwanza was able to regard the party and the gift of the refrigerator as the result of the shared work of all of the women in the church. She was able, in other words, to think of all women as having contributed, if not equally, then at least in keeping with their assigned roles, rather than being confronted with the reality that some women had given twice what was required of them while others had given nothing at all.

It is because of the efforts of the committee to shield Mrs. Mwanza from the divisions among her spiritual children by keeping her tuned into the official register of the event that she was able to regard the kitchen mending as a success. In our conversation on the day after the party she spoke confidently from within the official framework of spiritual parentage that had been carefully created for her by the super-members, Bana Chibale in particular. Although I am sure that Mrs. Mwanza was aware of the conflicts the kitchen mending caused, just as she was aware that a portion of the money used to pay for her refrigerator came not from the women of the congregation, but rather from a former church member living in the Congo, the work that Bana Chibale and the other committee members did to protect her nevertheless achieved its intended purpose. As a result, their spiritual mother was able to perceive the event in terms of Pentecostal relational ideals, confident that those who attended would be able to do the same.

Through their personal sacrifices and willingness to absorb those aspects of the exchange that threatened the social life of their congregation, then, super-members were able to produce an event in which these exchanges could be interpreted according to the official register alone.[7] The question that this analysis raises, of course, is why it was necessary for them to do so—why create a limited space that is governed by the official register when it is clear to so many of those involved that the unofficial register had been dominant all along? And why did they concentrate so much energy on protecting Mrs. Mwanza, in particular? In concluding this chapter I want to argue that the super-members' focus on Mrs. Mwanza is not only a function of their care for her as a parent, or of their desire to preserve their special relationship with their spiritual mother, though both of these factors are clearly in play. More importantly, the actions of Bana Chibale and her peers in preserving the official register point to the pivotal role of church leaders, especially during events like the kitchen mending, in moving by the Spirit. This is true not only because they are mediators of divine power but also because of their capacity to serve as icons of Pentecostal values.

PASTORS AS PENTECOSTAL ICONS

In her masterful study of value transformation on the tiny island of Gawa, Nancy Munn (1986) explores the symbolic aspects of value production—the mechanisms through which, as David Graeber puts it in his summary of Munn, "people represent the importance of their own actions to themselves" (Graeber 2001: 47). A key element of this process is what Munn calls "icons" of value. Icons in Munn's analysis are outcomes, such as a heavy body, which refer back to the actions that produced them, in this case the consumption of food rather than its distribution in relationally productive exchange. In Munn's best-known example, a witch's cannibalizing attacks target those who greedily hoard food, and the witch consumes the victim by making him ill. While the witch's greed for human flesh is the same in kind as the greed of her victim, it is vastly different in degree; it is greed in the extreme. Witchcraft therefore transforms an action into a commentary on itself, picking it up and revealing it for what it is. The process of iconicity, then, is one through which "the value of the act is concretized or given form" and thereby made "experientially available" (Munn 1986: 121, 271; also see Robbins 2015).

In the context of the kitchen mending, the most important outcome of the event was that through the successful actualization of Pentecostal exchange, believers at Key of David, particularly the super-members, were able to transform Mrs. Mwanza into an icon of moving by the

Spirit. During this event, Mrs. Mwanza emerged as someone in whom prosperity and charisma existed in a perfectly ordered relationship. Focused as the kitchen mending was on status-marking goods, especially the all-important upright refrigerator, this event was obviously one through which Mrs. Mwanza realized prosperity—that is, she became more prosperous. At the same time, the efforts of the committee to emphasize the official register, to foreground Mrs. Mwanza's status as a spiritual parent and therefore her charismatic authority, kept prosperity in its proper place. In the kitchen mending prosperity followed from and was therefore subordinated to charisma, thanks to continual reminders that Mrs. Mwanza was enjoying prosperity because she was a good spiritual parent, rather than the other way around. As a result, Mrs. Mwanza was transformed first and foremost into a symbol of charisma, while remaining a symbol of prosperity, and as such she became an icon of moving by the Spirit.

In the kitchen mending the value of Pentecostal exchange was therefore revealed in the person of Mrs. Mwanza. As we have seen, gifts to church leaders, whether seed offerings or contributions that demonstrate a believer's appreciation for a spiritual parent, are socially productive. These gifts form and strengthen ties to pastors, ties that in turn serve as mechanisms for moving by the Spirit. This means that the ultimate value of these exchanges and the social ties they produce is the same value that was realized by Mrs. Mwanza in the kitchen mending. Returning to the language developed in the introduction, we can say that by embodying value as a noun in this way, Mrs. Mwanza highlighted the process of value as a verb. The kitchen mending revealed the position of certain kinds of Pentecostal exchange and the relationships that these exchanges serve in the constellation of elements that make up the social world of Copperbelt Pentecostals. Put differently, the reason these exchanges and relationships are so important, so prominent, is because of their capacity to help people realize moving by the Spirit. They are valued by their connection to this value.

One further aspect of this process of valuation, which I return to in the conclusion, was the audience for the kitchen mending, especially visitors from outside the church. Guests at the kitchen mending who were not part of Key of David were, like Mrs. Mwanza, completely confined to the official register of the event. These outsiders were vital to the process of valuation that took place in this party because moving, like all values, is worked out in a wider social domain of perception and appreciation. Moving, we will recall, is *recognizable* progress, progress that, to invoke Jane Guyer's terms once more, is "graded and profiled," identified "in small nuances" (Guyer 2004: 147). Following Graeber (2001: 76–78; also see Haynes 2014), we can think of those engaged in this work of grading and profiling as "audiences" who recognize (or do not recognize) moving and in so doing ratify it (or not, as the case may be). In other words, it is before an audience like this that moving by the Spirit becomes meaningful as a new framework within which to realize an established Copperbelt value. The fact that this value emerged so clearly in the kitchen mending, in a moment where there was an extensive audience for its realization, means that with respect to the social processes I have been describing throughout this book, this event was especially significant. It is therefore no surprise that Mrs. Mwanza regarded it as a success.

While Mrs. Mwanza was very pleased with the outcome of her party, I should note that not everyone at Key of David was equally satisfied with the event. Certainly, some members of the church were able to see the work done in the party as benefiting them, as an opportunity to build their relationship with their spiritual parent, a relationship through which they hoped to realize moving by the Spirit just as Mrs. Mwanza had done. However, others involved in the kitchen mending were hurt and alienated, convinced that the outsized role played by the super-members pointed to serious problems in their church. Their experience with this large and expensive event felt like a variation on a common theme, namely that despite the equalizing language of spiritual parentage, church leaders were choosing, playing favorites in the congregation. While this concern usually remains in the background in Pentecostal churches on the Copperbelt, anxiety over the possibility of favoritism sometimes becomes too much for a believer to take. When that happens, she will look for new social networks through which she can move by the Spirit.

CHAPTER 8

The Circulation of Copperbelt Saints

If people do not welcome you, leave their town and shake the dust off your feet as a testimony against them.

—Luke 9:5

During my time in Nsofu, I came to rely on Bana Junior and her husband for patient explanations of Pentecostal practice, which was her specialty, and of mine politics, which was his. Bana Junior was a faithful member of Freedom Bible Church throughout my doctoral fieldwork, and though it was not unusual to run into her at other prayer meetings and fellowships, she remained committed to the congregation even during the scandals that drove so many others away. When I returned to Nsofu in 2013, however, I found that she was no longer part of Freedom and had instead started attending a different Pentecostal congregation. Sitting down with Bana Junior to discuss why she had changed churches took some doing, but finally she invited me to her house in a township adjacent to Nsofu, not far from where I had first met Pastor Ephraim. After being shown into her spotless front room—Bana Junior was a fastidious housekeeper—I settled as best I could into a precariously tippy wingback chair opposite Bana Junior, who sat on a single bed covered with a green blanket. The July morning was chilly, and Bana Junior served me cornflakes with hot milk along with the usual midmorning snack of bread and tea in an effort, she said, to warm me up.

In the period during which I had been away from Nsofu, Bana Junior's family had spent a couple of years living in the Copperbelt provincial capital of Ndola. When the family moved back to Kitwe, Bana Junior returned to Freedom Bible Church, only to be disappointed by what she found there. Bana Junior had expected that things would change in her absence; as she put it, after you have been away you imagine that there will have been some "development," that things will have moved (*ukusela*) in church. There ought to have been spiritual growth in the lives of church members, as well as visible (*ukumoneka*) changes in the church itself—its decor, meeting location, and so on. Instead, the number of congregants had declined, and those who remained didn't seem to have changed much. Meanwhile, the congregation was still meeting in a classroom, having failed at that point to move into a building of its own. In Bana Junior's telling, a church that didn't change could become toxic, and individual members could be negatively affected. Instead of helping congregants to go forward, the church might cause them to go backward (*ukubwelela inuma*), and going backward was not, in Bana Junior's Pentecostal turn of phrase, the "portion" of believers.[1]

In Bana Junior's account, the problem with Freedom Bible Church was not just that the congregation was not developing, but that this lack of progress could result in regression, in moving backward. Believers use the Bemba term for regression, *ukubwelela inuma*, to indicate apostasy, or "backsliding," as they put it in English, a concept that occupies a central place in the Pentecostal imagination. Those who have just begun to attend Pentecostal gatherings, in particular, make a point to regularly state that they could never backslide. Initially, I attributed these frequent declarations to the zeal of new church members. However, I have come to see the salience of backsliding for Copperbelt believers not only as a marker of religious fervor but also as a corollary of moving by the Spirit. If the appeal of Pentecostalism is largely bound up in the opportunities it presents for moving, the possibility that one might not move—indeed, might actually move backward—has a chilling effect. Backsliding in this context therefore refers both to the loss of religious commitment and to the absence of spiritual progress.

In this chapter I explore what happens when the promise of moving by the Spirit is not realized. As the experiences of people like Bana Junior, Moses, and the Zulus have already indicated, when people on the Copperbelt feel they are not moving by the Spirit, they will often leave the Pentecostal church they are attending and join another one where they feel they have a better chance of realizing this value. While the discussion that follows is about the breakdown of Pentecostal relationships, I don't want to belabor this point—in other words, I don't want to portray Nsofu's Pentecostal churches as excessively dysfunctional. Rather, my aim in exploring what happens when Pentecostal social relationships stop working is to further illuminate the process of valuation that animates religious adherence on the Copperbelt. As we will see, the shifting congregational affiliations of believers are a key point at which moving by the Spirit structures Pentecostal social life. The first step in this process is to explore the forces that act against believers' relationships.

CORRUPTION AND *JEALOUS:* TWO POINTS OF RELATIONAL BREAKDOWN

While walking one afternoon along one of the hundreds of dirt paths that crisscross Nsofu, I spied Bana James standing outside her home washing clothes. Bashi James was the groundskeeper at Key of David, and the family lived on the church property, which meant that Bana James's front door was also the back door of the church. I hopped over a trench cut for the footings of someone's new house, slipped through a gap in the plank fence around the church, and called out "*Odi,*" asking Bana James if I could enter the yard. She smiled and gestured to a wooden bench leaning against the cinderblock sanctuary. Leaving the washing to soak in a basin, Bana James dried her hands and sat down beside me in the shade of the church building. It was a few weeks before the kitchen mending, and our conversation soon turned to the growing tension among the women of Key of David. In Bana James's view, the blame for the divisions in the church fell on Mrs. Mwanza. Rather than treating all the members of her congregation equally, as she should, Bana James explained, Mrs. Mwanza appeared to favor those who "came in cars" and was likely to "baby" members of the church who displayed their wealth. This was why there was so much conflict among the women in the congregation.

Bana James's sentiments were by no means unique among Copperbelt believers. To return to Bana Chanda's discussion of Pentecostal corruption, which we looked at briefly in chapter 4, it is clear that many poorer church members perceived similar problems in their congregations. As Bana Chanda put it,

> There are some that are close [to the pastor] because of what we call *ukutula* [giving, or giving offering]. Let's say I have nothing, like right now I have nothing, I'm just staying at home [and not working]. There are others who have something, but I'm just sitting. There are some who go privately to our mother, to our *bafiyashi*. They may have bought Boom [detergent paste], they may have bought bread, sugar, food. They bring it to her. The next day, they go to town and ask, "Mother, what would you like?" They buy it whether

cooking oil, *citenge* material, soap, and bring it to her. That *bafiyashi* will think that the one who has considered her is the child who cares for her. You see? We don't care for her. Now, she doesn't know that the issue is simply that we don't have anything. Because if you have you can certainly give.

Both Bana Chanda's and Bana James's complaints offer strong indictments of church leaders, who they felt favored certain members of their congregations and who might be so disconnected from others that they could not understand why they were not giving as much as everyone else. At the risk of redundancy, I will here point out again that when religious kinship fails to act as an equalizing force, poorer church members like these women find themselves faced with structural barriers that keep them from developing relationships with their spiritual parents that can help them move by the Spirit. While the previous chapter pointed out that controversy in churches often crystalizes around supermembers, the experiences of Bana James and Bana Chanda point to the role of pastors in Pentecostal corruption. Although the language of corruption implies that some have tried to gain special access to spiritual resources through gifts to church leaders, the above accounts make it clear that in the eyes of believers the responsibility for this problem ultimately falls not on the laypeople who make these gifts, but rather on pastors. Super-members might be corrupting, but church leaders are corruptible, and that is worse. The central role played by pastors in every aspect of Copperbelt Pentecostalism therefore figures as much in the breakdown of church relationships as in their formation.

Both Bana James and Bana Chanda eventually left their Pentecostal fellowships. Bana James had a dramatic falling out with Mrs. Mwanza after her family was asked to move out of the church building. She remained a Pentecostal, however, and joined another Nsofu congregation. For her part, Bana Chanda's participation at Higher Calling began to taper off after Bana Mfuwe left. She stopped going altogether when Bana Chilomba was replaced by Pastor Conrad, who Bana Chanda said she found difficult (*ukushupa*, a verb that is used to describe a fussy child or an ill-fitting pair of shoes). Her main issue with Pastor Conrad was, again, his tendency to choose. While the experiences of Bana James and Bana Chanda illustrate the failure of vertical ties, horizontal relationships can also cause trouble for believers. As with the failure of spiritual parentage, the loss of connection to Pentecostal laypeople threatens to close off opportunities for moving by the Spirit.

While Bana Mfuwe was still living in Nsofu she was often found in the company of Bana Rachel, who lived on the opposite end of the township, roughly half an hour's walk away. Bana Rachel was an important member of Higher Calling, known for her faithful fasting and singing. Everyone in the group could recognize her voice, which seemed permanently hoarse—the result, I was told, of so many hours spent in prayer. In the months immediately following Bana Mfuwe's departure, Bana Rachel remained a fixture at Higher Calling, but as time went on she stopped coming to meetings. Rumors began to circulate that she was hosting prayer gatherings in her home, and a few believers confided in me that they had begun to seek out Bana Rachel for counseling and prayer.

One day I found myself in Bana Rachel's neighborhood and decided to pay her a visit. As I drew nearer to her house I heard the unmistakable sound of collective-personal prayer coming from inside. While it seemed clear that I had happened upon a Pentecostal meeting, the gate in Bana Rachel's fence was locked and the windows and curtains were shut. This was strange. At every other prayer meeting I had attended in Nsofu the door had been open as a way of welcoming visitors, and one almost never saw the windows of a house closed during the day unless it was raining or the occupants were away. Despite these indications that those inside did not want to be disturbed, I decided to see if they would let me in, and rapped on the gate to get their attention. Soon I saw Bana Rachel's face at the window, and a few minutes later she stepped out the front door, opened the gate, and let me inside. Half a dozen women, almost all of them people I recognized from my early attendance at Higher Calling, were pacing around Bana Rachel's living room praying. They eyed me warily as I slipped into a corner and sat quietly on a chair. After they had prayed for another hour or so, Bana Rachel decided to explain to me what they were doing. The group's only goal, she said, was to meet and pray. They wanted to keep their numbers small, she went on, so that they could focus on the spiritual practices that they thought were most important. This was why they hadn't invited others to their meetings. Having clarified the purpose of the group, Bana Rachel told me that I was free to go. I stood up to go—rather willingly, to be honest, as I found the entire experience rather disconcerting—leaving the women as I had found them, their voices blending with the familiar timbre of Bana Rachel's in prayer.

The meeting at Bana Rachel's house was perhaps the strangest Pentecostal gathering I have ever attended. Typically, Pentecostal events are expansive, welcoming newcomers without hesitation—a quality from which my research benefited. Up-and-coming pastors, in particular, are obviously more than happy to have visitors. The difference in Bana Rachel's case, of course, was that she was not an up-and-coming pastor. Despite the fact that a few people said they had gone to her for prayer, to my knowledge at least Bana Rachel had no designs on starting a church or fellowship. She certainly had not organized the prayer meetings at her house in a way that suggested that this was the case. Rather, the objective of her locked gate and closed windows was, as Bana Rachel put it, to allow a small group of believers the freedom to pursue the spiritual practices that they considered most important.

Although Bana Rachel did not elaborate on what these practices were, it is safe to assume that prayer was at the top of the list. In this regard, the women gathered at Bana Rachel's house were no different from most believers, who refer to prayer as a central part of their religious participation. If prayer was indeed their priority, this raises the question of why they felt the need to keep others away. Given that most Pentecostals attach a great deal of significance to collective-personal prayer, the women at Bana Rachel's house could be reasonably sure that anyone who came to join them would share their spiritual goals. The emphasis the group placed on prayer would therefore, at least in principle, not have been threatened by the addition of more people. Indeed, in the light of the power that comes with praying in the company of others, one would think that a group committed to prayer would be more than happy to see its numbers grow. Why, then, did Bana Rachel lock her gate?

I believe that the reason Bana Rachel kept her house closed up during prayer was that she was trying to protect the women gathered there from what people in Nsofu call "*jealous*." This English loanword carries a great deal of weight. The term does not just indicate the presence of jealousy, though that is certainly part of what it connotes. On the Copperbelt, *jealous* refers to the will to destroy (*ukuonaula*) others' advancements, to stop them from moving. More than mere verbal critique, *jealous* is active, taking the form of witchcraft, theft, gossip, or social sanctions (Ferguson 1999: 142–48). Writing about Botswana, Klaits (2010: 5) describes jealousy as "the antithesis of love," the cultural counterpoint to the mutuality that we have identified as the key to friendship on the Copperbelt. As such, *jealous* represents the inversion of a properly functioning relational world, antagonism and scheming where one hopes for cooperation and care. Indeed, according to my informants, *jealous* is what motivates most Copperbelt social ills. For example, Bana Chanda stated that the frequent theft of merchandise from the small kiosk she sometimes operated in her front yard was the result of *jealous*. If her neighbors saw her progressing, she said, they would deliberately act to foil her success by robbing her stand.[2]

While *jealous* is a salient term outside Pentecostal contexts, it is also used to explain conflicts within the church. This applies to all levels of the church hierarchy. *Jealous* laypeople are those who pray "dangerous prayers"—prayers that God would harm another person—against their fellow believers, trying to supernaturally hurt those in a congregation who have been successful.[3] Accounts of dangerous prayers offered by one layperson against another are rare. Far more frequent were accusations of *jealous* among pastors. At issue here was not dangerous prayers, but rather the propensity to schism. Pastoral *jealous* was often given as a response to my questions about why Pentecostal groups were so unstable. I was told many times that when one leader in a church sees another doing well, *jealous* will often compel him to leave and start his own fellowship rather than work with a more successful pastor. In sum, *jealous* undermines moving by threatening those who have realized this value, and, at least in the context of the church, keeps people from working effectively together in lateral relationships.

Returning to the secret prayer meeting at Bana Rachel's house, I would argue that it was *jealous* that the women were trying to keep out by closing the windows and locking the gate. By controlling attendance at the meetings, they were able to weed out those who might take offense at the progress of others, thereby shielding themselves from supernatural attacks that might set them back in their efforts to move by the Spirit. Since *jealous* also interferes with believers' ability to work well together in lateral networks, guarding against it was also a way of protecting the ritual energy produced by collective-personal prayer, ensuring that it would not be undermined by a lack of unity. Like anxieties about corruption, then, the fear of *jealous* demonstrates that what is at stake in the breakdown of Pentecostal relationships is the possibility of moving by the Spirit. When realizing this value begins to seem less possible, believers shake the dust of their feet, to employ a biblical expression, and move to one of the many other Pentecostal groups found in Nsofu.

I have so far explored the relational problems behind the movement of Copperbelt believers from one congregation to another; before going any further, I should point out that there are some Pentecostals who are very unlikely to leave their churches—namely, super-members. Given what we know about the relational lives of these believers, it is not difficult to see why. If circulation follows from a failure of Pentecostal social ties, a foreclosure of opportunities for moving by the Spirit, then those who are most successful at forming ties to church leaders and thereby realizing this value have no need to leave their churches. In the nine years during which I have followed Key of David, the Chibale family has remained a fixture in this congregation (the Phiris have since moved to Lusaka), despite having moved away from Nsofu to a low-density neighborhood in another part of Kitwe. The same is true of Freedom Bible Church, where Mr. Moyo, who has long been the most prominent member of the group, continues to serve as an elder. There are others in both of these congregations who have remained as well, but they are a small minority. Super-members are therefore the exception that proves the rule of changing religious affiliation, pointing to its roots in Pentecostal social life and moving by the Spirit.

Copperbelt believers often observe that shifting membership from one group to the next seems to be a uniquely Pentecostal practice. As they are quick to point out, you don't see Catholics or Anglicans jumping from church to church; why can't Pentecostals manage to stay put like these other Christians? In lamenting their tendency to move from one group to the next, believers imply that under ideal circumstances this sort of circulation would not be necessary. In a perfect world, the relationships they form in church would do what they're supposed to, making moving by the Spirit happen for every member of a congregation. While the shifting religious affiliations of believers in Nsofu fall short of the social ideal, their movement from church to church should nevertheless be understood as part of their efforts to create a good social world. This is because going from one congregation to another (and perhaps to another, and another . . .) draws Copperbelt Pentecostals into the process of valuation through which they seek to move by the Spirit.

SCHISM AS VALUE

As the foregoing discussion has shown, Copperbelt Pentecostalism is characterized by a large and ever-growing number of churches and the continual "circulation of the saints" (Bibby and Brinkerhoff 1973) among them, with believers regularly transferring their allegiance from one group to the next. It is possible to interpret these traits according to familiar social scientific models of schism. Here we might appeal to Weber's classic arguments about the unstable and ephemeral quality of charismatic leadership (see Weber 1946: 245–64; 1947: 358–86). Seen from this angle, Copperbelt churches expand, contract, or split apart because they are closely identified with pastors, whose position is easily challenged by the power of new charismatic leaders. In Weber's treatment, the counterpoint to charisma is bureaucracy, which is what happens when charismatic leadership becomes institutionalized, and which will in time be challenged by a new charismatic leader. This cyclical pattern is also reflected in sociological discussions of "churches" and "sects" (e.g., Niebuhr 1957). Here, schism is understood as a rejection of the bureaucratic establishment (the "church") in favor of charismatic power, which gives rise to a new movement or "sect"; as time goes on the sect turns into a church, which will eventually give rise to yet another sect. In contrast to these models, we might approach the changing composition of Copperbelt churches as a simple problem of competition or conflict. The religious "marketplace" of Nsofu, to use a metaphor common in sociology (e.g., Finke and Stark 2006), is extremely crowded, and church leaders are in a constant struggle for the allegiance of a relatively fixed number of believers. Framed in these terms, Pentecostal laypeople are effectively customers whose decision to attend a particular church is not much different from a decision to buy a particular brand of soap. Similarly, Courtney Handman (2014a) has identified a social scientific tendency to reduce schism to politics or interpersonal conflict. A schism is just what happens when a grab for power or breakdown in relationships happens in a church.

While each of these lines of interpretation can be made to speak to what is happening among Pentecostals on the Copperbelt, they do not go far enough in explaining why believers move so frequently from one church to the next, or why new fellowships continue to pop up in a religious context that is already saturated with Pentecostal groups. These dynamics do not constitute a rejection of institutional Christianity in favor of charismatic power—indeed, as their preference for hierarchies and titles suggests, believers on the Copperbelt are quite happy with what Kirsch (2008: 184) calls "bureaucracy in the Pentecostal-charismatic mode." Nor should the circulation of Pentecostal saints be read as cyclical, a moving back and forth between two poles, whether charisma and bureaucracy or sect and church. Here my thought follows an argument put forward by Jon Bialecki (2014) about the nature of denominational splits. The problem with models of church and sect or bureaucracy and charisma, according to Bialecki, is that they obscure the internal variation that schism produces, the efflorescence of forms through which Christians try to address the fundamental problem of religion—namely, how to connect with a divine entity who is simultaneously present and absent (Keane 1997). In Bialecki's treatment, these efforts do not cycle back and forth between churches and sects, but instead follow a linear process of "intensification" through which various mechanisms for resolving the "problem of presence" (Engelke 2007) are differentiated and purified. In other words, divisions among Christians are best understood as part of an ongoing effort to connect with the divine more effectively than others have done before. As Handman (2014a) points out, this is why we cannot reduce schism to politics or relational breakdown. Churches are not like other social groups because, as she puts it, they are sites of mediation—again, spaces within which people try to connect to God's presence and, I would add, power. This is certainly true in Nsofu, where the church represents a point of access to the divine power that drives moving by the Spirit, whether through the charismatic influence of pastors or the ritual energy of collective-personal prayer. The shifting membership of Pentecostal churches is therefore not simply an outgrowth of local political struggles, but is instead an indication that circumstances in a particular church have made access to the divine seem more difficult, and thereby made moving by the Spirit seem less possible. Taken together, these arguments allow us to approach the shifting religious membership of Pentecostals in Nsofu as a commentary on value.

Values are animating ideas that order the elements of a society, transforming what is theoretically a field of open-ended potential into a field with a differentiated topography. In our discussion thus far we have seen how the value of moving by the Spirit structures the relationships that believers pursue, the organization of their worship, and the relative position of charisma and prosperity. Each of these elements is ordered according to its capacity to realize moving by the Spirit. The same process of rank-ordering structures the positions of different Pentecostal groups on the religious landscape of Nsofu. In the years that I have been following the shifting composition of congregations in the township, I have observed the growth and decline of a number of churches. The changing fortunes of Higher Calling and Freedom Bible Church during my fieldwork are a case in point here. Both groups were bursting at the seams when I first arrived in Nsofu—that's one reason I chose them for my study—but lost more than half of their membership in the course of the following year. Other churches grew during the same period, including Key of David and the congregation that both Bana Junior and Bana James joined after leaving their churches. These changes in membership size were connected to changes in status, as groups rose or fell in the eyes of Pentecostals in Nsofu, gaining or losing a reputation for power.

By circulating among congregations, periodically transferring their loyalty from one church to another, believers were therefore engaged in a process of valuation, ranking Pentecostal groups according to the opportunities for moving by the Spirit they presented. Their shifting allegiance contours the religious landscape of Nsofu, elevating those communities in which people are moving by the Spirit and lowering those where they are not realizing this value.

Rather than an effect of the instability of charisma or the result of power struggles among church leaders, then, the circulation of believers among Nsofu's Pentecostal churches is best understood as part of the process of valuation through which moving by the Spirit structures Pentecostal social life on the Zambian Copperbelt. By raising and lowering the status of individual churches on the basis of how well these institutions help believers move by the Spirit, Pentecostals "intensify" their efforts at effective mediation by identifying the best social options for realizing this value. In this way, believers are working to create a good social world. As we will see in the conclusion, these efforts also constitute a claim about what constitutes the good in the first place.

Conclusion

Worlds That Flourish

We carry in our worlds that flourish
Our worlds that have failed

Christopher Okigbo, "Lament of the Silent Sisters"

What are we to make of the global expansion of Pentecostalism over the last three decades? I have argued that the key to understanding the meteoric rise of this form of Christianity, at least on the Copperbelt, is that it is "a site of *action*" (Marshall 2009: 22), a way of making life possible. In keeping with this emphasis, I have shown that a central component of Pentecostalism's attraction for people in Nsofu is its capacity to create a good social world by making relationships through which they are able to move by the Spirit. These relationships are not always easy to maintain, and indeed, keeping them strong and safe absorbs a great deal of people's time and energy. Nevertheless, Pentecostalism offers believers a powerful way of acting in the world, of realizing established values in new ways and of trying, as much as possible, to stay above the ebb and flow of the Copperbelt economy.

Why is Pentecostalism able to do this so effectively? What is it about this religion that enables it to not only help people create a good social world, but also, as I will argue below, to make claims about what constitutes a good social world in the first place? In this conclusion, I would like to turn my attention away from the particular context of the Copperbelt to explore those broad characteristics of Pentecostalism that make it especially effective at making claims about value. A claim about value is made when an alternative model of the good life—of what counts as a good relationship, or a good way of organizing one's resources, for instance—is put forward in a public context. These claims require a response, which may take one of several forms. The public or the "audience" for this claim may decide that it is invalid, that the proposed model of sociality or economy is not a good model. Alternately, they may decide to incorporate the new model into existing cultural frameworks, or to "adopt" (see Robbins 2004a) it whole cloth. By showing how Pentecostalism is uniquely structured to make these kinds of claims, my aim in the discussion that follows is to open up new lines of comparison that will allow us to better understand the global appeal of this religion. I argue that Pentecostalism's simultaneous processes of accommodation and critique have something fundamental to communicate about the way that value works, and as such represent the key to this religion's widespread popularity.

PENTECOSTALISM AS A SITE OF VALUE PRODUCTION

Over the course of the last ten years the core debate in the anthropology of Christianity has turned on the question of rupture. The terms of this debate have been largely framed by a seminal article by Joel Robbins (2007). Robbins argues that the reason anthropology has tended to ignore Christianity is that it is by and large a "science of continuity" (Robbins 2007: 6). Historically, anthropologists have focused primarily on those aspects of culture that have endured despite the influence of external forces like capitalism, development, or indeed Christianity. The more things change, the more they stay the same. According to Robbins, the tendency to look for continuity created a disciplinary blind spot that kept anthropologists from seeing change, perhaps especially when it came in the form of religious conversion. If, however, anthropologists would take seriously their informants' statements that their lives have been radically transformed since becoming Christians, they might begin to move beyond the "continuity thinking" (Robbins 2007: 5) that has held the discipline back and be able to engage more effectively with change across the board.

It is important to point out that Robbins never argued that continuity had no part to play in conversion. His analysis of Christian adherence among the Urapmin of highland Papua New Guinea employs a theoretical framework that draws extensively on the work of Marshall Sahlins. In particular, Robbins builds on Sahlins's (e.g., 1992) discussion of change to describe what he calls "adoption," the process through which people "reach out and take up a new culture in its own terms, without trying, at least in any concerted way, to work it into their traditional categories of understanding" (Robbins 2004a: 10). While this is an extreme form of cultural change, it nevertheless relies on extant cultural models to get off the ground. As Robbins puts it in his summary of Sahlins, "The stimulus for this kind of radical cultural change is itself cultural," and the motivations for taking up a new cultural framework "must themselves be made sensible in a particular cultural frame of reference" (Robbins 2004a: 9). Even radical transformation therefore hinges on a kind of engagement with the past, albeit an engagement with the past that treats it as an object of critique and scorn. Building on this discussion, I want to argue that Christianity's internal tension between continuity and change, especially in Pentecostal forms of this religion, structures its capacity to make claims about value.

In an article comparing the internal logics of Pentecostalism and anthropology, Simon Coleman argues that Pentecostal and charismatic forms of Christianity represent "part cultures" (2006b: 3). On the one hand, Pentecostal categories are "meant for export" and slot quite easily into a range of cultural contexts. On the other, despite the facility with which they are taken up, these same categories are "often in tension" with those of the "host society" in which they take root (Coleman 2006b: 3). In Coleman's analysis, Pentecostalism emerges as a religion with unfinished edges, easily sewn to an existing cultural fabric. While the seams that come to hold Pentecostalism into its place may be very neat, the Pentecostal material is often printed with a very different pattern, and (at the risk of stretching this metaphor too far) may even clash at points with the fabric it has been sewn into. In other words, Pentecostalism is both accommodating and critical, a religion that both resonates with local concerns and, at least sometimes, serves as a framework for calling local models into question (see Handman 2014b). In other words, in Pentecostalism believers are given resources to make claims about what constitutes the good. The critical aspects of Pentecostalism shape the content of these claims, orienting them around points of contrast between the Pentecostal world and the context that surrounds it. Where people were using their money in one way, for instance, Pentecostals are asking them to use it in another by giving seed offerings. At the same time, Pentecostalism's accommodating aspects ensure that these claims will be heard. Pentecostalism responds very well to preexisting local concerns, for instance, by addressing fears about malevolent spirits (Meyer 1999).

There is one more element to Pentecostalism's ability to make claims about the good. Pentecostalism, and particularly neo-Pentecostalism, does not call its adherents out of their communities. Believers are deeply embedded in their neighborhoods, families, workplaces, and schools. It is in these spaces that Pentecostals leverage their claims about what a good social world looks like. As I observed in chapter 7, these spaces are "audiences" (Graeber 2001: 76–78; also see Haynes 2014), sites of recognition and comparison. An audience inscribes value on action—whether relationships, rituals, or the purchase of an upright refrigerator—and places it in a larger framework that reveals how this action stacks up against others. The work of recognition and comparison is highly contested, a struggle over what values are (or should be) and how they are (or should be) realized. This struggle has real stakes in the way people use their resources, organize their relationships, and participate in the political life of their community. In the face of this contentious work, the audience for Pentecostal claims about value may choose to reject those claims, but it cannot ignore them completely, at not least in a place like Nsofu, which is saturated with Pentecostal believers and groups. In communities like these, as Harri Englund writes, Pentecostalism "is never confined to churches and congregations" but rather "occupies the public sphere as a possibility" (2007: 493).

In its balance between accommodation and critique, Pentecostalism tells us something about the way that value works. This is true because value is a relation. Value implies difference, rank, structure, and, as we have seen, struggle. Each of these terms implies one or several others against which an element is measured; more specifically, value connotes comparison, which in turn requires an examination of likenesses and differences. I think this is why Dumont (1980: 240) takes such care to define encompassment in terms of both similarity and distinction. An encompassed value is like an encompassing value in that it is consubstantial with it, part of the same whole; it is different in that it is the encompassing value's contrary. Value is always worked out on the basis of accommodation and contradiction, and that is never clearer than in situations in which the order of values and the appropriate framework for their realization—that is, the terms of the good—are up for debate. When a new claim about the good comes on the scene, its capacity to change things is predicated on the extent to which it is different from the model that is already in place. But the capacity of this claim to command a hearing hinges on its similarity, its overall salience in the community where it is being engaged.

If, as I have suggested, Pentecostalism is by definition marked by the very traits that characterize effective claims about the good, this goes a long way toward explaining its runaway success. In trying to understand Pentecostalism's popularity, scholars have long pointed out its simultaneously localizing and globalizing force, its capacity to address the specific concerns of a given community while at the same time extending that community beyond itself and into a worldwide body of Christ (e.g., Coleman 2000). This local/global framework may no longer be fashionable, but it still has something to say about what makes Pentecostalism so compelling. It is clear that analyses highlighting Pentecostalism's parallel engagement with the global and the local have hit on a more fundamental capacity in this religion to engage a particular audience and effectively present it with a new model of the good. The secret of Pentecostalism's global popularity, then, lies in the way its balance of continuity and critique structures claims about value, about what constitutes a good social world. Understood in these terms, it is not hard to see why Pentecostalism has been one of the most successful religious movements in recent history.

WORLDS THAT FLOURISH

In closing, I would like to briefly address one of the central questions that my analysis raises: what difference does Christianity make in the social situations I have described? (see Cannell 2006). This is a question to which one might imagine many different answers. Faced with the undeniable overlap between Pentecostal social life and the social life of the Copperbelt more generally, one might argue that this is a place where Christianity makes very little difference, that Pentecostal material has simply found its way into social processes that are always happening anyway (Scott 2005). Moreover, if the popularity of Pentecostalism on the Copperbelt follows from its relationship both to models of moving found outside the church and, to a lesser extent, to the impact of economic insecurity, might not these factors, rather than the presence of Christianity "per se," provide a more satisfying explanation of the social dynamics I have described here (Hann 2007; also see Hann 2014)? If this is the case, what is to be gained by situating the foregoing analysis within the broader intellectual debates of the anthropology of Christianity? (Comaroff 2010: 529).

Against this line of interpretation, I have argued that Christianity makes a great deal of difference in the social world I have just described. I have shown that while the new metric of moving that Pentecostalism provides, as well as the Pentecostal emphasis on moving more generally, resonates with cultural forms found outside the Pentecostal fold, it cannot be reduced to a slight modification of these forms. That said, while I have argued against a reductive reading of the Pentecostal relational world as I have presented it here, it should also be clear that we cannot go too far in the other direction and suggest that the social or political economic context within which Pentecostalism is practiced is irrelevant to the religious lives of Copperbelt believers. Rather, in keeping with the model of Pentecostalism I have just developed, I hope it is clear that moving by the Spirit is a value, an animating idea, that is part moving and part Spirit—part extant cultural ideas and part emerging Pentecostal models. We might therefore say that it is an elective affinity between religion and Copperbelt social life that allows Pentecostalism to be both culturally meaningful and socially productive, while at the same time challenging and expanding cultural and social paradigms by leveraging new claims about what constitutes the good.

Weber's point in bringing the notion of elective affinity into social science was, famously, to argue against what he found to be a vulgar materialist reading of history that could not recognize the power of ideology (Weber 2010). Weber understood that ideology, including religion, was not simply a tool of obfuscation, but was rather an animating force with consequences that even the most committed materialist could not help but acknowledge. Nearly a century later this argument is still relevant, perhaps especially to the efforts of the anthropology of Christianity. As a subdiscipline that has sought to put this religion back on the analytical map in places where it has been "[airbrushed] out" (Robbins 2007: 8), the anthropology of Christianity has had its work cut out for it. Arguably, there will always be those who refuse to see Christianity as a driving force in its own right; for some, the answer to the question, "What difference does Christianity make?" will always be, "None at all"—or at least, "Not nearly so much as other things," whether traditional practices or neoliberalism.[1] While I do not wish to dispute the possibility that in some ethnographic contexts this will indeed be the case, this is a conclusion that must be demonstrated ethnographically, rather than assumed theoretically.

In response to the tension between materialist and idealist readings of Pentecostalism, I have chosen in this book to employ a framework focused on value. My argument has been idealist in orientation, showing how the animating idea of moving by the Spirit reverberates through the social world of Pentecostals. That said, I hope that I have also demonstrated the very real impact that the political economy of the Copperbelt has on believers. This is true on both a small and large scale, as believers negotiate differences in economic status among themselves and navigate the alternating cycles of boom and bust that are a fact of life in a globalized extraction economy. It would be impossible to understand Pentecostal adherence on the Copperbelt if we did not attend to the ebbs and flows of the world beyond the church, the context in which Christianity is practiced. Believers carry bits of this world—perhaps especially its shortcomings—into the social relationships that form in their congregations, just as they carry bits of Pentecostal ties that have broken down into their new churches and fellowships. These bits shape new relationships and structure institutions, making the worlds that have failed an integral part of the worlds the flourish, to borrow some turns of phrase from Christopher Okigbo's poem "Lament of the Silent Sisters." For many people on the Copperbelt, Pentecostalism represents an important site for the construction of social relationships that can make moving possible. It provides a model of a good social world, a world in which everyone is moving by the Spirit. As we have seen, this world is as fragile as any other, susceptible to forces both beyond and within the church that can easily break it down. It is not a perfect world, and certainly not a world that insulates people from the many difficulties that life in urban Africa presents. Against the odds, however, it is a world that flourishes.

Notes

INTRODUCTION

1. I spent more than twenty-two months living in this township, first in 2008–2009 and then on return trips in 2013 and 2014. Before that I spent fourteen months in the nearby city of Chingola working with a local NGO, and later doing preliminary research for my doctorate. In both locations I always lived with Pentecostals and almost always in the homes of Pentecostal pastors.

2. Indeed, a number of scholars have connected the exponential growth of Pentecostalism, particularly in its prosperity gospel guise, to the expansion of capitalist interests (Martin 1995, 1998; Ukah 2005; Nolivos 2012; CDE 2012).

3. In addition to the ethnographic observations noted in this paragraph, arguments about the social corrosiveness of Pentecostalism are also shaped by classic social scientific discussions that connect the Protestant emphasis on personalized salvation to the rise of individualism in the West (e.g., Dumont 1986, Mauss 1985).

4. While "informants" is a vexed term in anthropology, I employ it from time to time in an effort to highlight the unique relationship an anthropologist has with those she studies. My aim in using what some will take to be an anachronistic term is, first, to emphasize the expertise of the people that I studied. Second, while I admit that "informants" sounds rather awkward, I find it preferable to most alternatives, for instance, "interlocutors," which problematically privileges the role of speech in participant observation. As Marilyn Strathern puts it, "People are more than respondents answering questions; they are informants in the fullest sense, in control of the information they offer. I mean this in the sense that the ethnographer is often led to receive it as information, that is, as data which has become meaningful, by putting it into the context of general knowledge about these people's lives and situations and thus the context of its production" (Strathern 1999: 7).

5. For example, in his description of the consumption patterns of urban residents in colonial Broken Hill (today the city of Kabwe), a mining town in Zambia's Central Province, Godfrey Wilson noted the high demand for enduring prestige goods, citing clothing as an especially important example (Wilson 1942: 15–18; also see Mitchell and Epstein 1959: 32; Hansen 1992: 275; Parpart 1994: 250). Similarly, in a longer discussion of what she identified as emerging social stratification on the colonial Copperbelt, Hortense Powdermaker (1962: 94–96) wrote that clothing was a key marker of prestige, a tendency that she, following Audrey Richards (1995: 216–17), connected to an earlier pattern of social differentiation, display, and prestige among the Bemba.

6. The idea of play is also central to Wariboko's discussion—a notion that he notes is elemental to Pentecostalism, a movement that takes its name from a festival (Wariboko 2011: 161).

7. For example, "When you ask, you do not receive, because you ask with wrong motives, that you may spend what you get on your pleasures" (James 4: 3).

CHAPTER 1. BOOM AND BUST, REVIVAL AND RENEWAL

1. Although Chinese investment in Zambia is often characterized as positive, it has also encountered public oppposition (e.g., Hess and Aidoo 2015).

2. To make matters worse, many of those who were laid off had outstanding debt of some sort; when the balance of that debt was deducted from their termination benefits, most were left with little or no take-home pay at all (Ndulo et al. 2009: 21).

3. This would potentially have benefited the export market; however, the fall in the price of raw materials likely prevented this from happening.

4. In the 2010 census the population of Kitwe was recorded as 501,360. Ndola, the provincial capital of the Copperbelt, was slightly smaller, with a population of 451,246.

5. The Lumpa Church came to symbolize opposition to the mission churches, to the colonial administration, and to President Kenneth Kaunda's United National Independence Party (Hinfelaar 1994: 73–100). This conflict came to a head in the months before independence in 1964, when at least one thousand people were killed in a violent conflict between Lumpa adherents and government troops.

6. For a more detailed discussion of Pentecostal expansion in Zambia, see Burgess and van der Maas 2010.

7. While, as we will see, the movement from classical to neo-Pentecostalism represents an important benchmark in the development of this religion on the Copperbelt, the distinction I am drawing between the older and newer forms of this religion is not one that I heard most of my informants make. Indeed, people on the Copperbelt will call members of both missionary-established and more recent independent congregations "Pentecostals," or *bapente* in Bemba. The general irrelevance of this distinction reflects the extent to which neo-Pentecostalism has encompassed all Pentecostal practice in Zambia.

8. Other key indicators of Pentecostal expansion in Zambia include the opening of the Trinity Broadcasting Network (a Christian television station

with mostly Pentecostal content) in 1998, and the establishment of the Independent Churches Organization of Zambia to incorporate emerging Pentecostal groups in 2001 (Cheyeka 2008). Perhaps the most famous marker of the rising prominence of Pentecostalism was President Frederick Chiluba's 1991 declaration of Zambia as a "Christian nation" (see Gifford 1998, Phiri 2003, Haynes 2015). Chiluba, whose election marked the end of one-party rule in Zambia, was outspoken about his "born-again" faith. While he remained a member of the mainline United Church of Zambia, his Pentecostal loyalties were well known, and Pentecostal leaders happily claimed him as one of their own (e.g., Mumba 1994: 42).

CHAPTER 2. MAKING MOVING HAPPEN

1. While the alimentary metaphor of "eating" money often refers to corruption, in this case it connotes the immediate consumption of money, often literally through the purchase of food, rather than using it to buy something of more enduring value.

2. In this way, my analysis reflects discussions of personhood in southern Africa, which have shown that individual identity is produced through relationships with others, and especially through relationships of exchange (e.g., Comaroff and Comaroff 2001, Durham 1995, Klaits 2011).

3. "Banukulu" and "Bashikulu" are the teknonyms used for grandparents, which often replace those of parentage.

4. As a female researcher, I have a better sense of what friendship looks like between women than between men. However, I believe that many of my observations hold for both women and men.

5. Kate Crehan (1997: 202–7) describes a similar model of exchange among Kaonde speakers living in Zambia's Northwestern Province. One person's agricultural surplus was always channeled toward a kinsperson whose crops had been poor. Later, when the person who had previously enjoyed extra grain found himself in need, a similar exchange of resources might be made.

6. At that time, $2 USD. On 1 January, 2013, the Zambian government rebased its currency, knocking three zeros off the end of its value. So, 1,000 kwacha (ZMK) = 1 kwacha (ZMW) under the new configuration. In June of 2013, when this transition took place, people were still adjusting to the new numbers, which sounded impossibly low. By the time I returned to Zambia in 2014, however, the change was more or less complete and everyone had adjusted to the rebased currency. Since my research spanned this period, I have kept amounts of money in the currency used at the time an event took place.

7. We can compare this arrangement to the "alternating inequality" that characterizes some Melanesian exchanges (McDowell 1990: 181; Robbins 1994: 41), particularly those "replacements" in which one partner "replaces resources previously received from the other [partner] while committing the recipient [partner] to replace these resources again in the future" (Foster 1995: 143). Here, as Anthony Forge puts it, "equal exchange is, in fact, a system of alternating seniority" (1972: 535).

8. For a detailed study of Copperbelt kitchen parties, see Rasing 2002.

9. Mr. Zulu was not the only person who told me that in the past wage labor enabled people to support a larger number of dependents than it could today. At a funeral in Nsofu a woman who looked to be in her early seventies told me that one of her primary recollections of the postindependence period was, as she put it, that if your uncle worked at the mine every child in your family went to school. While comments like these almost certainly reflect an idealized vision of the past, it is clear that in the eyes of at least some people opportunities for dependence on the Copperbelt have been dramatically reduced.

10. At that time, $40 USD.

CHAPTER 3. BECOMING PENTECOSTAL ON THE COPPERBELT

1. In fact, I have only ever met two people over the age of thirty who were brought up in Pentecostal churches.

2. Describing the convention in these terms doesn't quite do it justice. Some Pentecostals will distinguish between their "spiritual" father or mother—that is, the person who first brought them into Pentecostalism—and others who also serve as religious parents. I have also heard Pentecostals frame these discussions in terms of generations, referring to spiritual "grandparents," by which they mean those who brought their spiritual parents into Pentecostalism. These conventions mirror the classificatory kinship systems of many of Zambia's ethnic groups, in which a person has many mothers and fathers and, if necessary, distinguishes among them by indicating the one who gave birth to her.

3. I return to this exchange in chapter 7.

4. As Ruth Marshall (2009: 199) has pointed out, this aspect of Pentecostalism's appeal is in part the consequence of a missionary legacy in which Christianity was presented as more powerful than traditional spiritual beliefs. It can also be interpreted in the light of a more general tendency, evident throughout Africa, to engage with the supernatural in a quest for finding an ever-greater source of power (e.g., Kirsch 2004).

5. This was a noteworthy experience, as glossolalia is a rather rare event in Copperbelt Pentecostal fellowships.

6. Although prayer is the primary space in which the shared efforts of a relatively egalitarian group help each person move forward, there are other examples of this kind of collective effort that are worth pointing out. On the Copperbelt, church groups are responsible for providing the necessary resources for major rituals, especially funerals, but also weddings and kitchen parties. While believers often complained that Pentecostal congregations were not as good at facilitating these events as their counterparts in mainline churches, the ritual and relational (if not necessarily material) efforts of Pentecostals can be an important part of making sure that a funeral or wedding is successful. When this happens, the status of both the family at the center of an event and the status of the church that helps out are raised.

7. There have been a number of good scholarly treatments of the prosperity gospel, including the work of Simon Coleman (2000), Kate Bowler (2013), and Katherine Attanasi and Amos Yong (2012).

8. Here it is worth pointing out that, with the exception of Bible study, most Pentecostal practices are almost impossible to carry out in private. In particular, because believers prefer to pray aloud, even individual petitions offered at home are easily overheard by one's neighbors (see Haynes 2016).

9. Toward this end, a friend of mine, a non-Pentecostal who found formal titles rather silly, once quipped that soon "bishop" would not be enough for people and that they would have to start calling themselves "trishops" and "quadrishops."

10. For further discussions of young men seeking status through the pastorate, see van Dijk 1992, Werbner 2011.

CHAPTER 4. RITUAL AND THE (UN)MAKING OF THE PENTECOSTAL RELATIONAL WORLD

1. While to a certain extent these contrasting emphases have to do with differences in the places being examined—differences between suburban America and an African urban center like Accra, for example—I do not think they can be explained by appeals to sociocultural factors alone. Not only do we find references to communitas in non-Western contexts where we might expect to find hierarchy (e.g., Robbins 2009b, Smilde 2011), but we also find discussions of hierarchy among Pentecostal and charismatic Christians in the individualized, egalitarian West (e.g., Coleman 2000, Csordas 1997). This suggests that more is happening in these cases than a simple reflection of, or even a challenge to, predominating social or cultural patterns.

2. Joel 2: 28–29.

3. John 3: 8.

4. Many Pentecostal pastors preach in English, and some therefore employ an interpreter to translate their sermons into Bemba.

5. It is extremely rare for Pentecostals on the Copperbelt to celebrate communion. In the hundreds of Pentecostal meetings I have attended over the years I have only observed the Eucharist twice, and only once in Nsofu, when Key of David members took communion on Easter. As Pastor Mwanza and Mr. Chibale prepared bread and grape squash the night before, I commented on how infrequently Pentecostals took communion in comparison with other Christians, who will often have Eucharist on a weekly or monthly basis. Mr. Chibale replied that having communion so often would only create problems in a place like Nsofu. As he explained, if word got out that bread and "drink," as squash is called on the Copperbelt, were on offer every week at church, many people would come just for that.

6. In fact, whenever an "Amen" or "Alleluia" is spoken from the front of the church, it requires a response, usually another "Amen" from the congregation. These rhetorical cues serve as a way for a speaker to gauge whether the group is paying attention. A weak "Amen" will usually prompt the speaker to repeat the original request more loudly and pointedly, perhaps by turning it into a question: "Amen?!"

7. In an especially extreme example of this, Pastor Conrad, who took over Higher Calling after Bana Chilomba left to start her own church, would not

allow members of the group to sit down until they could answer detailed questions about his sermon from the previous week. I was quite shaken by this experience—the room was very hot and people had been fasting all day—and related it to several Pentecostal friends. To my surprise, most of them felt that Pastor Conrad had done a good thing, "That way, people will remember what they've been taught," one person said.

8. The former president of the Kitwe pastors' association, a group of church leaders from around the city that meets weekly for prayer and Bible study, conducted a survey to help him understand how pastors were living. In summarizing the results of his project to me, he said that his findings indicated that the vast majority did not own their own homes, did not own cars, and were not able to send their children to private schools—key markers of middle-class status in Zambia. In short, most of Kitwe's pastors were not living terribly well.

CHAPTER 5. PROSPERITY, CHARISMA, AND THE PROBLEM OF GENDER

1. While there are almost no Pentecostal women who serve as pastors or bishops on their own, there are a number who hold this position alongside their husbands. The authority of these women is largely an extension of their husbands' positions rather than something that belongs to them alone, and in many cases I do not think that the women who serve as pastors alongside their husbands would continue in this capacity if their husbands were no longer involved in ministry (though, as we will see in the example of Bishop Nelly Chikwanda, below, such a situation is not unheard of).

2. To be sure, these fellowships can become churches: this happened at Higher Calling, and Pastor Janice, another leader whom I discuss below, was also working to turn her fellowship into a church when I interviewed her in 2014.

3. In focusing on the church in my discussion of gender, I do not wish to suggest that the home is not important. Many analyses of Pentecostalism contrast the domestic and religious spheres as a way of teasing apart the contradictory discourses surrounding female submission. While this can be a productive move, I have found that it eclipses some important aspects of the gender dynamic found in Copperbelt Pentecostal churches (see Haynes n.d.). My focus on church leadership here should therefore not imply that the domestic domain is separate from the issue of church authority.

4. Although this observation shares much with the rich literature on gender performance, I prefer to make my point using Strathern because of the centrality of relationality in her work. In Strathern's treatment the Melanesian person is, famously, not an individual, but a dividual—that is, a bundle of relations. Although personhood in the Zambian context is by no means identical to this reading of Melanesian personhood, the centrality of relationships for my analysis—particularly with regard to moving—makes the comparison between these two models a productive one.

5. This observation adds another dimension to the fact that women tend to lead fellowships rather than churches, as the former are often referred to simply as "prayers" (*amapepo*).

6. At the same time, Pastor Janice was engaged in a process of identification with characters in the Old Testament, Sarah and Hannah, another exercise in collapsing the distinction between persons that is key to Pentecostal practice (Haynes forthcoming; also see Harding 2000: 105–24)

7. There was some confusion in our conversation as to the number of female bishops in Zambia and what that title really means. While Bishop Nelly is by all accounts the first, she suggested both that the number of female bishops has increased dramatically and that there are still very few who hold this title. When I asked her to clarify what she meant by this, she said that these days there were many women who were called bishop, but that was only because their husbands were also bishops. She could only think of one other woman who, like her, was in this position on her own (i.e., independent of her husband).

CHAPTER 6. ON THE POTENTIAL AND PROBLEMS OF PENTECOSTAL EXCHANGE

1. Luke 6: 38.

2. The massive Filipino prosperity gospel movement known as "El Shaddai" is similarly oriented around the leadership of Mike Velarde, a charismatic man known to his followers as "Brother Mike" who believers expect will personally pray for their requests when seed offerings are received (Wiegele 2005). Here again, the charismatic power of a prosperity gospel leader is understood to be central to the blessings that follow seed offerings.

3. In the particular case of the Copperbelt, seed offerings can be thought of as sacrifices not only because their aim is to compel God, but also because seed offerings often stretch a believer financially. In at least some people's interpretation, this is precisely what they should do: seed offerings are only demonstrations of faith if one gives more than he feels he can afford, sacrificing because he knows that God will bless him in return (see Harding 2000: 105–24).

4. Likewise, Coleman's discussion of seed offerings in Sweden emphasizes generalized reciprocity, an open-ended network of transactions in which a return gift might come from anywhere, including outside the church. At the same time, Coleman also demonstrates that although these gifts do not create relationships between believers and church leaders (the congregation is too large to make that a realistic possibility for most people), seed offerings do produce a strong sense of connection and loyalty to individual pastors.

5. I should note that reaction to this scandal was likely fueled by some cultural prejudice. There is a significant Congolese population on the Copperbelt, and Congolese people have a reputation as skilled traders who are at times also hucksters. This is especially true of Congolese pastors, who are often regarded with suspicion.

6. Although the primary thing that believers expect to receive from their pastors in return for seed offerings are spiritual services, they may also hope for some material assistance from their Pentecostal congregation. This is particularly true in crisis situations like funerals, for which mainline congregations often provide food, firewood, and transportation. Such gifts are not always

forthcoming from Pentecostal groups, at least those in my study, primarily because their budgets do not allow for it.

7. Key of David was not the only Nsofu congregation to use eponymous envelopes for tithes and offerings. Indeed, the practice has become more and more widespread since I first began working on the Copperbelt. A print shop located in the Kitwe city center advertised that in addition to wedding invitations and business brochures they also made tithing cards, which suggested that there was enough demand to register with local businesses. Keeping records of giving has long been common in mainline churches, and it is safe to assume that on one level the use of envelopes in Pentecostal churches is another example, along with the order of worship, of the Pentecostal appropriation of established Christian forms. However, in the light of the important role that tithing envelopes have in shaping the religious obligations of church leaders, it appears that this technology has taken on a new role in Pentecostal churches, one that reflects the particular social dynamics of these congregations.

8. During my fieldwork I would regularly invite women from different Pentecostal congregations to visit me during the week so that we could talk about a sermon. I would play recordings of the message, which all of us had heard before, while we drank tea together. The women would discuss the sermon and analyze its content, sometimes disagreeing with what a pastor had said and other times comparing it with other Pentecostal messages.

9. While I would argue that this example does an especially good job of teasing apart the various levels present in ritual exchange, as well as the risks that exchange often entails, I should point out that this type of analysis can be found in studies of Christian communities as well. To take two examples from North America, Jon Bialecki (2008) has shown that members of Southern California Vineyard churches move back and forth among what he identifies as different spheres of exchange as they negotiate the use and sacrifice of their material resources. Similarly, my argument in this chapter dovetails well with Omri Elisha's (2011) study of conservative Protestants in Tennessee, who simultaneously employ what they refer to as "compassion" and "accountability" in their efforts at social engagement. Elisha argues that each of these concepts carries with it a model of exchange that is in turn grounded in a theological paradox, which ultimately leaves believers trying to pursue both a free gift and a reciprocal relationship at the same time.

CHAPTER 7. MENDING MOTHER'S KITCHEN

1. Rent in Nsofu is collected in lump sums at intervals of three, or occasionally six, months.

2. At that time around $50 USD.

3. Around $20 USD.

4. The Bemba term *mayo*, which translates as "my mother," can refer not only to one's biological mother, but also, in the classificatory kinship terminology of Northern Zambia, to one's mother's sisters.

5. While I do not doubt that this is a reflection on the capacity of the church to attract more big people and to facilitate the moving of its members—and that

is certainly how people in Nsofu saw it—I should also note that the period of my absence saw a sharp increase in the number of cars in Zambia.

6. This is especially true when, as in the case of the kitchen mending, everyone in a congregation is told to contribute a set amount, which is often determined by lay leaders whose financial circumstances are very different from those of other church members. This was certainly this case for the kitchen mending, and some of the women at Key of David complained to me that while it might be easy for people like Mrs. Phiri to give several hundred thousand kwacha, for some families, even the lowest required contribution represented a third or more of their monthly income, and therefore an amount they could not possibly afford to give.

7. Here, the example of the South Asian *dan* is again instructive, as it is the job of ritual specialists to absorb the "poison" in this gift (Raheja 1988), a task that in this example is performed by the super-members.

CHAPTER 8. THE CIRCULATION OF COPPERBELT SAINTS

1. The word "portion" occurs often in the Old Testament as a description of one's lot in life. For Copperbelt believers, whose expectations of blessing have been shaped by the prosperity gospel, knowing what is and what is not one's portion is an important part of prayer and spiritual discernment.

2. In the eyes of many people on the Copperbelt, *jealous* was the particular province of Africans (see Ferguson 2006; Vigh 2006)—perhaps especially Zambians. Mr. Zulu described *jealous* to me as "a problem with Zambian culture," and Pastor Mwanza once noted in a sermon that the success of Indian, Chinese, or Nigerian business owners could be linked to their lack of concern for what others were doing, to the fact that they seemed immune to *jealous*.

3. Not all Pentecostals agree that dangerous prayers are something believers should engage in—indeed, some would certainly reject this idea as unorthodox. Even those who consider dangerous prayers an option generally treat them as a last resort, the sort of thing that one would only use against a person who is causing deep personal or physical harm, such as a relative who is using witchcraft to make a believer ill.

CONCLUSION

1. As Robbins has recently pointed out (2014: S163) these conflicting approaches are ultimately a reflection of the longstanding dispute between cultural and materialist interpretations in anthropology.

References Cited

Agha, Asif. 2001. Register. In *Key terms in language and culture,* edited by A. Duranti, pp. 212–15. Oxford: Wiley-Blackwell.

Ajibade, Babson. 2012. Lady no be so: The image of women in contemporary church posters in Nigeria. *Visual Studies* 27(3): 237–47.

Albrecht, Daniel E. 1999. *Rites in the spirit: A ritual approach to Pentecostal /charismatic spirituality.* Sheffield: Sheffield Academic Press.

Apter, Andrew H. 2005. *The Pan-African nation: Oil and the spectacle of culture in Nigeria.* Chicago: University of Chicago Press.

Ardener, Shirley. 1964. The comparative study of rotating credit associations. *Journal of the Royal Anthropological Institute* 94(2): 201–29.

Assimeng, J.M. 1970. Sectarian allegiance and political authority: The Watch Tower Society in Zambia, 1907–35. *Journal of Modern African Studies* 8(1): 97–112.

Attanasi, Katherine. 2012. Introduction: The plurality of prosperity theologies and pentecostalisms. In *Pentecostalism and prosperity: The socio-economics of the global charismatic movement,* edited by A. Yong and K. Attanasi, pp. 1–14. New York: Palgrave Macmillan.

Attanasi, Katherine, and Amos Yong, eds. 2012. *Pentecostalism and prosperity: The socio-economics of the global charismatic movement.* New York: Palgrave Macmillan.

Bialecki, Jon. 2008. Between stewardship and sacrifice: Agency and economy in a Southern California charismatic church. *Journal of the Royal Anthropological Institute* 14(2): 372–90.

———. 2011. No Caller ID for the soul: Demonization, charisms, and the unstable subject of Protestant language ideology. *Anthropological Quarterly* 84(3): 679–703.

———. 2014. After the denominozoic: Evolution, differentiation, denominationalism. *Current Anthropology* 55(S10): S193–S204.
Bialecki, Jon, and Girish Daswani. 2015. Introduction: What is an individual? The view from Christianity. *HAU: Journal of Ethnographic Theory* 5(1): 271–94.
Bialecki, Jon, Naomi Haynes, and Joel Robbins. 2008. The anthropology of Christianity. *Religion Compass* 2(6): 1139–58.
Bibby, Reginald W., and Merlin B. Brinkerhoff. 1973. The circulation of the saints: A study of people who join conservative churches. *Journal for the Scientific Study of Religion* 12(3): 273–83.
Bloch, Maurice, and Jonathan P. Parry. 1989. Money and the morality of exchange: Introduction. *Money and the morality of exchange,* edited by M. Bloch and J. P. Parry, pp. 1–32. Cambridge: Cambridge University Press.
Bloemen, Shantha. 2016. *Debt relief and HIPC: Zambia.* Initiative for Policy Dialogue Case Studies. http://policydialogue.org/publications/backgrounders/casestudies/debt_relief_and_hipc_zambia/en/#/.
Blunt, Robert. 2004. "Satan is an Imitator": Kenya's recent cosmology of corruption. In *Producing African futures: Ritual and reproduction in a neoliberal age,* edited by B. Weiss, pp. 294–328. Leiden: Brill.
Bolt, Maxim. 2014. The sociality of the wage: Money rhythms, wealth circulation, and the problem with cash on the Zimbabwean–South African border. *Journal of the Royal Anthropological Institute* 20(1): 113–30.
Bowler, Kate. 2013. *Blessed: A history of the American prosperity gospel.* New York: Oxford University Press.
Brusco, Elizabeth. 2010. Gender and Power. In *Studying global Pentecostalism: Theories and methods,* edited by A. Anderson, M. Bergunder, A. F. Droogers and C. Van der Laan, pp. 74–92. Berkeley: University of California Press.
Burgess, Stanley M., and Eduard M. van der Maas. 2010. *The new international dictionary of Pentecostal and charismatic movements.* Grand Rapids: Zondervan.
Burlington, Robert Gary. 2004. "I love Mary": Relating private motives to public meanings at the genesis of Emilio's Mutima Church. PhD diss., School of Intercultural Studies, Biola University.
Cannell, Fenella. 2006. Introduction: The anthropology of Christianity. In *The anthropology of Christianity,* edited by F. Cannell, pp. 1–50. Durham, NC: Duke University Press.
Carsten, Janet. 2000. Introduction: Cultures of relatedness. In *Cultures of relatedness: New approaches to the study of kinship,* edited by J. Carsten, pp. 1–36. Cambridge: Cambridge University Press.
Central Statistical Office, Republic of Zambia. 2006. www.zamstats.gov.zm.
Centre for Development and Enterprise (CDE), South Africa. 2012. Under the radar: Pentecostalism in South Africa and its potential social and economic role. In *Pentecostalism and prosperity: The socio-economics of the global charismatic movement,* edited by A. Yong and K. Attanasi, pp. 63–86. New York: Palgrave Macmillan.
Cheyeka, Austin M. 2006. Charismatic churches and their impact on mainline churches in Zambia. *Journal of Humanities, University of Zambia* 5: 54–71.

———. 2008. Toward a history of the Charismatic churches in post-colonial Zambia. In *One Zambia, many histories: Towards a history of post-colonial Zambia*, edited by J.-B. Gewald, M. Hinfelaar, and G. Macola. Leiden: Brill.

Cole, Jennifer, and Lynn Thomas. 2009. Introduction: Thinking through love in Africa. In *Love in Africa*, edited by J. Cole and L. Thomas, pp. 1–29. Chicago: University of Chicago Press.

Coleman, Simon. 2000. *The globalisation of charismatic Christianity: Spreading the gospel of prosperity*. Cambridge Studies in Ideology and Religion. Cambridge: Cambridge University Press.

———. 2004. The charismatic gift. *Journal of the Royal Anthropological Institute* 10(2): 421–42.

———. 2006a. Materializing the self: Words and gifts in the construction of charismatic Protestant identity. In *The anthropology of Christianity*, edited by F. Cannell, pp. 163–84. Durham, NC: Duke University Press.

———. 2006b. Studying "global" Pentecostalism: Tensions, representations and opportunities. *PentecoStudies* 5(1): 1–17.

———. 2011. Prosperity unbound? Debating the "sacrificial economy." *Research in Economic Anthropology* 31: 23–46.

Comaroff, Jean, and John L. Comaroff. 1999. Occult economies and the violence of abstraction: Notes from the South African postcolony. *American Ethnologist* 26(2): 279–303.

———. 2000. Millennial capitalism: First thoughts on a second coming. *Public Culture* 12(2): 291–343.

Comaroff, John. 2010. The end of anthropology, again: On the future of an in/discipline. *American Anthropologist* 112(4): 524–38.

Comaroff, John L., and Jean Comaroff. 2001. On personhood: An anthropological perspective from Africa. *Social Identities* 7(2): 267–83.

Corten, André, and Ruth Marshall-Fratani. 2001. Introduction. In *Between Babel and Pentecost: Transnational pentecostalism in Africa and Latin America*, edited by A. Corten and R. Marshall-Fratani, pp. 1–21. Bloomington: Indiana University Press.

Crehan, Kate. 1997. *The fractured community: Landscapes of power and gender in rural Zambia*. Berkeley: University of California Press.

Csordas, Thomas J. 1997. *Language, charisma, and creativity: The ritual life of a religious movement*. Berkeley: University of California Press.

Daswani, Girish. 2011. (In-)dividual Pentecostals in Ghana. *Journal of Religion in Africa* 41(3):256–79.

———. 2015. *Looking back, moving forward: Tranformation and ethical practice in the Ghanaian Church of Pentecost*. Toronto: University of Toronto Press.

de Boeck, Filip , and Marie-Françoise Plissart. 2004. *Kinshasa: Tales of the invisible city*. Ghent: Ludion.

Derrida, Jacques. 1992. *Given time: I. Counterfeit money*. Chicago: University of Chicago Press.

Dillon-Malone, Clive M. 1978. *The Korsten basketmakers: A study of the Masowe Apostles, an indigenous African religious movement*. Manchester: Manchester University Press.

Dumont, Louis. 1977. *From Mandeville to Marx: The genesis and triumph of economic ideology.* Chicago: University of Chicago Press.

———. 1980. *Homo hierarchicus: The caste system and its implications.* Complete rev. English ed. Chicago: University of Chicago Press. Original edition, 1970.

———. 1986. *Essays on individualism: Modern ideology in anthropological perspective.* Chicago: University of Chicago Press.

Durham, Deborah. 1995. Soliciting gifts and negotiating agency: The spirit of asking in Botswana. *Journal of the Royal Anthropological Institute* 1(1): 111–28.

Elisha, Omri. 2011. *Moral ambition: Mobilization and social outreach in evangelical megachurches.* Berkeley: University of California Press.

Engelke, Matthew. 2007. *A problem of presence: Beyond Scripture in an African church; The anthropology of Christianity.* Berkeley: University of California Press.

———. 2010. Past Pentecostalism: Notes on rupture, realignment, and everyday life in Pentecostal and African independent churches. *Africa* 80(2): 177–99.

Englund, Harri. 2007. Pentecostalism beyond belief: Trust and democracy in a Malawian township. *Africa* 77(4): 477–99.

Epstein, A. L. 1958. *Politics in an urban African community.* Manchester: Manchester University Press.

———. 1961. The network and urban social organization. *Human Problems in British Central Africa: The Rhodes-Livingston Journal* 29: 29–62.

———. 1981. *Urbanization and kinship: The domestic domain on the copperbelt of Zambia, 1950–1956.* New York: Academic Press.

Eriksen, Annelin. 2009. Gender and value: Conceptualizing social forms on Ambrym, Vanuatu. In *Hierarchy: Persistence and transformation in social formations,* edited by K. M. Rio and O. H. Smedal, pp. 89–112. New York: Berghahn Books.

———. 2012. The pastor and the prophetess: An analysis of gender and Christianity in Vanuatu. *Journal of the Royal Anthropological Institute* 18(1): 103–22.

———. 2014. Sarah's sinfulness: Egalitarianism, denied difference, and gender in Pentecostal Christianity. *Current Anthropology* 55(S10): S262–70.

Errington, Frederick Karl, and Deborah B. Gewertz. 1995. *Articulating change in the "last unknown."* Boulder: Westview Press.

Evans, Alice. 2014. Women can do what men can do: The causes and consequences of growing flexibility in gender divisions of labour in Kitwe, Zambia. *Journal of Southern African studies* 40(5): 981–98.

Ferguson, James. 1999. *Expectations of modernity: Myths and meanings of urban life on the Zambian Copperbelt.* Perspectives on Southern Africa. Berkeley: University of California Press.

———. 2006. *Global shadows: Africa in the neoliberal world order.* Durham, NC: Duke University Press.

———. 2013. Declarations of dependence: Labor, personhood, and welfare in southern Africa. *Journal of the Royal Anthropological Institute* 19: 223–42.

Finke, Roger, and Rodney Stark. 2006. *The churching of America, 1776–2005: Winners and losers in our religious economy*. New Brunswick, NJ: Rutgers University Press.

Forge, Anthony. 1972. The Golden Fleece. *Man* 7(4): 527–40.

Foster, Robert J. 1995. *Social reproduction and history in Melanesia: Mortuary ritual, gift exchange, and custom in the Tanga Islands*. Cambridge: Cambridge University Press.

Foucault, Michel. 2008. *The birth of biopolitics: Lectures at the College de France, 1978–79*. New York: Palgrave Macmillan.

Frahm-Arp, Maria. 2010. *Professional women in South African Pentecostal Charismatic churches*. Leiden: Brill.

Ganti, Tejaswini. 2014. Neoliberalism. *Annual Review of Anthropology* 43: 89–104.

Gifford, Paul. 1998. Chiluba's Christian nation: Christianity as a factor in Zambian politics 1991–1996. *Journal of Contemporary Religion* 13 (3):363–381.

———. 2004. *Ghana's new Christianity : Pentecostalism in a globalizing African economy*. Bloomington: Indiana University Press.

Gill, Lesley. 1990. "Like a veil to cover them": Women and the Pentecostal movement in La Paz. *American Ethnologist* 17(4): 708–21.

Gordimer, Nadine. 1958. *A world of strangers*. New York: Simon and Schuster.

Graeber, David. 2001. *Toward an anthropological theory of value: The false coin of our own dreams*. New York: Palgrave.

———. 2013. It is value that brings universes into being. *Hau: Journal of Ethnographic Theory* 3(2): 219–43.

Green, Maia, and Simeon Mesaki. 2005. The birth of the "salon": Poverty, "modernization," and dealing with witchcraft in southern Tanzania. *American Ethnologist* 32(3): 371–88.

Gregory, C.A. 1980. Gifts to men and gifts to God: Gift exchange and capital accumulation in contemporary Papua. *Man* 15(4): 626–52.

Guest, Peter. God save the Kwacha: Zambia will pray for recovery this Sunday. *Forbes*. October 16, 2015. http://www.forbes.com/sites/peteguest/2015/10/16/god-save-the-kwacha-zambia-will-pray-for-recovery-this-sunday/print/.

Guyer, Jane I. 1995. *Money matters: Instability, values, and social payments in the modern history of West African communities*. Social History of Africa. London: Heinemann, James Currey.

———. 2004. *Marginal gains: Monetary transactions in Atlantic Africa*. Chicago: University of Chicago Press.

Guyer, Jane I., and Samuel M. Eno Belinga. 1995. Wealth in people as wealth in knowledge: Accumulation and composition in equatorial Africa. *Journal of African History* 36(1): 91–20.

Handman, Courtney. 2014a. Becoming the body of Christ: Sacrificing the speaking subject in the making of the colonial Lutheran Church in New Guinea. *Current Anthropology* 55(S10): S205–15.

———. 2014b. *Critical Christianity: Translation and denominational conflict in Papua New Guinea*. Oakland: University of California Press.

Hann, Chris. 2007. The anthropology of Christianity per se. *European Journal of Sociology* 48(3): 383–410.

———. 2014. The heart of the matter: Christianity, materiality, and modernity. *Current Anthropology* 55(S10): S182–92.

Hansen, Karen Tranberg. 1985. Budgeting against uncertainty: Cross-class and transethnic redistribution mechanisms in urban Zambia. *African Urban Studies* 21: 65–73.

———. 1992. *African encounters with domesticity.* New Brunswick, NJ: Rutgers University Press.

———. 1997. *Keeping house in Lusaka.* New York: Columbia University Press.

Harding, Susan Friend. 2000. *The book of Jerry Falwell: Fundamentalist language and politics.* Princeton, NJ: Princeton University Press.

Hasu, Päivi. 2006. World Bank and heavenly bank in poverty and prosperity: The case of Tanzanian faith gospel. *Review of African Political Economy* 33(110): 679–92.

Haynes, Naomi. 2012. Pentecostalism and the morality of money: Prosperity, inequality, and religious sociality on the Zambian Copperbelt. *Journal of the Royal Anthropological Institute* 18(1): 123–39.

———. 2014. Afterword: Affordances and audiences; Finding the difference Christianity makes. *Current Anthropology* 55(S10): S357–65.

———. 2015. "Zambia shall be saved!": Prosperity gospel politics in a self-proclaimed Christian nation. *Nova Religio* 19(1): 5–24.

———. 2016. Learning to pray the Pentecostal way: Language and personhood on the Zambian Copperbelt. *Religion.* http://dx.doi.org/10.1080/0048721X.2016.1225906

———. Forthcoming. Theology on the ground: Pentecostals and the expansive present. In *Theologically engaged anthropology: Social anthropology and theology in conversation,* edited by J. Derrick Lemons. Oxford: Oxford University Press.

———. n.d. Getting beyond the "Pentecostal gender paradox": Domestic life and Pentecostal ministry on the Zambian Copperbelt. Unpublished manuscript.

Haynes, Naomi, and Jason Hickel, eds. 2016a. Special issue: Hierarchy, values, and the value of hierarchy. *Social Analysis* 60(4).

———. 2016b. Introduction: Hierarchy, values, and the value of hierarchy. *Social Analysis* 60(4): 1–20.

Hess, Steve, and Richard Aidoo. 2015. *Charting the roots of anti-Chinese populism in Africa.* Cham: Springer.

Hickel, Jason. 2012. Neoliberal plague: The political economy of HIV transmission in Swaziland. *Journal of Southern African Studies* 38(3): 513–29.

———. 2015. *Democracy as social death: The making of anti-liberal politics in neoliberal South Africa.* Berkeley: University of California Press.

Hinfelaar, Hugo F. 1994. *Bemba-speaking women of Zambia in a century of religious change (1892–1992).* Leiden: Brill.

Hoch, E. 1960. *Bemba pocket dictionary: Bemba-English and English-Bemba.* Abercorn, Northern Rhodesia: White Fathers.

Hubert, Henri, and Marcel Mauss. 1964. *Sacrifice: Its nature and function.* Chicago: University of Chicago Press.

Hunt, Stephen. 2002. "Neither here nor there": The construction of identities and boundary maintenance of West African Pentecostals. *Sociology* 36(1): 147–69.

James, Deborah. 2015. *Money from nothing: Indebtedness and aspiration in South Africa*. Palo Alto, CA: Stanford University Press.
Johnson, Todd M., and Gina A. Zurlo, eds. 2014. *World Christian database*. Leiden: Brill.
Jules-Rosette, Bennetta. 1975. *African apostles: Ritual and conversion in the Church of John Maranke*. Ithaca, NY: Cornell University Press.
Kapferer, Bruce 2010. Louis Dumont and a holist anthropology. In *Experiments in holism: Theory and practice in contemporary anthropology*, edited by T. Otto and N. Bubandt, pp. 187–208. Malden, MA: Wiley-Blackwell.
Kärkkäinen, Veli-Matti. 2010. Pneumatologies in systematic theology. In *Studying global Pentecostalism: Theories and methods*, edited by M. Bergunder, A. F. Droogers, C. v. d. Laan and A. Anderson, pp. 223–44. Berkeley: University of California Press.
Keane, Webb. 1997. *Signs of recognition: Powers and hazards of representation in an Indonesian society*. Berkeley: University of California Press.
———. 2007. *Christian moderns: Freedom and fetish in the mission encounter*. Berkeley: University of California Press.
Killick, Evan, and Amit Desai. 2010. Introduction: Valuing friendship. In *The ways of friendship: Anthropological perspectives*, edited by A. Desai and E. Killick, pp. 1–19. New York: Berghahn Books.
Kirsch, Thomas G. 2004. Restaging the will to believe: Religious pluralism, anti-syncretism, and the problem of belief. *American Anthropologist* 106(4): 699–709.
———. 2008. *Spirits and letters: Reading, writing and charisma in African Christianity*. New York: Berghahn Books.
Klaits, Frederick. 2010. *Death in a church of life: Moral passion during Botswana's time of AIDS*. Berkeley: University of California Press.
———. 2011. Introduction: Self, other and God in African Christianities. *Journal of Religion in Africa* 41(2): 143–53.
Laidlaw, James. 1995. *Riches and renunciation: Religion, economy, and society among the Jains*. Oxford: Clarendon Press.
———. 2000. A free gift makes no friends. *Journal of the Royal Anthropological Institute* 6(4): 617–34.
Lash, Scott, and John Urry. 1994. *Economies of signs and space*. London: Sage.
Lauterbach, Karen. 2010. Becoming a pastor: Youth and social aspirations in Ghana. *Young* 18(3): 259–78.
Lindhardt, Martin. 2009. More than just money: The faith gospel and occult economies in contemporary Tanzania. *Nova Religio* 13(1): 41–67.
———. 2010. "If you are saved you cannot forget your parents": Agency, power, and social repositioning in Tanzanian born-again Christianity. *Journal of Religion in Africa* 40(3): 240–72.
———. 2011. Introduction. In *Practicing the faith: The ritual life of Pentecostal-charismatic Christians*, edited by M. Lindhardt, pp. 1–48. New York: Berghahn Books.
Lorentzen, Lois, and Rosalina Mira. 2005. El milagro está en casa: Gender and private/public empowerment in a migrant Pentecostal church. *Latin American Perspectives* 32(1): 57–71.

Luhrmann, T.M. 2012. *When God talks back: Understanding the American evangelical relationship with God.* New York: Alfred A. Knopf.

Lynn, Christopher Dana. 2013. "The wrong Holy Ghost": Discerning the apostolic gift of discernment using a signaling and systems theoretical approach. *Ethos* 41(2): 223–47.

Macmillan, Hugh. 1993. The historiography of transition on the Zambian Copperbelt—Another view. *Journal of Southern African Studies* 19(4): 681–712.

Marshall, Ruth. 2009. *Political spiritualities: The pentecostal revolution in Nigeria.* Chicago: University of Chicago Press.

Martin, Bernice. 1995. New mutations of the Protestant ethic among Latin American Pentecostals. *Religion* 25(2): 101–17.

———. 1998. From pre- to postmodernity in Latin America: The case of Pentecostalism. In *Religion, modernity, and postmodernity,* edited by P. Heelas, D. Martin, and P. Morris, pp. 102–46. Oxford: Blackwell.

———. 2001. "The pentecostal gender paradox: A cautionary tale for the sociology of religion." In *The Blackwell companion to sociology of religion,* edited by Richard K. Fenn. *Blackwell Reference Online.* http://www.blackwellreference.com/subscriber/tocnode.html?id=g9780631212416_chunk_g978063121241 66.

Mate, Rekopantswe. 2002. Wombs as God's laboratories: Pentecostal discourses of femininity in Zimbabwe. *Africa* 72(4): 549–68.

Mauss, Marcel. 1954. *The gift: Forms and functions of exchange in archaic societies.* Glencoe, IL: Free Press.

———. 1985. A category of the human mind: The notion of person; The notion of self. In *The Category of the person: Anthropology, philosophy, history,* edited by M. Carrithers, S. Collins and S. Lukes, pp. 1–25. Cambridge: Cambridge University Press.

Maxwell, David. 2006. *African gifts of the spirit: Pentecostalism and the rise of a Zimbabwean transnational religious movement.* Athens: Ohio University Press.

McCulloch, Neil, Bob Baulch, and Milasoa Cherel-Robson. 2000. *Poverty, inequality, and growth in Zambia during the 1990s.* Institute of Development Studies Working Paper 114. http://www.ids.ac.uk/files/wp114.pdf.

McDowell, Nancy. 1990. Competitve equality in Melanesia: An exploratory essay. *Journal of the Polynesian Society* 99(2): 179–204.

Mbembe, Achille. 2001. *On the postcolony.* Berkeley: University of California Press.

Meyer, Birgit. 1998. "Make a complete break with the past": Memory and postcolonial modernity in Ghanaian Pentecostal discourse. In *Memory and the postcolony: African anthropology and the critique of power,* edited by R.P. Werbner, pp. 182–208. London: Zed Books.

———. 1999. *Translating the devil: Religion and modernity among the Ewe in Ghana.* Trenton, NJ: Africa World Press.

———. 2010. Pentecostalism and globalization. In *Studying global Pentecostalism: Theories and methods,* edited by A. Anderson, M. Bergunder, A.F. Droogers and C. Van der Laan, pp. 113–32. Berkeley: University of California Press.

Mitchell, James Clyde, and A. L. Epstein. 1959. Occupational prestige and social status among urban Africains in northern Rhodesia. *Africa* 29(1): 22–40.

Mukuka, L., W. Kalikiti, and D. Musenge. 2002. Phase II: Chilimba and market associations. *Journal of Social Development in Africa* 17(2): 97–105.

Mumba, Nevers. 1994. *Integrity with fire: A strategy for revival.* Tulsa: Vincom.

Munn, Nancy. 1986. *The fame of Gawa: A symbolic study of value transformation in a Massim (Papua New Guinea) Society.* Durham, NC: Duke University Press.

Ndulo, Manenga, Dale Mudenda, Lutangu Ingombe, and Lillian Muchimba. 2009. *Global financial crisis discussion series paper 10: Zambia.* London: Overseas Development Institute.

Newell, Sasha. 2007. Pentecostal witchcraft: Neoliberal possession and demonic discourse in Ivoirian Pentecostal churches. *Journal of Religion in Africa* 37(4): 461–90.

Niebuhr, H. Richard. 1957. *The social sources of denominationalism.* New York: Meridian Books.

Nielsen, Morten. 2011. Futures within: Reversible time house-building in Maputo, Mozambique. *Anthropological Theory* 11(4): 397–423.

Nolivos, Eloy H. 2012. Capitalism and Pentecostalism in Latin America: Trajectories of prosperity and development. In *Pentecostalism and prosperity: The socio-economics of the global charismatic movement,* edited by A. Yong and K. Attanasi, pp. 87–107. New York: Palgrave Macmillan.

Okigbo, Christopher. 1971. *Labyrinths, with "Path of Thunder."* New York: Africana Publishing.

Ong, Aiwa. 1987. *Spirits of resistance and capitalist discipline: Women factory workers in Malaysia.* Albany: SUNY Press.

O'Reilly, Caroline. 1996. Urban women's informal savings and credit systems in Zambia. *Development in Practice* 6(2): 165–73.

Otto, Ton, and Rane Willerslev, eds. 2013. Special issue: Value as theory (part I). *Hau: Journal of Ethnographic Theory* 3(1).

Parpart, Jane L. 1994. "Where is your mother?": Gender, urban marriage, and colonial discourse on the Zambian Copperbelt, 1924–1945. *International Journal of African Historical Studies* 27(2): 241–71.

Parry, Jonathan. 1986. The gift, the Indian gift and the "Indian gift." *Man* 21(3): 453–73.

———. 1989. On the moral perils of exchange. In *Money and the morality of exchange,* edited by J. Parry and M. Bloch, pp. 1–32. Cambridge: Cambridge University Press.

Peacock, Vita. 2015. The negation of hierarchy and its consequences. *Anthropological Theory* 15(1): 3–21.

Pedersen, David, ed. 2008. Special issue: Toward a value theory of anthropology. *Anthropological Theory* 8(1).

Peterman, Gerald W. 1997. *Paul's gift from Philippi: Conventions of gift exchange and Christian giving.* Cambridge: Cambridge University Press.

Pfeiffer, James, Kenneth Gimbel-Sherr, and Orvalho Joaquim Augusto. 2007. The Holy Spirit in the household: Pentecostalism, gender, and neoliberalism in Mozambique. *American Anthropologist* 109 (4): 688–700.

Phiri, Isabel Apawo. 2003. President Frederick J.T. Chiluba of Zambia: The Christian nation and democracy. *Journal of Religion in Africa* 33(4): 401–28.
Powdermaker, Hortense. 1962. *Copper town: Changing Africa*. New York: Harper and Row.
Pritchett, James A. 2001. *The Lunda-Ndembu: Style, change, and social transformation in South Central Africa*. Madison: University of Wisconsin Press.
———. 2007. *Friends for life, friends for death: Cohorts and consciousness among the Lunda-Ndembu*. Charlottesville: University of Virginia Press.
Raheja, Gloria Goodwin. 1988. *The poison in the gift: Ritual, prestation, and the dominant caste in a north Indian village*. Chicago: University of Chicago Press.
Rasing, Thera. 2002. *The bush burnt, the stones remain: Female initiation rites in urban Zambia*. Leiden: African Studies Centre.
Reece, Koreen M. . 2015. An ordinary crisis? Kinship in Botswana's time of AIDS. PhD diss., University of Edinburgh.
Richards, Audrey I. 1982. *Chisungu: A girls' initiation ceremony among the Bemba of Zambia*. 2nd ed. New York: Tavistock.
———. 1995. *Land, labour and diet in Northern Rhodesia: An economic study of the Bemba tribe*. Hamburg: LIT with the IAI.
Rio, Knut. 2007. Denying the gift: Aspects of ceremonial exchange and sacrifice on Ambrym Island, Vanuatu. *Anthropological Theory* 7(4): 449–70.
Rio, Knut Mikjel, and Olaf H. Smedal. 2009. Hierarchy and its alternatives: An introduction to movements of totalization and detotalization. In *Hierarchy: Persistence and transformation in social formations*, edited by K.M. Rio and O.H. Smedal, pp. 1–64. New York: Berghahn Books.
Robbins, Joel. 1994. Equality as a value: Ideology in Dumont, Melanesia, and the West. *Social Analysis* 36: 21–70.
———. 2002. My wife can't break off part of her belief and give it to me: Apocalyptic interrogations of Christian individualism among the Urapmin of Papua New Guinea. *Paideuma* 48: 189–206.
———. 2004a. *Becoming sinners: Christianity and moral torment in a Papua New Guinea society*. Berkeley: University of California Press.
———. 2004b. The globalization of Pentecostal and charismatic Christianity. *Annual Review of Anthropology* 33: 117–43.
———. 2007. Continuity thinking and the problem of Christian culture: Belief, time, and the anthropology of Christianity. *Current Anthropology* 48(1): 5–38.
———. 2009a. Conversion, hierarchy, and cultural change: Value and syncretism in the globalization of Pentecostal and charismatic Christianity. In *Hierarchy: Persistence and transformation in social formations*, edited by K.M. Rio and O.H. Smedal. New York: Berghahn Books.
———. 2009b. Pentecostal networks and the spirit of globalization: On the social productivity of ritual forms. *Social Analysis* 53(1): 55–66.
———. 2013a. Beyond the suffering subject: Toward an anthropology of the good. *Journal of the Royal Anthropological Institute* 19(3): 447–62.
———. 2013b. Monism, pluralism and the structure of value relations: A Dumontian contribution to the contemporary study of value. *Hau: Journal of Ethnographic Theory* 3(1): 99–115.

———. 2014. The anthropology of Christianity: Unity, diversity, new directions: An introduction to supplement 10. *Current Anthropology* 55(S10): S157–71.

———. 2015. Ritual, value, and example: On the perfection of cultural representations. *Journal of the Royal Anthropological Institute* 21(S1): 18–29.

Roeber, Carter Alan. 1995. Shylocks and mabisinesi: Trust, informal credit and commercial culture in Kabwe, Zambia. PhD diss., Northwestern University.

Roitman, Janet L. 2005. *Fiscal disobedience: An anthropology of economic regulation in Central Africa.* Princeton, NJ: Princeton University Press.

Rose, Nikolas S. 1999. *Powers of freedom: Reframing political thought.* Cambridge: Cambridge University Press.

Rudnyckyj, Daromir. 2010. *Spiritual economies: Islam, globalization, and the afterlife of development.* Ithaca, NY: Cornell University Press.

Sahlins, Marshall. 1976. *Culture and practical reason.* Chicago: University of Chicago Press.

———. 1992. The economics of develop-man in the Pacific. *Res: Anthropology and Aesthetics* 21: 12–25.

Scherz, China. 2014. *Having people, having heart: Charity, sustainable development, and problems of dependence in central Uganda.* Chicago: University of Chicago Press.

Schumaker, Lyn. 2001. *Africanizing anthropology: Fieldwork, networks, and the making of cultural knowledge in central Africa.* Durham, NC: Duke University Press.

Schuster, Ilsa M. Glazer. 1979. *New women of Lusaka.* Palo Alto, CA: Mayfield.

Scott, Michael. 2005. "I Was Like Abraham": Notes on the anthropology of Christianity from the Solomon Islands. *Ethnos* 70(1): 101–25.

Shipley, J.W. 2010. Africa in theory: A conversation between Jean Comaroff and Achille Mbembe. *Anthropological Quarterly* 83(3): 653–78.

Sichone, Owen. 2001. Pure anthropology in a highly indebted poor country. *Journal of Southern African Studies* 27(2): 369–79.

Sinyangwe, Binwell. 2000. *A cowrie of hope.* Oxford: Heinemann.

Smilde, David. 2011. Public rituals and political positioning: Venezuelan evangelicals and the Chávez government. In *Practicing the faith: The ritual life of Pentecostal-charismatic Christians,* edited by M. Lindhardt, pp. 306–29. New York: Berghahn Books.

Smith, Daniel Jordan. 2007. *A culture of corruption: Everyday deception and popular discontent in Nigeria.* Princeton, NJ: Princeton University Press.

Smith, James H. 2011. Tantalus in the digital age: Coltan ore, temporal dispossession, and "movement" in the eastern Democratic Republic of the Congo. *American Ethnologist* 38(1): 17–35.

Smith, James K.A. 2010. *Thinking in tongues: Pentecostal contributions to Christian philosophy.* Grand Rapids: Eerdmans.

Soothill, Jane E. 2007. *Gender, social change and spiritual power: Charismatic Christianity in Ghana.* Leiden: Brill.

Spitulnik, Debra, and Mubanga Kashoki. 2001. Bemba. In *Facts about the world's languages: An encyclopedia of the world's major languages, past and present,* edited by J. Garry and C.R.G. Rubino, pp. 81–85. New York: H.W. Wilson.

Spronk, Rachel. 2012. *Ambiguous pleasures: Sexuality and middle class self-perceptions in Nairobi*. New York: Berghahn Books.

Stasch, Rupert. 2011. Ritual and oratory revisited: The semiotics of effective action. *Annual Review of Anthropology* 40: 159–74.

Strathern, Marilyn. 1988. *The gender of the gift: Problems with women and problems with society in Melanesia*. Berkeley: University of California Press.

———. 1999. *Property, substance, and effect: Anthropological essays on persons and things*. London: Athlone.

Street, Alice. 2010. Belief as relational action: Christianity and cultural change in Papua New Guinea. *Journal of the Royal Anthropological Institute* 16(2): 260–78.

Sumich, Jason. 2016. The uncertainty of prosperity: Dependence and the politics of middle-class privilege in Maputo. *Ethnos* 81(5):1–21.

Szymborska, Wislawa. 1995. *View with a grain of sand*. Translated by Stanslaw Baranczak and Clare Cavanagh. New York: Harcourt.

Taylor, John Vernon, and Dorothea A. Lehmann. 1961. *Christians of the copperbelt*. London: SCM Press.

te Velde, Dirk Willem, Medani M. Ahmed, Getnet Alemu, Lawrence Bategeka, Massimiliano Calí, Carlos Castel-Branco, Frank Chansa, Shouro Dasgupta, Marta Foresti, M. Hangi, Lutangu Ingombe, Ashiq Iqbal, and Hossein Jalilian. 2010. *The global financial crisis and developing countries*. London: Overseas Development Institute.

Travisano, Richard. 1981. Alternation and conversion as qualitatively different transformations. In *Social psychology through symbolic interaction*, edited by G. Stone and H. Faberman, pp. 237–48. New York: Wiley.

Turner, Victor Witter. 1969. *The ritual process: Structure and anti-structure*. The Lewis Henry Morgan Lectures. Chicago: Aldine.

Ukah, Asonzeh F-K. 2005. "Those who trade with God never lose": The economies of Pentecostal activism in Nigeria. In *Christianity and social change in Africa: Essays in honor of J.D.Y. Peel*, edited by J.D.Y. Peel and T. Falola. Durham, NC: Carolina Academic Press.

van de Kamp, Linda. 2010. Burying life: Pentecostal religion and development in urban Mozambique. In *Development and politics from below: Exploring religious spaces in the African state*, edited by B. Bompani and M. Frahm-Arp, pp. 152–71. New York: Palgrave Macmillan.

van Dijk, Rijk. 1992. Young Puritan preachers in post-independence Malawi. *Africa* 62(2): 159–81.

———. 1998. Pentecostalism, cultural memory and the state: Contested representations of time in postcolonial Malawi. In *Memory and the postcolony: African anthropology and the critique of power*, edited by R.P. Werbner, pp. 155–81. London: Zed Books.

———. 2009. Social catapulting and the spirit of entrepreneurialism: Migrants, private initiative, and the Pentecostal ethic in Botswana. In *Traveling spirits: Migrants, markets and mobilities*, edited by G. Hüwelmeier and K. Krause, pp. 107–17. New York: Routledge.

Vigh, Henrik. 2006. The colour of destruction. *Anthropological Theory* 6(4): 481–500.

von Doepp, Peter. 2002. Liberal visions and actual power in grassroots civil society: Local churches and women's empowerment in rural Malawi. *Journal of Modern African Studies* 40(2): 273–301.
Wariboko, Nimi. 2011. *The Pentecostal principle: Ethical methodology in new spirit*. Grand Rapids: Eerdmans.
Weber, Max. 1946. *From Max Weber: Essays in sociology*. Translated by H. H. Gerth and C. W. Mills. New York: Oxford University Press.
———. 1947. *The theory of social and economic organization*. Translated by A. M. Henderson and T. Parsons. New York: Oxford University Press.
———. 2010. *The Protestant ethic and the spirit of capitalism*. Translated by T. Parsons. London: Routledge.
Werbner, Richard P. 1984. The Manchester School in south-central Africa. *Annual Review of Anthropology* 13: 157–85.
———. 2011. *Holy hustlers, schism, and prophecy: Apostolic reformation in Botswana*. Berkeley: University of California Press.
Wiegele, Katharine L. 2005. *Investing in miracles: El Shaddai and the transformation of popular Catholicism in the Philippines*. Honolulu: University of Hawai'i Press.
Wilson, Godfrey. 1941. *An essay on the economics of detribalization in northern Rhodesia (part 1)*. Livingstone: Rhodes-Livingstone Institute.
———. 1942. *An essay on the economics of detribalization in northern Rhodesia (part 2)*. Livingstone: Rhodes-Livingstone Institute.
Zafar, Ali. 2007. The growing relationship between China and Sub-Saharan Africa: Macroeconomic, trade, investment, and aid links. *World Bank Research Observer* 22(1): 103–30.

Index

Note: Names of the study township and congregations in quotation marks are pseudonyms. Page numbers in italics denote illustrations.

Accra, 171n1
African Independent Churches, 28, 75
alternation, conversion versus, 59–60
amaka (power or strength), 105
Ambrym Island, 94–96, 105
American Protestants, 171n1, 174n9
Anglicans, 59, 80, 154
Apostolic Church of Pentecost of Canada, 28
Attanasi, Katherine, 170n7
Azusa Street Revival, 28

bafyashi (spiritual parents), 61–62
bakalamba ("big" people), 138
balungami (righteous people), 118
Bantu languages, xvii
Baptists, 29, 59, 104–5
Barclays Bank, 69, 138
Belinga, Samuel, 138
Bemba language and people, xvii, 62, 63, 69, 78, 127, 148, 168nn5,7, 171n4
Bemba Pocket Dictionary (Hoch), xvii
Benares (India), 123
Bialecki, Jon, 155–56, 174n9
"big" people (*bakalamba*), 138
Botswana, 152
Bowler, Kate, 170n7
Brahmins, 123

bridewealth, 141
Britain, African protectorates of, 27
Broken Hill, 168n5
Buchi township, 20
bupe (gift), 105

call-and-response singing, 78, 82, 86, 98
Canadian missionaries, 28
Catholics, 28, 60, 63, 80, 154; charismatic, 29
Chikwanda, Bishop Matthews, 104, 105
Chikwanda, Bishop Nelly, 103–6, 108, 172n1, 173n7
chilimba (credit associations), 49–56, 89
Chiluba, Frederick, 169n8
China, 22, 168n1, 175n2
Chingola, 22, 138, 167n1
Christianity, 1, 57–60, 72, 121, 163–65, 171n1, 174nn7,9; anthropology of, 6, 10, 18, 160, 164; gender concerns in, 93–95; of majority of Zambians, 28–29, 169n8; missionaries and conversion to, 10, 27–28, 170n4; order of worship in, 80, 174; prosperity gospel in, 4–5, 12, 68, 109, 114–16; schism in, 155–56; social relationships in, 57, 62, 76, 163–64; theology of, 2
CiBemba, xvii

191

Coleman, Simon, 114, 161, 170n7, 173n4
collective-personal prayer, 63–67, 72, 78, 82–83, 151–53, 156; breakthroughs through, 87; egalitarianism of, 81–82, 90–91
Comaroff, Jean and John, 4
Congo, Democratic Republic of, 117, 134, 143, 173n5
consumption, 1, 4, 120, 123, 144, 168n5, 169n1; conspicuous, 28, 127
conversion, 10, 27–28, 170n4; versus "alternation," 58–60
Cowrie of Hope, A (Sinyangwe), 21–22
credit associations (*chilimba*), 49–56, 89
Crehan, Kate, 169n5

dan ("Indian Gift"), 122–24, 175n7
Daswani, Girish, 62
deliverance, 30, 34, 57, 61, 63, 75, 96
devil (Satan), 4, 74–75, 78, 84, 117
Dubai, 26
Dumont, Louis, 9–10, 95, 107, 162
Durkheim, Émile, 66
Dutch Reformed Church, 29

ecstatic experiences, 57, 69, 78
Elisha, Omri, 174n9
"El Shaddai," 173n2
English language, 78, 148, 171n4; loanwords from, 152
Englund, Harri, 162
Epstein, A. L., 38
Eriksen, Annelin, 94–96
Eucharist, 80, 171n5
exorcism, 103
Expectations of Modernity (Ferguson), 21, 38

fasting, 65, 69, 85, 97, 102, 110, 151, 172n7
fee-for-service religions, 4. *See also* prosperity gospel
Ferguson, James, 3–4, 15, 21, 23, 38, 47
Filipinos, 173n2
fintu filesela ("things are moving"), xxii
Forbes magazine, 23
Forge, Anthony, 169n7
"Freedom Bible Church," 31–34, 43, 48, 61, 67, 74, 156; chapel built by, 32, 32, 33; elders of, 71, 154; meeting sites of, 34, 116–17; scandals at, 31, 117, 147–48, 173n5; seed offerings to leaders of, 117–19

Gawa, 8, 144
GDP, 22

Ghana, 62, 75, 93
Gifford, Paul, 75
glossolalia, 78
good soil, sowing in, 116–19, 124
Gordimer, Nadine, 37
Graeber, David, 8, 102, 103, 144
greeting, refusal of, xx–xxi
Guyer, Jane, 7, 46, 138, 146

Handman, Courtney, 155, 156
healing, 1, 12, 103; traditional, 60
"health and wealth" gospel. *See* prosperity gospel
"Higher Calling," 34, 53, 61, 97–98, 151, 172n2; collective prayer at, 63, 66, 97; excessive praying at, 83–84; loss of membership of, 156; popularity of, 32–33
Hinfelaar, Hugo, 41
HIV, 3
Hoch, E., xvii
Holy Spirit, 1, 8, 76, 95, 99, 105; access to power of, 71, 76, 82–86, 90, 103
Hubert, Henri, 114–15

Independent Churches Organization of Zambia, 169n8
"Indian gift" (*dan*) 122–24, 175n2
India, 95, 122–23, 175n2
individualism, 1, 8, 58, 167n3
informal trade, 23, 26, 56
intercession, 63–65, 70, 77–78, 81–82, 86, 97, 138
International Phonetic Alphabet, xvii
intersubjective spacetime, 8

Jainism, 122–23, 125
James, Epistle of, 168n7
Jehovah's Witnesses, 28, 63
Jesus Christ, 28, 101, 163
Joel, Book of, 74
John, Gospel of, 74

Kabwe, 168n5
Kaonde language, 169n5
Kaunda, Kenneth, 168n5
"Key of David Pentecostal Church," 71, 100, 105, 149, 154, 171n5, 175n2; believers overcome by Holy Spirit at, 83–84; breakthroughs of members of, 61–62, 67; conflicts in, xix–xxi, 35–36, 69–70, 150; disruption by devil of service at, 74–75; financial concerns at, 88–90; kitchen mending party for wife

of pastor of, 17–18, 52, 128–46, *129*, 175n6; meeting space of, 34–35, *35;* pastor and wife as icons of, 144–46; receiving line at, *81;* super-members of, 137–41; thanksgiving service at, 110–13, *111*, 115; tithing envelopes of, 120, *120, 174n7
Kirsch, Thomas, 60, 62, 75, 155
Kitwe, 32, 45, 26, 104, 147, 168n4, 172n8, 174n7; City Council of, 25, 31; Ferguson's fieldwork in, 3–4, 15, 21; neighborhood status in, 20, 43, 127; townships on outskirts of, 2, 20, 24, 147 (*See also* "Nsofu"); "Women of Influence" conference in, 92
Klaits, Frederick, 152

Laidlaw, James, 122–23, 125
"Lament of the Silent Sisters" (Okigbo), 159, 165
laypeople, 16, 34, 63, 85–87, 120, 128, 155. *See also* super members; gender issues and, 92, 96, 98, 100, 106, 108–9; Jain, 122, 124; relationships between church leaders and, 17, 34, 58–62, 66, 70–72, 75, 89, 118
Lenshina, Alice, 28
Levites, 116–17
Life Chapel, 29
Lindhardt, Martin, 115–16
Los Angeles, 28
low density neighborhoods, 20, 104
Lumpa Church, 27–28, 168n5
Lunda-Ndembu, 13–14
Lusaka, 26, 69, 104, 135, 154; Bible college in, 34–35

Malagasy, 102
Malaysia, 83
Manchester School, 19
Marian apparitions, 4
Marshall, Ruth, 13, 14, 170n4
Massim, 8
Mauss, Marcel, 114–15
Mbembe, Achille, 1
Melanesia, 8, 94, 169n7, 172n4
Meyer, Birgit, 77
middle class, xix, 20, 26, 36, 140, 182n8
mining townships, 20, 22
Munn, Nancy, 144

Ndola, 103, 147, 168n4
neoliberalism, 1, 3–6
New Guinea, 8, 58, 160

New Life Ministries International, 103
New Year, preparing for, 110–11
Nigeria, xix, 175n2
Nkana mine, 24
"Nsofu," xix, 47, 57, 98, 150, 157, 162, 174n1. *See also* "Freedom Bible Church," "Higher Calling," "Key of David Pentecostal Church"; change and progress in, 11–12; charisma and prosperity in, 15, 72; religious "marketplace" in, 155; collective-personal prayer in, 91, 156; continuity of Christianity in, 60, 80; economic conditions in, 23, 53–56, 72–73, 88, 175n5; gender in, 92, 96, 100; middle class in, xix, 20, 26, 36; population of, 2; portrait of, 24–27; seed offerings in, 117–19; social relations in, 128, 150, 152–53, 159
Nyanja, 38, 69

occult economies, 4–5
offerings, 39, 80, 83, *111,* 111–12, 138, 140, 149. *See also* seed offerings
Okigbo, Christopher, 159, 165
Old Testament, 173n6, 175n1; Joel, 74; Samuel, 110

Papua New Guinea, 8, 58, 160
Parklands neighborhood (Kitwe), 20
Parry, Jonathan, 123–24
Paul, Saint, 115
Pentecostal Assemblies of God, 35; Canada, 28; Zambia, 117
petitions, 78, 81, 84, 97, 132, 171n87
Politics in an Urban African Community (Epstein), 38
poverty, 15, 21
Powdermaker, Hortense, 168n5
praise and worship, 78, 82, 85–86, 90, 138
Presbyterianism, 28
Pritchett, James, 13–14
prophecy, 1, 12, 30, 31, 69, 75, 76, 83, 96, 102, 108
prosperity gospel, 4–5, 12–18, 28, 68, 109, 173n2. *See also* seed offerings; capitalistic framework of, 114–16, 167n2; thanksgiving service derived from, 112–13
Protestantism, 58, 80, 167n3, 174n9. *See also specific denominations*

Rasing, Thera, 127
"Reality Demands" (Szymborska), 1

Index

religious affiliation, shorthand term for (*ukupepa*), 63
Renewalists, 29
Rhodes-Livingstone Institute (RLI), 19
Rhodesia, 27
Richards, Audrey, 168n5
righteous people (*balungami*), 118
Riverside neighborhood (Kitwe), 20
Robbins, Joel, 13, 160–61, 175n1

Sahlins, Marshall, 160–61
Samuel, Book of, 110
Satan. *See* devil
Saul, King, 119
seed offerings, 121, 128, 132, 145, 161, 173nn2–4,6; good soil for, 117–19, 124; moral ambiguity of, 122–25; of super members, 141
Seventh Day Adventists, 29, 59
shantytowns, 20, 98
Sichone, Owen, 23
singing, 12, 30, 57, 70, 75, 83, 116, 134, 151; call-and-response, 78, 82, 86, 98
Sinyangwe, Binwell, 21–22
Smith, James K. A., 14
Soothill, Jane, 93
South Africa, 33, 96, 99
Southern California Vineyard churches, 174n9
"Spirit disco" ritual, 8
spiritual parents (*bafyashi*), 61–62
Strathern, Marilyn, 17, 94, 167n4, 172n4
Street, Alice, 58
super-members, 17–18, 137–44, 146, 150, 153–54, 175n7
Sweden, 173n4
Sweetheart Church, 28
Szymborska, Wislawa, 1

Tanzania, 115
thanksgiving services, 110–13, *111*, 115, 131, 138

tithing envelopes, *120*, 174n7
"Tiyende Pamodzi (Let Us Go Forward)" (independence anthem), 38
Town Bemba, xvii
trade, 5, 47, 49, 73, 173n5; informal, 23, 26, 56
traditional healers, 60
Travisano, Richard, 60
Trinity Broadcasting Network, 168–69n8
Turner, Terry, 8
Turner, Victor, 75

ukukana ukuposha (refusal to greet), xx–xxi
ukupepa ("to pray"), 63
ukupokelela (receiving), 42, 105
Union Church of the Copperbelt, 27, 29
United Church of Zambia, 29, 63
United National Independent Party, 168n5
Urapmin, 8, 160

Vanuatu, 94–96

wage labor, 19, 56, 170n9
Wariboko, Nimi, 14, 168n6
Weber, Max, 10, 71, 90, 154–55, 164
Wilson, Godfrey, 168n5
witchcraft, 4, 144, 152, 175n3
"Women of Influence" conference (Kitwe), 92
World of Strangers, A (Gordimer), 37
worship, 16, 31, 33, 69, 77–91, 156; from egalitarianism to hierarchy in, 81–87; order of, 77–81, 174n7; praise and, 78, 82, 85–86, 90, 138; satanic hindrances to, 74–75, 84
Wuzakile township, 20

Yong, Amos, 170n7

ZamTel, 53
zombies, 28